GALATIANS

Paul's Charter of Christian Freedom

Leon Morris

InterVarsity Press
Downers Grove, Illinois

Published in the United States of America by InterVarsity Press, Downers Grove, Illinois, with permission from Universities and Colleges Christian Fellowship, Leicester, England.

InterVarsity Press® is the book-publishing division of InterVarsity Christian Fellowship®, a student movement active on campus at hundreds of universities, colleges and schools of nursing in the United States of America, and a member movement of the International Fellowship of Evangelical Students. For information about local and regional activities, write Public Relations Dept., InterVarsity Christian Fellowship, 6400 Schroeder Rd., P.O. Box 7895, Madison, WI 53707-7895.

Unless otherwise noted, scriptural translations are the author's own.

Cover illustration: Scala/Art Resource, NY: Michelangelo Buonarroti. Conversion of St. Paul. Cappella Paolina, Vatican Palace, Vatican State.

ISBN 0-8308-1420-5

Printed in the United States of America ∞

Library of Congress Cataloging-in-Publication Data

Morris, Leon, 1914-
   Galatians: Paul's charter of Christian freedom / by Leon Morris.
      p.   cm.
   Includes bibliographical references.
   ISBN 0-8308-1420-5 (cloth: alk. paper)
      1. Bible.   N.T.   Galatians—Commentaries.   I. Title.
   BS2685.3M67   1996
   227'.407—dc20   96-17460
                                                          CIP

16	15	14	13	12	11	10	9	8	7	6	5	4	3	2	1
09	08	07	06	05	04	03	02	01	00	99	98	97	96		

PREFACE

The epistle to the Galatians has exercised a great influence on the Christian church through the centuries. It has made very clear the importance of some of the central teachings of the faith. Through the years it has been my privilege to lecture on this letter and to preach on it. Now in retirement I have the opportunity of putting on paper some of the important teachings I find in it.

I have made my own translation of the letter (as well as of other Bible passages I quote, unless otherwise stated). It is not that I am dissatisfied with the many excellent translations that are available, but simply to help the reader see some of the teachings I see in the Greek that Paul wrote. The commentary is meant for the general reader rather than the specialist, but in the footnotes I have tried to take notice of some of the more scholarly writing I have encountered.

Leon Morris

CHIEF ABBREVIATIONS

Citations are *ad loc.* unless a page reference is given.

Abbott-Smith	G. Abbott-Smith, *A Manual Greek Lexicon of the New Testament* (Edinburgh, 1954)
Allan	John A. Allan, *The Epistle of Paul the Apostle to the Galatians* (London, 1951)
AV	Authorized (King James) Version of the Bible
BAGD	Walter Bauer, *A Greek-English Lexicon of the New Testament and Other Early Christian Literature*, revised and augmented by William F. Arndt, F. Wilbur Gingrich and Frederick W. Danker from the 5th edn. (Chicago, 1979)
Barclay	William Barclay, *The Letter to the Galatians*, The Daily Study Bible (Edinburgh, 1958)
BDF	F. Blass and A. Debrunner, *A Greek Grammar of the New Testament and Other Early Christian Literature, A Translation and Revision* by Robert W. Funk (Cambridge, 1961)
Betz	Hans Dieter Betz, *Galatians* (Philadelphia, 1979)
BJRL	*Bulletin of the John Rylands Library*
Boice	James Montgomery Boice, *Galatians*, in The Expositor's Bible Commentary, vol. 10 (Grand Rapids, 1976)
Bruce	F. F. Bruce, *The Epistle to the Galatians*, The New International Greek Testament Commentary (Grand Rapids, 1982)
Burton	E. de W. Burton, *A Critical and Exegetical Commentary on the Epistle to the Galatians*, The International Critical Commentary (Edinburgh, 1921)
Burton, *Moods*	E. de W. Burton, *Syntax of the Moods and Tenses in New Testament Greek* (Edinburgh, 1955)
Calvin	Calvin's Commentaries, *The Epistles of Paul the Apostle to the Galatians, Ephesians, Philippians and Colossians*, translated by T. H. L. Parker (Grand Rapids, 1965)
Chamberlain	W. D. Chamberlain, *An Exegetical Grammar of the Greek New Testament* (New York, 1951)

Chrysostom	Cited from *Nicene and Post-Nicene Fathers,* first series, ed. P. Schaff, vol. 13 (Grand Rapids, 1956)
Cole	R. A. Cole, *The Letter of Paul to the Galatians* (Leicester, 1989)
Cousar	Charles B. Cousar, *Galatians* (Louisville, 1982)
Duncan	George S. Duncan, *The Epistle of Paul to the Galatians* (London, 1934)
Dunn	James D. G. Dunn, *The Epistle to the Galatians* (Peabody, Mass., 1993)
EQ	*The Evangelical Quarterly*
Fung	Ronald Y. K. Fung, *The Epistle to the Galatians,* The New International Commentary on the New Testament (Grand Rapids, 1988)
GNB	Good News Bible
Grammar	N. Turner, *A Grammar of New Testament Greek* (Edinburgh, 1963)
Guthrie	Donald Guthrie, *Galatians,* The New Century Bible Commentary (London, 1973)
Hamann	H. P. Hamann, *Galatians* (Adelaide, 1976)
Hendriksen	William Hendriksen, *New Testament Commentary, Exposition of Galatians* (Grand Rapids, 1976)
IB	*The Interpreter's Bible,* vol. 10, *Galatians:* exegesis, T. Stamm; exposition, O. F. Blackwelder (Abingdon, 1978)
IBD	*The Illustrated Bible Dictionary,* ed. J. D. Douglas (Leicester, 1980)
IDB	*The Interpreter's Dictionary of the Bible* (Abingdon, 1962)
JB	Jerusalem Bible
JBL	*Journal of Biblical Literature*
Lenski	R. C. H. Lenski, *The Interpretation of St Paul's Epistles to the Galatians, to the Ephesians and to the Philippians* (Minneapolis, 1961)
Lightfoot	J. B. Lightfoot, *Saint Paul's Epistle to the Galatians* (London, 1902)
Loane	Marcus L. Loane, *This Surpassing Excellence* (Sydney, 1969)
Longenecker	Richard N. Longenecker, *Galatians,* Word Biblical Commentary, vol. 41 (Dallas, 1990)
LSJ	H. G. Liddell and R. Scott, *A Greek-English Lexicon,* revised by H. S. Jones and R. McKenzie (Oxford, n. d.)

Lührmann	Dieter Lührmann, *Galatians* (Minneapolis, 1992)
Luther	Martin Luther, *A Commentary on St Paul's Epistle to the Galatians* (London, 1953)
MI	J. H. Moulton, *A Grammar of New Testament Greek*, vol. I, *Prolegomena* (Edinburgh, 1906)
MII	*Ibid.*, vol. II, *Accidence and Word-Formation*, ed. W. F. Howard (Edinburgh, 1919)
MIII	*Ibid.*, vol. III, *Syntax*, by Nigel Turner (Edinburgh, 1963)
MIV	*Ibid.*, vol. IV, *Style*, by Nigel Turner (Edinburgh, 1976)
Machen	J. H. Skinner ed., *Machen's Notes on Galatians* (Nutley, NJ, 1977)
Meyer	H. A. W. Meyer, *Critical and Exegetical Commentary on the New Testament*, Part VII, *The Epistle to the Galatians* (Edinburgh, 1880)
MM	J. H. Moulton and G. Milligan, *The Vocabulary of the Greek Testament* (London, 1914–29)
Moffatt	James Moffatt, *The New Testament, A New Translation* (London, n. d.)
Moule	C. F. D. Moule, *An Idiom Book of New Testament Greek* (Cambridge, 1953)
NEB	New English Bible
New Documents	*New Documents Illustrating Early Christianity*, vols. 1–5 by G. H. R. Horsley, vol. 6 by S. R. Llewelyn and R. A. Kearsley (Sydney, 1981–92)
NIDNTT	C. Brown, ed., *The New International Dictionary of New Testament Theology*, 3 vols. (Exeter, 1975–78)
NIV	New International Version of the Bible
NRSV	New Revised Standard Version of the Bible
NTS	*New Testament Studies*
Osiek	Carolyn Osiek, *Galatians* (Wilmington, 1980)
Phillips	J. B. Phillips, *Letters to Young Churches* (Melbourne, 1952)
Ramsay	W. M. Ramsay, *A Historical Commentary on St Paul's Epistle to the Galatians* (Minneapolis, 1978)
REB	Revised English Bible
Ridderbos	Herman N. Ridderbos, *The Epistle of Paul to the Churches of Galatia* (London, 1954)
Robertson	A. T. Robertson, *A Grammar of the Greek New Testament in the Light of Historical Research* (London, n. d.)

RSV	Revised Standard Version of the Bible
SBk	H. L. Strack and P. Billerbeck, *Kommentar zum Neuen Testament aus Talmud und Midrasch* (München, 1922–28)
Schmoller	Otto Schmoller, *The Epistle of Paul to the Galatians* (Edinburgh, 1871)
Stott	John R. W. Stott, *The Message of Galatians* (Leicester, 1968)
Synonyms	R. C. Trench, *Synonyms of the New Testament* (London, 1880)
TDNT	G. Kittel, ed., *Theological Dictionary of the New Testament*, translated by G. W. Bromiley (Grand Rapids, 1964–76)
Theology	James D. G. Dunn, *The Theology of Paul's Letter to the Galatians*, (Cambridge, 1993)
Turner	N. Turner, *Grammatical Insights into the New Testament* (Edinburgh, 1965)
Warren	M. A. C. Warren, *The Gospel of Victory* (London, 1955)

Statistics are taken from R. Morgenthaler, *Statistik des Neutestamentlichen Wortschatzes* (Zürich, 1958).

INTRODUCTION

'It is a great pity that Paul's letters were ever called *epistles*. They are in the most literal sense *letters*' (Barclay, p. xiv). In this way William Barclay brings out the fact that what Paul wrote was a series of genuine letters addressing specific situations in which he and his converts found themselves. He was not setting himself to produce literary works. Each of these missives was clearly written in the light of what was needed in a given situation; none was written with a view to adding to the stock of Jewish literature. They all focus on the situation confronting Paul at the time he wrote them.

But, as Barclay further reminds us, 'a thing need not be a transient thing because it was written to meet an immediate situation. All the great love songs of the world were written for one person, but all the world loves them' (p. xvii). So with Paul's letters. The apostle did not write to meet the needs of the church through the ages, but what he has written speaks to believers in every age, to us as well as to those in previous days. Galatians takes us to the very heart of the Christian faith.

Galatians is one of the shortest of Paul's letters, but we should not regard it as therefore unimportant. It deals with great themes, themes to which the Christian church must always give heed and which affect the daily life of every Christian. As Longenecker puts it, 'Historically, Galatians has been foundational for many forms of Christian doctrine, proclamation, and practice. And it remains true today to say that how one understands the issues and teachings of Galatians determines in large measure what kind of theology is espoused, what kind of message is proclaimed, and what kind of lifestyle is practiced' (p. xliii).[1]

The author

The letter opens with the claim that it comes from Paul and there is no serious reason for doubting this. Hendriksen points out that 'as soon

---

[1]Cole can say, 'Galatians is not primarily a pastoral letter like the Corinthian letters, dealing with the questions and problems of a struggling local church, but a theological refutation of a heresy that, if accepted, would have destroyed the whole church' (p. 57). Duncan sees it as a great epistle, 'the Magna Charta [*sic*] of Evangelical Christianity. It shows how Paul saved Christianity from sinking to be a mere sect of Judaism, or, as he himself felt, degenerating into a form of paganism' (p. xvii).

as this epistle was ascribed to anyone, it was ascribed to Paul'.[2]
Actually the opening runs, 'Paul . . . and all the brothers who are with
me' (1:1), but this does not mean that 'the brothers' actually took part
in the writing of the letter. There is no serious reason for doubting that
Paul was the author. It has all the marks of his style and it fits into
what we know of his situation. But the apostle often associates others
with him in the writing of a letter, and in each case it is generally
agreed that this is no more than a courtesy. This letter (like the others
with several names in the address) bears the hallmarks of Paul's style.
No doubt 'the brothers' would have agreed with what was written,
but that does not mean that they took any active part in writing it.
Towards the end Paul's letters usually have some greetings sent by
those with him to the church to which he is writing, but this letter has
none. This may be a mark of the speed at which it is written, or
perhaps of a disapproval in Pauline circles of positions taken up by the
Galatians.

Letters in the first century were usually dictated. Most people were
not literate and scribes wrote what the authors wanted. One of them
comes to our notice when we read towards the end of Romans, 'I,
Tertius, who wrote the letter, greet you' (Rom. 16:22). Though the
scribe does not reveal himself elsewhere in the New Testament, we
need not doubt that the use of a scribe was customary. There is an
unusual feature when we read towards the end of this letter, 'You see
with what big letters I am writing to you in my own hand' (6:11). This
probably means that at this point in the letter Paul took over from the
amanuensis and finished the letter in his own handwriting. It appears
from 2 Thessalonians 3:17 that this was the apostle's custom,[3] but in
Galatians he seems to have taken the pen a little earlier than was

---

[2]He goes on, 'That has been the belief of the church throughout the centuries and is
its conviction today. No argument of any merit has ever been presented to show that
this view is in error' (Hendricksen, p. 21). A few radical German and Dutch scholars
have disputed this view, but not many have followed them. Guthrie points out that 'at
no time have any other of Paul's epistles been accepted and this rejected' (p. 7). If any
of the letters attributed to Paul are authentic, then Galatians certainly is one of them.
M. S. Enslin insists on the genuineness of this letter: 'Forgery is out of the question.
The obvious excitement under which it was written; the passionate form of
expression; the sudden changes of front – all these are quite unlike the work of a
later Christian essaying to write in Paul's manner' (*Christian Beginnings* [New York
and London, 1938], p. 216).

[3]He could do this even if he did not draw his readers' attention to the fact. A.
Deissmann reproduces a letter dated in AD 50 on our reckoning of time, written by an
olive-planter named Mystarion, in which the body of the letter is in one handwriting
(clearly that of the scribe) and the conclusion in another (that of Mystarion) (*Light from*

usual. He may have felt that the situation was so serious that he wanted to underline the importance he attached to the great truths he has dictated. He closes with an emphasis on them in his own handwriting.

The destination of the epistle

Galatia was the name of an area in what we now call Asia Minor. During the third century BC some Celtic peoples (or Gauls) migrated to this area and, after some fighting with the people they encountered, they settled in the northern part of Asia Minor. In due course they came into conflict with the Romans, who defeated them, and from this time they remained under the authority of the Romans as a dependent kingdom. The name 'Galatia' covered the territory settled by the Gauls but also included other adjacent areas. In 64 BC the Romans recognized the area as a client kingdom, but when its king died in 25 BC they added areas such as Pamphylia to it and made the whole into a province. The question arises whether the New Testament applies the term to the kingdom of Galatia proper (the area settled by the Gauls), as Lightfoot, for example, argued,[4] or whether it follows the Roman practice and includes the southern districts, Lycaonia, *etc.*, which the Romans incorporated in the province they called 'Galatia'. Perhaps we should notice here that in AD 137 Lycaonia was taken away from the province and added to Cilicia, while late in the third century the rest of the southern part of Galatia was added to Pisidia to form a new province, leaving only the northern area in Galatia. When writers in the early centuries of the church speak of Galatia they have this situation in view, and see the letter of Paul as written to Christians in the northern part of the province. It seems not to have occurred to them that 'Galatia' in New Testament times may well have differed

---

the *Ancient East* [London, 1927], pp. 170–172). The writer says nothing about it; he just does it. The fact that Paul does not draw attention to his handwriting in some letters does not mean that he did not end the letter in this way. Mystarion shows that this was done in instances other than the letters of Paul.

[4]He says, 'There are many reasons which make it probable that the Galatia of St Paul and St Luke is not the Roman province of that name, but the land of the Gauls' (Lightfoot, p. 19). He thinks that Paul may have founded churches in Ancyra, in Pessinus, in Tavium, perhaps also in Juliopolis (p. 20). There is, of course, no evidence for this. Perhaps we should notice also that Lightfoot, in arguing for the Gauls, puts a good deal of emphasis on the fickleness of the recipients of the letter. But many others than the Gauls were fickle, and when Lightfoot can argue that changing a view over a period of 'five or ten years' (or 'a whole decade of years') shows fickleness (p. 42), the argument ceases to have value.

from the 'Galatia' of their day. But from them the church seems to have taken the idea that the Galatians of the New Testament came from the northern area, an idea that was rarely doubted until recent times.[5]

In support of the view that the term is to be confined to the northern area, considerations such as the following are adduced.

1. *The strict meaning of 'Galatia'.* It is pointed out that in Acts the Antioch in which Paul preached on his first missionary journey (as opposed to Antioch in Syria from which he started his trip) is called 'Antioch in Pisidia', while Lystra and Derbe are called cities 'of Lycaonia', not of Galatia. Luke does not use the term 'Galatia' for the location of these southern cities.[6]

2. *Geographical expressions.* Terms such as 'Mysia', 'Phrygia', 'Pisidia', *etc.*, are geographical expressions, not designations of Roman provinces. It is alleged accordingly that we would expect the same to be true of 'Galatia'.[7]

3. *Popular usage.* Luke speaks of Lystra and Derbe as 'cities of Lycaonia' (Acts 14:6), and of 'Pisidian Antioch' (Acts 13:14). He does not apply 'Galatia' to any of them.

4. *The Phrygio-Galatic region* (Acts 16:6) 'shows that the district intended was not Lycaonia and Pisidia, but some region which might be said to belong either to Phrygia or Galatia, or the parts of each contiguous to the other' (Lightfoot, p. 20).

5. *Paul's second visit to Jerusalem* (Gal. 2:1–10) is to be taken as a reference to the Jerusalem Council (Acts 15). Paul's two visits to Galatia will be those of Acts 16:6 and 18:23.

6. *The Christians of Phrygia and Lycaonia* were not Galatians by race

---

[5]Curiously, R. M. Grant says, 'In modern times the question of the addressees of the letter has often been discussed, chiefly because scholars have realized that if they could be located in "south Galatia" the letter could be dated earlier than the other Pauline epistles' (*A Historical Introduction to the New Testament* [London, 1963], p. 184). I do not know of anyone who starts with the date and then tries to find evidence of location to support it.

[6]Thus W. G. Kümmel argues that '1) . . . Paul would not have said: "Then I went into the regions of Syria and Cilicia" (1:21), but something like this: Then I went to Syria, Cilicia, and to you. 2) Paul could not possibly have addressed Lycaonians or Pisidians "O foolish Galatians"' (*Introduction to the New Testament* [London, 1966], p. 193). But this overlooks Ramsay's point that 'Galatians' was the only term that covered all the people in the province.

[7]Meyer finds evidence for the North Galatian view in Acts 14:6 (together with 16:6; 18:23), 'in which the universally current popular mode of designation, not based on the new provincial arrangements, is employed' and in Paul's usage in 1:2 (p. 3). But evidence for the so-called 'popular mode of designation' is lacking, and it is curious to describe as 'new' provincial arrangements that had been in place for 70 years or so.

but only because they had been incorporated into the Roman province. It would be curious (and undiplomatic) for Paul to address them as 'Galatians'. Thus the letter to the Galatians was not addressed to these people.

7. *Ancient authors* often speak of the Gauls (in North Galatia) as fickle, and that fits what Paul says of his addressees.

There are however a number of reasons for holding that this letter is directed to churches in the southern part of the province.

1. *Development*. The northern part of Galatia was not as well developed as the southern region. A continual stream of commerce passed through the cities of the south but there was not nearly as much in the rougher country of the north. It is unlikely that when he was ill (Gal. 4:13–14) Paul would have ventured into this northern area.[8] Nor is it likely that the Judaizers would have followed him into such places, especially as it would have meant passing by the flourishing towns of the south, where churches had been established. Luke says that Paul and Barnabas founded churches in Pisidian Antioch, Iconium, Lystra, *etc.* (Acts 13 – 14), but he mentions no northern city. It cannot be shown that Paul was ever in the cities of the northern area (Ancyra, Pessinus, *etc.*). Indeed none of the cities in the northern area is ever mentioned in the New Testament.[9]

2. *Barnabas* is mentioned as one familiar to the readers of the epistle (Gal. 2:1, 9, 13; note 'even Barnabas' in 2:13). This is especially significant if the epistle is early, *i.e.* not far in time from Paul's labours in Galatia. Barnabas separated from Paul after the first missionary journey (Acts 15:36–41). Some of the force of this argument is perhaps taken away by the fact that Barnabas is mentioned in 1 Corinthians 9:6, although we have no evidence that he was personally known to the Corinthians.

3. *Paul's silence about northern Galatia*. We may put this in Lightfoot's words. Though he favours the view that the Galatians to whom Paul writes were in the north of the province, he yet can say: 'It is strange

---

[8]'It is incredible that he would have chosen the long unhealthy journey to North Galatia when he was ill. But it is extremely probable that he left the damp lowlands of Pamphylia for the bracing air of Pisidian Antioch' (Leighton Pullan, *The Books of the New Testament* [London, 1926], p. 152).

[9]'The strength of the South Galatian view is its identification of the recipients of Gal with churches where we know Paul founded. It is most unlikely that he ever penetrated so far as Ancyra in North Galatia' (R. H. Fuller, *A Critical Introduction to the New Testament* [London, 1966], p. 25). He also says, 'The motive, conscious or unconscious, behind the North Galatian theory seems to be the desire to avoid making Gal the earliest Pauline letter' (*ibid.*).

that while we have more or less acquaintance with all the other important Churches of St Paul's founding, with Corinth and Ephesus, with Philippi and Thessalonica, not a single name of a person or place, scarcely a single incident of any kind, connected with the Apostle's preaching in Galatia, should be preserved in either the history or the epistle' (p. 21).[10] His words should be taken more seriously than advocates of the northern cities usually take them. Acts, of course, gives us information about southern Galatian cities, but not those in the north. This may well imply that Paul's work was confined to the southern regions. It is not too much to say that we have no knowledge of any North Galatian church in New Testament times.[11]

4. 'Galatians' was the only comprehensive term to cover the citizens of all the cities, such as Antioch, Lystra, Iconium and Derbe. Moreover, the practice appears to have been that people were designated by their province in the Empire rather than their nation.[12]

5. *The collection.* Paul gives directions for a collection to help the poor saints in Jerusalem and informs the Corinthians that he has already told the Galatian churches what to do (1 Cor. 16:1–4). The churches were to send representatives to accompany the collection to Jerusalem and if possible Paul would go with them. Acts gives us the names of a Berean, two Thessalonians, two South Galatians and two Asians (Acts 20:4), and this looks suspiciously like the relief party. But no representatives of North Galatia are included in the list. We must not, of course, put too much emphasis on this, for there is no representative named from Corinth, although we know from the letters to the Corinthians that this church took part in the collection.

6. *Galatia and Phrygia.* Paul and his party travelled through 'the Phrygian and Galatic region' (Acts 16:6), which probably refers to that part of Phrygia that is in Galatia, while 'the Galatian region and

[10]S. A. Cartledge puts a related argument this way: 'In Acts 15 the controversy over circumcision took place at the Jerusalem Council, and there is no indication that the controversy ever broke out again, the Southern theory can date the Epistle early and make it fit into this background; the Northern theory must date the Epistle later and must assume that the controversy broke out again after having once been settled, which is possible but not probable' (*A Conservative Introduction to the New Testament* [Grand Rapids, 1957], p. 109).

[11]*Cf.* Ridderbos, 'It ought to be evident . . . that any founding and existence of churches in North Galatia can be inferred from the Acts with only very meager certainty' (p. 28).

[12]Lenski cites as 'a valuable observation' that 'when Luke speaks of Asia Minor and of other districts he employs the old ethnographic names without regard to the boundaries of the Roman provinces; Paul, however, employs the names of the Roman provinces regardless of the nationalities inhabiting them' (p. 10).

Phrygia' (Acts 18:23) appears to mean that they went through districts in the province of Galatia and that part of Phrygia which was in Asia. It is not easy to see North Galatia in either expression.[13]

7. *No record of preaching in North Galatia.* We know from Acts that Paul preached in some of the cities in the southern part of this Roman province (in Pisidian Antioch, in Iconium, Lystra, Derbe),[14] but there is no record of Christian preaching in the north (in Ancyra, Pessinus, Tavium, Juliopolis, *etc.*).[15] It is not too much to say that solid evidence that Paul was ever in North Galatia has not been cited.

8. *In Lystra* Paul was taken to be the god Hermes come to earth (Acts 14:12). Paul's words, 'You received me as an angel of God, as Christ Jesus' (4:14), may be an echo of this. Some have thought that 'the marks of Jesus' (6:17) may be a reference to the stoning at Lystra (Acts 14:19).

9. *Paul's second visit to Jerusalem* (Gal. 2:1–10) is surely to be identified with the famine visit (Acts 11:30). This, it is urged, is too early to allow a visit to North Galatia before it.

10. *Historical geography.* W. M. Ramsay urged that Christianity spread along the main roads to the principal centres. There was a road to the north, but the north was not developed before AD 292, when Diocletian made Nicomedia the centre for imperial administration. The Christian message would have gone along the more southerly routes to Iconium and Ephesus and that proceeding by Philadelphia to Troas.

Longenecker also finds four biographical matters which, though not proving the South Galatian hypothesis, combine to lend support to it. The first is the fact that Timothy is not mentioned in Galatians, though he is spoken of in all Paul's other letters except Ephesians and Titus: 'It is virtually unthinkable that Paul would have addressed a letter to Christians in an area that included Lystra without sending news or

---

[13]Moffatt takes the former expression to mean 'Phrygia and the region of Galatia' and the latter 'the region of Galatia and Phrygia' (*An Introduction to the Literature of the New Testament* [Edinburgh, 1918], pp. 93, 95). But in neither passage is there an indication of the major journey that would be involved in travelling to the kingdom of Galatia proper.

[14]'It would be surprising if the apostle wrote to converts in the north of whom the *Acts* relates nothing, and made not the slightest reference in his epistles to his work and sufferings nearer home in the region of Antioch, Iconium, Lystra, and Derbe, which figure prominently in St. Luke's narrative' (A. H. McNeile, *An Introduction to the Study of the New Testament* [Oxford, 1927], pp. 131–132).

[15]Allan points out that in addition to the fact that Acts has no record of churches being founded in this region, it is also the case that 'archaeology provides no evidence of the existence of Christianity in the region until comparatively late' (p. 25).

making mention of their native son' (p. lxxi). This means that the letter must have been written before Timothy joined Paul's party. The second is that Barnabas is mentioned three times in Galatians, which presumes that he was known to the recipients of the letter. The third is Titus, who was not constrained to be circumcised, though certain 'false brothers' urged that this be done. Longenecker finds it difficult to hold that this would be done at the time of the Council of Jerusalem. The fourth concerns Peter at Antioch, where he ate with Gentiles, but when some people came from James he withdrew. It is not easy to see this happening after the Jerusalem Council (pp. lxxi-lxxii).

Thus, while there are some quite good arguments for holding that the letter was written to churches in the northern part of Galatia, they do not seem strong enough to counter those considerations that point to those in the south of the area, churches that Paul is known to have visited and indeed to have founded.[16]

The date of the letter

In this letter Paul speaks of two visits he paid to Jerusalem (Gal. 1:18; 2:1–2). The most natural way of understanding this is that the two visits are the one he paid to that city after his time in Arabia, subsequent to his conversion (Gal. 1:17; Acts 9:25–26), and the visit he made to bring famine relief (Acts 11:29–30). Some hold that the second visit was to attend the Council (Acts 15), but that does not account satisfactorily for the omission of the 'famine' visit. It will not do to lay it down that the 'famine' visit was unofficial and therefore is not to be counted. There was nothing 'official' in Paul's first visit when he simply had a couple of weeks getting to know Peter (Gal. 1:18). If he includes such a private visit, why would he not include a reference to the 'famine' visit? And in any case if a visit to present to the Jerusalem church a sum of money subscribed by a number of Gentile churches, and in which Paul was accompanied by representatives of at least some of those churches, is not official, then what is? We should also bear in mind that Paul put himself on oath before God as he was detailing his contacts with the apostles (Gal. 1:20). He could not have omitted reference to one of his visits. Merrill C. Tenney points out that

---

[16]K. and S. Lake conclude their discussion of the problem by saying: 'The point which seems too often overlooked is that the identification of the church of Galatia is not the same problem as the exegesis of Acts xvi.6. Ramsay seems to us clearly wrong as to Acts xvi.6, but he may be right as to the locality to which the Epistle to the Galatians was addressed' (*An Introduction to the New Testament* [London, 1938], p. 130).

'Paul reviewed his biography up to the time of writing. He spoke of his conversion and call (1:15, 16), his stay in Damascus (1:17), his first visit to Jerusalem (1:18), his ministry in Syria and Cilicia (1:21), and the visit to Jerusalem with Barnabas (2:1–10)'. If this last mentioned were the Acts 15 visit, 'there is a strange silence of Galatians concerning many of its important features that would have been quite pertinent to the argument of the letter'.[17]

Thus the Council discussed the position taken up by some that it was necessary to circumcise new believers and have them keep the law of Moses (Acts 15:1, 5). It is noteworthy that its decision was that circumcision and the keeping of the Mosaic law were not necessary for the Gentiles who were turning to God (as the resolution of the Council makes clear, Acts 15:19–21). It is not easy to see why Paul should have omitted all reference to the Council in this letter if it had already taken place, for, in addition to the fact that he has sworn he is telling the truth (1:20), it would have given him splendid support. Specifically, it is difficult to see why he should have failed to quote the decrees of the Council which had direct reference to the question of circumcision (Acts 15:19–21). His opponents in Galatia were clearly arguing that Peter (among other people) was in favour of circumcising new Christians, a position at variance with the Council's position that Gentile converts need not be circumcised. The obvious conclusion is that the Council had not yet taken place.[18]

We should not minimize the seriousness of the problem facing those early Christians. As far as we know, Jesus had never ministered among Gentiles apart from the occasional contacts narrated in the gospels, but had lived all his life as a faithful Jew among other Jews. We have no record of his ever querying the necessity for circumcision, a basic requirement for Jewish males. And the gospels show that he kept Jewish feasts. The Judaizers could appeal to his example and argue that it was necessary for all his followers to do as he did with regard to circumcision and the Jewish festal year. It would not have been easy for people to take the Pauline line in such matters.

We should bear in mind Ralph Martin's point that 'a discussion on the admissibility of the Gentile believers and the terms of their

[17]*New Testament Survey* (London, 1961), p. 267.

[18]We should also bear in mind the point made by A. Robert and A. Feuillet, who find it 'strange that as solemn and unanimous a decision as that of the Council of Jerusalem could have been followed by issue-dodging of Peter, of Barnabas, and of the Judeo-Christians of Antioch in the essential problem of the relationships between converted Galatians and the Law' (*Introduction to the New Testament* [New York, 1965], p. 411.

inclusion in the church is more appropriate *before* the first missionary journey'. He sees this as having taken place during the famine visit of Acts 9:26–30.[19] It is hardly likely that Christian preachers should have ventured into Gentile territory to preach the gospel without some idea about how their converts were to be integrated into the church. This may not have been a problem for the church in Judea, but when Paul and Barnabas went off from Antioch on their missionary journey, they must have had some idea of what they would demand from those who believed as the result of their preaching. All the more would they have been ready to accept Gentile converts without circumcision because of Peter's contact, including table fellowship, with Cornelius and other Gentiles in that man's house (Acts 10). The innovators were the Judaizers, not Paul and his companions.

It is also difficult to see why Paul should have omitted all reference to the Council's verdict that it was not to be required of Gentile converts to Christianity that they be circumcised and taught to keep the law of Moses (Acts 15:5, 19–21, 28–29). At the highest level Christians had decided that these basic Jewish requirements were not to be imposed on converts. That Paul did not mention this decision surely means that it had not yet taken place, and that in turn means that Galatians is early, probably the first of Paul's surviving letters.[20] It is not easy to put a date on it, and discussion of such matters would take us far afield. Suffice to say that some time in the late 40s or early 50s of our era is not improbable. G. Ogg dates the conversion of Paul in AD 35 or 34,[21] and Paul's reference to going up to Jerusalem 'after fourteen years' (Gal. 2:1) takes us on to AD 49 (or 48). If he wrote shortly after this visit we again come to the early 50s (or possibly 49). B. W. Bacon thought of a date around 50;[22] S. A. Cartledge suggests 'about 48 AD' (*op. cit.,* p. 112). Somewhere about AD 50 is about as close as we can get.

---

[19]*New Testament Foundations,* II (Exeter, 1978), p. 150.

[20]F. F. Bruce argues that 'Galatians is the earliest among the extant epistles of Paul'. He goes on, 'I know of no evidence to make this conclusion impossible, or even improbable. Even on this early dating, Paul has been a Christian for at least fifteen years, and the main outlines of his understanding of the gospel would have been as well defined as ever they were likely to be' (*BJRL,* 54, 1972, p. 267). For an impressive list of scholars who have supported this dating, see his commentary on Galatians, p. 55, n. 56.

[21]*The Chronology of the Life of Paul* (London, 1968), p. 30.

[22]*The Making of the New Testament* (London, n. d.), p. 56.

The nature of the opposition to Paul

Paul refers to people who opposed him in every chapter of this letter (1:6–7; 2:4–5; 3:1; 4:17; 5:7–12; 6:12–13). It is clear that he was very perturbed by this opposition, but it is not so clear exactly who these people were whom Paul castigates as those 'who trouble you' (1:7; *cf.* 5:10) or precisely how we should understand the positions they took up. We can say the following things about them.

1. They were people who professed to be believers but whom Paul saw as 'false brothers' who 'infiltrated' the group of Christians to spy out the freedom they had in Christ. They aimed at bringing these believers into bondage (2:4).

2. They preached 'a different gospel' which Paul rejected as no gospel at all. He saw it as an attempt to trouble the believers and to overthrow the gospel of Christ (1:7). He invokes a curse (*anathema*) on anyone who preaches any other gospel, be it one of his party or an angel from heaven (1:6–9).

3. The false teachers were intent on detaching the believers from their allegiance to Paul so that they might become zealous for these new teachers (4:17).

4. This activity looked like a bewitching of the believers (3:1). In the face of this, Paul reminds them that they have received the gift of the Holy Spirit, given to them because they believed and not on account of any keeping of the law. Having begun with the Holy Spirit, he asks whether they can go on in the flesh to completeness (3:1–3).

5. Paul asks what has hindered his converts from obeying the truth and says that the persuasion the converts have been receiving is not 'from him who called you' (1:6). He reminds them that a little leaven works its way through the whole mass of dough (5:9). He goes on to ask why he is persecuted if he preaches circumcision (which makes it appear that he had been accused of this). If he did preach circumcision, then 'the offence of the cross has ceased' (5:11), and this leads into the wish that those who were troubling the converts would mutilate themselves.

6. The last passage dealing with the false teachers accuses them of wishing to make a good impression and of circumcising believers, but only in order to avoid being persecuted for the cross of Christ (6:12–13). Paul says that those who are advocating circumcision do not in fact keep the law but wish to boast in the converts' flesh. The apostle refuses to boast except in the cross of Christ and goes on to say that there is no particular merit in either circumcision or uncircumcision.

7. Some passages show that the false teachers were trying to introduce Jewish teachings, such as the necessity for circumcision (6:12–13; *cf.* 5:2–3). The reference to keeping days, months, *etc.* (4:10), appears to refer to the Jewish sacred calendar.

A number of suggestions have been made as to the identity of these opponents of the apostle. Some have seen the local Jews, others a group of Jews who originated in Judea. Some have seen more than one group of opponents, part of the opposition being from Jewish converts and part from Gentile converts. And there are other views.[23]

The traditional view is that the trouble began with converts to Christianity who felt that people like Paul were going too far from Judaism. After all, the sacred books of the Christians were those that the Jews accepted as authoritative, and these books did things like command circumcision. There is quite an emphasis on 'flesh' in the latter part of the letter (5:13, 16–17, 19; 6:12–13), and it is not unlikely that Paul's opponents suggested that in view of the difficulty of living the Christian life it would be well to place themselves under the shelter of the Sinai covenant by accepting the law with its demand for circumcision.[24] It would seem that they taught that it was all very well to listen to Paul as a first step. But to go on in the Christian way meant, for them, the acceptance of such Old Testament commands as that to circumcise their members. Paul saw that to add obedience to the ritual commands of the Old Testament was to make a mockery of the Christian teaching that the cross of Christ is the means of bringing salvation to all who believe.[25]

It seems that Paul was also accused of being inconsistent: he called on the Galatians to have nothing to do with Jewish practices, but he himself was a Jew and sometimes conformed to Jewish customs. Thus at a later time than this the leaders of the church in Jerusalem

[23]Cousar lists five potential groups: Jewish Christians from Jerusalem, Jewish Christians with no support from Jerusalem, Jewish Christians with gnostic views, Gentile Christians who felt that Paul's teaching had departed from its Jewish base, and the final group composed partly of Judaizers who wanted submission to the law and partly of radicals who 'felt themselves exempt from moral issues' (Cousar, p. 5).

[24]*Cf.* Betz, 'The Galatians had been given the "Spirit" and "freedom," but they were left to that Spirit and freedom. There was no law to tell them what was right or wrong. There were no more rituals to correct transgressions' (p. 9). Such considerations may have helped them look favourably on Judaism.

[25]'The picture we get of the Judaizers from all parts of the New Testament is one of a sincere, zealous, energetic (and, it must be said, unscrupulous) group of men, bent on carrying through their conviction at all costs. The only possible position to take which was true to the Christian Gospel was the one taken by St Paul, which was, in effect, that the Jewish law had no claim of any kind on Christians' (Hamann, p. 9).

suggested that Paul conform to Jewish custom in order to refute a slander that he taught apostasy from Moses, and the apostle agreed to take part in a Jewish ceremonial that involved his joining in purification rites with four men who were under a vow (Acts 21:21ff.). Something like this may be behind his words in 5:11, 'If I still preach circumcision, why am I still being persecuted?' Apparently his adherence to some Jewish practices on occasion was made the point of sharp criticisms by his opponents. As Bruce puts it, 'Jewish worship in the pre-Christian stage of God's dealings with men was far from being culpable – it was divinely instituted – but it had the character of infancy and immaturity as compared with the coming of age into which men were introduced by faith in Christ' (p. 30). It was this that Paul's opponents could not see.

The literary genre

Galatians comes to us in the form of a letter. In antiquity, however, the letter could be a recognized form of writing when there was no serious intention of making it a true letter, sent to real people. It might serve to convey teaching meant for a wide circle and not merely for the person or persons to whom it was nominally addressed. But by common consent Galatians is a real letter, sent to real people. The fact that we may study it to our profit centuries after it was written is evidence of the continuing value of the instruction it conveys to people far removed from its first recipients. But it does not alter the fact that it is a real letter.

Serious writing from antiquity brings us many letters, but so do the papyri which contain letters from poor people, often with no literary skills. Some things are common to letters generally, for example, the fact that a letter in the area in which we are interested began with the name of the writer, followed by 'to' plus the name of the recipient (occasionally these appear in the reverse order). There could be brief descriptions of the writer or the recipient or both, especially if the letter was to go to an important person. Before the communication the writer wishes to convey there might be a little prayer.

A. Deissmann made a close study of the letters in the papyri, which, of course, are originals, not copies made later by scribes as is the position with other works that come down to us from antiquity. There are quite a few of these literary letters, and scholars have debated how far Paul conforms to this model. Perhaps we could sum it up by saying that he uses the letter form that was common among ordinary people, but modifies it in ways that bring out important spiritual truths.[26]

The contribution of Galatians to Christian thought

Galatians is a passionate letter, the outpouring of the soul of a preacher on fire for his Lord and deeply committed to bringing his hearers to an understanding of what saving faith is. Together with Barnabas, Paul had been responsible for founding the Christian congregations to which he is writing, and it grieved him beyond measure when some of those churches departed or were in the process of departing from the essentials of the gospel.[27] We discover from this letter that, after Paul and his helpers went away from Galatia, other people came in professing to be Christian teachers and able to take the new converts along to a further stage in their Christian career and to a better understanding of what faith in Christ means. They apparently taught the new converts (with their imperfect understanding of the Christian way) that they had made a good start, but that to progress in the Christian faith they must follow the example of the original apostles. That meant, as they taught it, that believers must be circumcised as all the apostles were (even Paul!), and that they must take seriously the law revealed in the Old Testament. The gospel Paul had preached was all right as a beginning, they apparently said, but to be mature Christians the law in all its fullness must be followed. Was not the law clearly laid down in the Old Testament, the holy Scripture that even Paul held to be inspired and sacred?

We do not know how or when Paul heard what was going on. But from the white-hot tone of Galatians it was not long before he wrote this letter. It was crystal clear to the apostle that these new teachings cut at the very heart of the gospel. So without delay he wrote this letter to make it very plain that the gospel is not another way of imposing the law on people. Apparently the teachers Paul was opposing placed the keeping of the law revealed in Scripture as at the heart of the Christian way, whereas Paul saw the gospel as emphasizing the

[26]Longenecker has a valuable discussion and a useful bibliography in a section of his commentary entitled 'Epistolary and Rhetorical Structures' (pp. c–cxix).

[27]Galatians 'is the passionate outpouring of the Apostle's soul in vindication of the Gospel, which he has been commissioned to preach, and of the faith, which has made all things new for himself' (F. B. Clogg, *An Introduction to the New Testament* [London, 1940], p. 42).

reception of God's free gift. The gospel is about the faith that means trusting God and not relying on our own efforts.[28]

Throughout the epistle Paul points the Galatians to the centrality of the cross. He cannot wait to make this plain, and we find a reference to it in his very first sentence. After the usual words about the sender and the recipients, Paul goes on, 'Grace to you and peace from God our Father and the Lord Jesus Christ, who gave himself for our sins' (1:3–4). And as he comes close to the end of his letter he declines to boast 'except in the cross of our Lord Jesus Christ, through whom the world has been crucified to me and I to the world' (6:14). Right through his letter he insists that the cross is central to the Christian message. Paul does not object to Jewish Christians keeping the law as part of the way they served God. Indeed, on occasion he himself could comply with its provisions (Acts 21:20–26). But insisting on the law as binding on Gentile converts was quite another thing.

That the cross is absolutely central means that the keeping of the law cannot be imposed on Gentile believers. The teachers Paul was opposing apparently did not grasp this. They were insisting that all converts must keep the whole law. The law was part of revealed Scripture and they saw it as binding on all. The law was at the heart of God's purpose, they thought, and this for Gentile believers as for Jews.[29] Paul does not denigrate the law. It was divinely given and it was regarded as a great treasure by Israelites in general, and Paul in particular. Paul sees it as very important. But it is not the way to salvation.[30] To see the law as divinely given and as an incomparable guide to the way we should live out our salvation is one thing, but it is quite another to affirm that anyone's salvation hangs on the way he or she keeps the law.

Circumcision evidently loomed large in the discussions. Paul uses the noun 7 times in this letter, and the verb 'to circumcise' 6 times. It was not that he had anything against the practice. He himself was circumcised, of course, and we find from Acts that he circumcised Timothy (Acts 16:3). But this was not a way of winning salvation for

---

[28]'The Law could not bring men to God; indeed, the Law is an afterthought in the working-out of the divine purpose. It is no positive aid to righteousness, it puts men under condemnation and a curse' (Clogg, *ibid.*, p. 44).

[29]'Law' is a principal concern throughout the letter. Paul uses the term *nomos*, 'law', 32 times in these 6 chapters, a total exceeded in the New Testament only by Romans (which has it 72 times in its 16 chapters). Clearly it had a great deal of importance for the Galatians.

[30]'The Letter to the Galatians is the one that most clearly makes the antithesis between law and faith in Christ the standard for Christianity' (Lührmann, p. 4).

that disciple. It was a means of commending him among Jewish hearers of the gospel when they heard it proclaimed by a young man whose mother was Jewish. It was not to be understood as meaning that circumcision was necessary for Christians. Paul insisted that 'in Christ Jesus neither circumcision nor uncircumcision is of any force' (5:6; *cf.* 6:15). He points out that important apostles, 'James, Peter and John', gave to him and Barnabas 'the right hands of fellowship' that they should go to the Gentiles (2:9). These leaders did not see circumcision as necessary for Gentile converts.

In this letter Paul uses the word for 'flesh' 18 times, which is quite a lot in 6 chapters. Sometimes he uses it in a neutral fashion, as when he says that he lives 'in the flesh' (2:20), but more often he employs it pejoratively: for example, 'having made a beginning in the Spirit, are you now being perfected in the flesh?' (3:3). Relying on the Spirit and relying on the flesh are mutually exclusive (5:17). The 'fruit of the Spirit' is contrasted with 'the works of the flesh' (5:19–23), which, as Paul lists them, are all evil. It is clear that Paul sees this bodily life as necessarily subjected to temptations from 'the flesh'. But it is equally clear that he sees that anyone who believes has victory over such temptations because the Spirit of God dwells in every believer.

Paul not only opposes evils like 'the flesh', but throughout this epistle he exults in the glorious victory that Christ has won for all the faithful. He has several ways of doing this. Thus he keeps referring to 'faith', and uses the term 22 times, which is more than in any other New Testament book except Romans (which has it 40 times) and Hebrews (32 times). He quotes Habbakuk (as also in Rom. 1:17), 'he that is just by faith will live', or, 'he that is just will live by faith' (3:11; the quotation is from Hab. 2:4). This puts justification by faith right at the centre of Christian thinking and living. In chapter 3 he has the noun 'faith' 14 times, a striking concentration on the importance of faith for those who wish to live the Christian life.

As he does this he seizes on the example of Abraham (3:7, 9) who is for Paul a striking example of the importance of faith (*cf.* Rom. 1:17). Nine times in this short epistle he appeals to the example of the patriarch (the same number as in Romans; it is a striking number in so short a letter). He draws attention to Abraham's faith rather than to any of the deeds of this great man. Paul leaves the reader in no doubt as to the importance of living by faith.[31]

---

[31]Brevard S. Childs argues for a 'canonical' approach to this letter as to other parts of Scripture, as a result of which he comes up with two important conclusions: 'The Galatians are historical representatives of an erroneous alternative offered by the law.

With this we should take the idea of justification, which, of course, for Paul is by faith. The apostle insists that no-one is justified by 'works of law' but only 'through faith in Jesus Christ' (2:16). In this one verse, Paul twice says that people are not justified 'by works of law' and insists that 'we' ('we' is emphatic) 'believed in Christ Jesus so that we might be justified by faith in Christ', and goes on to say that 'by works of law shall no flesh be justified'. He later makes reference to the faith of Abraham and draws the conclusion that it is those who believe who are justified. He says that Scripture foresaw that God would justify the Gentiles by faith and promised beforehand that all the nations would be blessed through him (3:6–8). It is 'those who are of faith' who 'are blessed with faithful Abraham' (3:9).

Another way of bringing out the freeness of the gift of God is to speak of promise, and this Paul does eight times in chapter 3 and twice elsewhere. He speaks of the promises made to Abraham (3:16), and points out that a promise made 430 years before the giving of the law is not rendered void by the coming of the law (3:17). He tells his readers that law and promise are contradictory: if the inheritance were to be by law-keeping it would no longer be due to a promise, but God has given it freely to Abraham by a promise (3:18). The gift of the Holy Spirit is another example of the fulfilling of a promise of God (3:14). He strings together a number of important concepts when he says, 'If you are Christ's then you are Abraham's seed, heirs according to promise' (3:29).

They have embraced a way of salvation through works of the law which is opposite in principle from the faith in God who justifies the ungodly . . . By grounding his argument in the faith of Abraham, Paul removes the debate from the sphere of merely contingent history . . . Secondly, Paul's letter sets forth positively the truth of the Gospel, which is constitutive of the Christian faith.' (*The New Testament as Canon* [London, 1984], pp. 308f.).

ANALYSIS

I. Introduction, 1:1–5

II. The gospel, 1:6 – 2:21
  1. The 'different' gospel the Galatians preached, 1:6–10
  2. Paul's experience of the gospel, 1:11–24
  3. Paul's agreement with the Jerusalem church, 2:1–10
  4. Paul's clash with Peter, 2:11–14
  5. Justification by faith alone, 2:15–21

III. A Christian view of the law, 3:1 – 4:31
  1. The experience of the Galatian Christians, 3:1–5
  2. Abraham, 3:6–9
  3. No-one is justified by the law, 3:10–14
  4. Covenant, 3:15–22
  5. The law our tutor, 3:23–29
  6. Sons of God, 4:1–7
  7. The beggarly elements, 4:8–11
  8. Paul's perplexity, 4:12–20
  9. Two covenants, 4:21–31

IV. Christian freedom, 5:1 – 6:10
  1. Freedom and the bondage of circumcision, 5:1–12
  2. Love, 5:13–15
  3. The Spirit and the flesh, 5:16–26
  4. Mutual helpfulness, 6:1–10

V. Conclusion, 6:11–18

GALATIANS 1

I. Introduction, 1:1–5

[1]*Paul an apostle, not from men or through a man but through Jesus Christ and God the Father who raised him from the dead,* [2]*and all the brothers who are with me, to the churches of Galatia:* [3]*Grace to you and peace from God our Father and the Lord Jesus Christ,* [4]*who gave himself for our sins, in order that he might deliver us from the present evil age according to the will of our God the Father,* [5]*to whom be glory for ever and ever, amen.*

Every age has had its conventions about letter writing. For example, we begin a letter with our address and the date and end it by assuring our correspondent that we are 'yours faithfully' or 'yours sincerely' or the like before we append our signature. In the first-century Roman Empire the custom was to begin with the name of the writer and proceed with the name of the recipient and a greeting: 'A to B, greeting'. There is an example in Acts 23:36. There might be a short description of either or both, especially of the recipient. Sometimes this was followed by a short prayer.

1. Paul generally follows the usual pattern, but he makes his own modifications. Thus in the present letter he opens in the first person (*Paul ... and all the brothers who are with me*), whereas normally correspondents used the third person. As a Roman citizen, Paul would have had three names, but he never uses the other two and we do not know what they were. Longenecker points out that this use of one name 'would have been acceptable to both Greeks and Romans without bringing in any nuance as to status'. His Hebrew name was Saul (Acts 13:9), but in his letters he always has the form Paul.

He generally uses the conventional framework to bring out significant Christian teaching, and he does that here. Thus he qualifies his name by describing himself as *an apostle*.[1] The word means 'someone sent', 'a messenger'. It was used of an ordinary messenger

---

[1]I have examined the term *apostle* in *Ministers of God* (London, 1964), pp. 39–61. Many commentators draw attention to the Jewish *šālîaḥ* and even see the origins of the Christian apostolate there. But we should be clear that there is no good reason for seeing this Jewish messenger as behind the apostolate. Despite the confident assertions of some, it is not at all certain that the *šālîaḥ* was as early as New Testament

but also of an ambassador, an envoy, the commander of a naval force or the naval squadron itself (see LSJ). In the Christian church it was applied first to the twelve whom Jesus called to be his close associates. In due course the church recognized a few more such as James, the brother of Jesus (see 1:19). But the important thing about the apostolate is not any ecclesiastical recognition (some of the Galatians did not recognize Paul's apostleship), but the fact that its members owed their position to divine appointment. Paul says plainly that he was an apostle *not from men or through a man*, and he goes on, *but through Jesus Christ and God the Father*. It was vital for Paul that he owed his position to divine initiative and action. Being an apostle was important. Perhaps we should add that there is a reference to apostles 'of the churches' (2 Cor. 8:23), which probably means emissaries sent out on behalf of a church or churches. They do not seem to have been apostles in the sense in which Paul normally uses the term. Clearly there were not many apostles with divine appointment, and those few were highly esteemed.

We do not know exactly when Paul became an apostle but it must have been very early. His conversion seems to have taken place in AD 34 or 35,[2] which is pretty close to the time of the death of Jesus. He must have become an apostle not long after that. He uses the term of himself 15 times, and clearly he saw the word as important for an understanding of what he was doing for Christ. In addition to these 15 uses he often refers to the apostles generally. In all he uses the word 34 times, which is more than any other New Testament writer. (It is found 79 times in the New Testament, Acts, with 28, being next to Paul.) Paul mostly treats the word as well known and does not say who did the sending, but here he makes something of an explanation. His apostleship, he says, was *not from men or through a man*. It is important for him that apostleship was not of human origin.[3] Not only did apostleship not originate from a human source, but it is not *through a*

---

times (for this term see my *Ministers of God*, pp. 114–118). And in any case there were significant differences. A *šālîaḥ* was not a religious functionary, but a secular one, a person sent on a specific errand; once that task was fulfilled his commission was finished. There is nothing like the lifetime commitment of the New Testament apostle. Nor is there anything of the missionary about the *šālîaḥ*, as there was about the apostle.

[2]George Ogg surveys the evidence and concludes, 'Paul's conversion can hardly have taken place later than AD 35 and must be dated either in that year or, less probably, in AD 34' (*The Chronology of the Life of Paul* [London, 1968], p. 30).

[3]*From men, ap' anthrōpōn*, would signify that apostleship was of human appointment. It is this that Paul denies.

man,[4] which negates any view that the divine gift might be conveyed through some human channel. Paul is emphatically repudiating any idea that apostleship was inextricably tied to any human source. We are not to think of any man or men as originating apostleship. Nor, after Jesus originated it, was it conveyed by any human agency.

Apostleship then is of divine origin. It is not *through* any man *but*[5] *through Jesus Christ and God the Father*. Right at the outset Paul wants there to be no doubt about his credentials; he had been appointed to his place as apostle by none less that *Jesus Christ and God the Father*. The preposition *through* covers both divine persons, and the use of one preposition emphasizes the unity of the Father and the Son in making the gift.[6] We should probably relate this insistence of his divine appointment to the situation in Galatia. Clearly some in the Galatian churches had belittled Paul, and he begins his letter by reminding them of his credentials.[7] Barclay conjectures that some of the Galatians had heard of Paul's life when he 'had been the most savage of all persecutors of the Church'; such a man, they would think, could never become a Christian preacher. But God had done what humanity could never do: he had transformed this persecutor and made an apostle out of him. Stott points out that Paul's vigorous defence of his apostleship arose not from vanity or pique but 'because the gospel that he preached was at stake' (p. 14). The denial that Paul was an apostle meant also the denial that the gospel he preached was from God.

The unanswerable response to this was that it was Christ who had called him to be an apostle. Paul uses the word *Jesus* 213 times (18 in Galatians) and *Christ* 379 times (37 in this letter). The combination of the two divine names emphasizes his point that his apostleship did not originate in any human activity. Some people in the church were

---

[4]*Di' anthrōpou* (which we could, of course, translate as 'through man'), where there is a change from plural to singular as well as a change of preposition. Robertson says that here 'Paul covers source and agency in his denial of man's control of his apostleship by the use of *apo* and *dia*' (p. 567).

[5]*But* is the strong adversative, *alla*. Machen draws attention to the importance of 'not through a man but through Jesus Christ' (pp. 13ff.). This is not argued but taken for granted. Paul can assume that the Galatians, though in his view in error in important matters, would yet agree that Jesus Christ was more than a mere man.

[6]Burton points out that had he written *apo Iēsou Christou kai theou patros*, this would have conveyed the meaning of the joint source, but 'it would have left open the possibility of a human channel'. *Dia* makes it clear that the gift was direct from God and Christ and that there was no human channel.

[7]Hendriksen sees here the meaning that 'Jesus Christ *in person* had invested him with this high distinction. Hence, Paul is an apostle *through* – not only *from* – Jesus Christ.'

strongly opposed to Paul, and he loses no time in this letter in making it clear that he did not owe his position to them or to any human appointment, but to God alone. 'Jesus' is of course the human name, the name the angel told Joseph to call the baby (Mt. 1:21). It is the Greek form of Joshua, a Hebrew name meaning 'Yahweh is salvation'; the name stresses his function as Saviour (*cf.* Mt. 1:21). 'Christ' means 'anointed' and is equivalent to 'Messiah', the one chosen out by God for important work. Paul uses the term 379 times, out of 529 times in the New Testament. He is thus far and away the most frequent user of the term, and it is to Paul that we owe our habit of referring to our Saviour simply as 'Christ'. His greeting then makes it clear that he writes in full consciousness that he has been given a divine commissioning of the highest order. *Who raised him from the dead* points to the central importance of the resurrection.[8] At the heart of Christianity is the atonement that Christ wrought in his death to put away sins, and the resurrection is part of that atoning work: the Father set the seal on the atoning work of the Son in that he raised him from the dead. This emphasis on the divine origin of his apostolate is important for Paul, and it may here reflect the contention of his opponents that he was commissioned only by human authority.

2. Paul joins with him in his opening salutation *all the brothers who are with me. Brother* was the term used for a fellow Christian, but unfortunately we do not know who these *brothers* were or even where they were. But evidently the Galatians could be trusted to know and to value greetings from the people in question. Fung thinks that the expression reflects 'Paul's desire to indicate to the Galatians that his gospel is no personal idiosyncracy, but something shared by his colleagues.' Paul mostly associates others with him in his opening salutations (the exceptions are Romans, Ephesians and the very personal pastoral epistles). *All* makes it comprehensive; quite a few people would have been included. This does not mean that they had a hand in composing the letter; we need not doubt that it was written by Paul himself. But they would have approved what Paul was doing and doubtless were pleased to be associated with the great apostle. It is usually agreed that the expression refers to the group of fellow workers associated with Paul, but Ramsay argues that the expression

---

[8]Hamann finds Paul's reference to the resurrection natural, 'for not only would there be no apostles – in fact, no Christ, no Christianity at all – without the resurrection; what made any one an apostle was just this: he had seen the risen Christ, and could bear witness to the resurrection (Acts 1:22)'.

points to a whole church, and, further, that in this case the church was that at Antioch (p. 242). This, however, seems unlikely. Paul's immediate associates are much more probable.[9]

To the churches[10] *of Galatia* indicates that there were quite a few recipients of the letter. As we do not know which Galatian centres had churches at this time, or even how many churches there were in that area, we do not know precisely who the recipients were. But it is clear that Paul intended his words to have a wide circulation in the region of Galatia. The letter would be taken to each centre and read there, or several copies would be made and one taken to each church. But perhaps Paul's reference to the 'large letters' he wrote (6:11) indicates that the one copy went round all the churches rather than that several copies were made and one sent to each church. Paul normally says something complimentary in his opening greeting to a church, but there is here no reference to the faithful brothers or the like. The absence of such an expression probably reflects the difficulties that had arisen between him and the churches of Galatia. 'He is too deeply distressed for compliments' (Allan).

3. Paul commonly links *grace* and *peace* in his epistolary salutations. Both are important words for the apostle. He uses the word *grace* 100 times, whereas it occurs in all the rest of the New Testament only 55 times. It is very much a Pauline word. It is akin to that for 'joy',[11] and fundamentally means 'that which brings about joy'. In the Christian context there is nothing that brings joy like what God has done in Christ for us, so grace has become a very important Christian concept. Sometimes grace is associated with Christ, as in the well-known and well-used blessing, 'The grace of our Lord Jesus Christ and the love of God . . .' Sometimes it is linked with the Father, as in the expression 'the grace of God' (Acts 11:23; Gal. 2:21). Here we are reminded that the Father and the Son are united in the grace they exercise towards us.[12]

---

[9]REB has 'I and all the friends now with me send greetings', to which the comment of Betz on the similar NEB is applicable: 'This paraphrase has changed the text and has assimilated it to Greek style and culture.'

[10]*Ekklēsia* was not a religious term, but the word for a secular assembly (*cf.* Acts 19:39, 41). The regular use of this term by the Christians sets them apart from the usual run of religious gatherings.

[11]'Joy' is *chara* and 'grace' *charis*. Paul uses *chara* 21 times out of a New Testament total of 59. It is found only once in Galatians, but *charis* occurs 7 times in this epistle.

[12]The MSS are divided as to whether we should read *hēmon* with *patros* or with *kyriou*, and there is a good manuscript support for each reading. As the term is more commonly associated with 'Lord' in the New Testament, we should probably take it

With 'grace' Paul links *peace*. This was the normal Jewish greeting, but Paul uses the term more widely than as a formula of greeting. He has it more than anyone else in the New Testament (43 times, out of 91 in the New Testament; next is Luke with 13), and he makes it one of the great Christian words. 'The peace of God' meant a great deal to this apostle, drawing attention as it does to the truth that those who trust in Christ are no longer the objects of the divine wrath. As Christ has put away our sins he has made peace for us, peace with God and peace with our fellows. Paul's use of peace reminds us that sinners are opposed to God and are the objects of his wrath. But Jesus has put away that wrath in bringing about propitiation for our sins (Rom. 3:25). Now we enjoy peace with God and from that there flows peace with people. The believer, trusting God for full salvation, no longer fears to face God and no longer cherishes wrath against other people. Peace flows through the life of those who trust Christ for full salvation.[13]

Paul speaks of Jesus Christ as 'Lord'. This is another Pauline word (275 times), and the frequency with which the apostle used it shows us something of the importance he attached to it. The word was used in a variety of ways. It could denote the owner of slaves, or it could be used in ordinary society as a polite form of address (like our 'sir'). It was the right way to address a noble or any other exalted person. In the society in which Paul moved, it was used of gods, and indeed in the translation of the Old Testament into Greek it was a word used for the divine name.[14]

4. *Who gave himself for our sins* succinctly refers to the central truth of the gospel. In an opening salutation Paul does not have room for much doctrinal matter and it is revealing that he chooses this as the

---

here with 'Father', reasoning that a scribe would be more likely to move it from 'Father' to 'Lord' than to alter 'our Lord' to 'our Father'.

[13]Luther comments, 'These two words, grace and peace, do contain in them the whole sum of Christianity. Grace containeth the remission of sins, peace a quiet and joyful conscience.'

[14]Some hold that in the earliest days scribes wrote the Hebrew name without translating it. But it seems more likely that 'Lord' was used. Joseph A. Fitzmyer argues that the evidence shows that the Palestinian Jews did use 'Lord' when referring to Yahweh. He says, 'the transfer of that title to Jesus undoubtedly took place on Palestinian soil itself. It would thus mean that the primitive confession "Jesus is Lord" (1 Cor 12:3; Rom 10:9) was a response to the early kerygma itself and was not then a product of missionary activity during the evangelization of the eastern Mediterranean' (*The Gospel According to Luke [I–IX]* [New York, 1981], p. 202). In verse 1 Paul has the order 'Jesus Christ and God the Father', but here he inverts it, which, Boice says, 'heightens the effect' and is 'a good statement of the full divinity of Jesus'.

truth to emphasize. In this letter we may be right in discerning an early blow against legalists.[15] The essential Christian message is concerned with Christ's sacrifice of himself, not with our conformity to the law. Paul does not say when or how Jesus *gave himself*, but clearly he is referring to Jesus' laying down of his life on Calvary's cross. That was the central truth of the gospel and Paul does not miss any opportunity to emphasize it. From another angle he can say that God gave him up (Rom. 8:32), or that Christ 'was given up' (Rom. 4:25). *For our sins* points us to the purpose of Christ's sacrifice of himself. It was to deal with the problem posed by our wrongdoings. By dying in the place of sinners Jesus took away our sins. Cousar speaks of 'the extraordinary radicality' of this expression and says that it implies 'among other things, that as our representative he has actually taken our place and assumed the responsibility for our irresponsibility, our complicity in the oppression of the weak, all our personal failures'.

The purpose of that sacrifice of himself was *in order that*[16] *he might deliver*[17] *us from the present evil age*. The Jews had the idea of two ages, the present age and the age to come, and the Christians took over this idea.[18] The deliverance is seen as thoroughgoing (*cf*. Rom. 12:2). Paul regards the 'age' in which he lived as evil; we should probably see this as referring not to the precise first-century years in which the apostle lived, but to this present world system, the present age in contrast to the age to come (so BAGD; *cf*. Jn. 5:19). Christians are not meant to live in bondage to the ideas and the manner of life of those among whom they find themselves. Christ died to deliver them from such bondage. And he did it in full accordance with *the will of our God and Father*. The atoning death of Jesus 'was not merely something which God had *permitted*, it was something which God the Father had *willed*' (Duncan). God wills something better for his people than an unthinking conformity to the worldliness of the age in which they find themselves.

Bruce points out that this is probably the earliest written statement in the New Testament about the significance of Christ's death. He

---

[15]Osiek begins her commentary on this epistle by saying, 'Galatians is a letter that is concerned from start to finish with a question that is timely in any age; the freedom of the Christian.'

[16]*Hopōs*. Paul mostly uses *hina*, but there seems no appreciable difference. The conjunction denotes purpose.

[17]The verb is *exaireō*, here only in Paul. It is used of plucking out the right eye in Mt. 5:29, and of Yahweh's deliverance of the nation in Acts 7:34.

[18]H. Sasse has a very useful discussion of the two ages, *TDNT*, I, pp. 204–207.

points out also that as early as AD 50 Paul 'delivered' to the Corinthians 'as part of the gospel which he had "received" and which he shared with the leaders of the Jerusalem church, "that Christ died for our sins in accordance with the Scriptures" (1 Cor. 15:3)'. We should be clear that this teaching is not a late development, but is found as early as we can discern what the message was that the Christians proclaimed.

5. Paul finishes his opening with a little doxology (the only doxology in Paul's openings to letters). To the Father of whom he has been speaking he ascribes *glory*, a concept of which he is fond (he uses it in all 77 times), but this is the only time he uses it in this epistle. Here it refers to the majesty, the splendour, of God. Its permanence is brought out with the conclusion, *for ever and ever, amen.* This is often the conclusion to a prayer, and it makes a very suitable conclusion to this introduction to the epistle. *Amen* is the participle from the Hebrew verb meaning 'to confirm'. It is taken over by the New Testament writers as a suitable way of bringing a prayer to its close. As we notice what Paul has said in this opening,[19] it is proper that we should also notice what is not said. Paul usually has a thanksgiving for some aspect of the life of the churches to which he writes, and its absence from this opening is perhaps due to his concern over what was amiss in Galatia.

II. The gospel, 1:6 – 2:21

For Paul, what was at stake was the very heart of the gospel. It was clear to him that what the Galatians were doing meant abandoning the gospel of grace and substituting for it a religion of good works. He begins his argument then by showing that what the Galatians were putting forward as the essence of Christianity was not the gospel the apostles proclaimed but 'a different gospel'. Then he goes on to show that he is in agreement with the apostles in Jerusalem on the essentials of the genuine gospel. Specifically he makes it plain that the gospel message is not an exhortation to earn one's salvation by keeping the law.

---

[19]Boice says of the opening to this epistle, 'In these few verses the three major themes of the letter – the source of authority in religion, the doctrine of grace, and the promise of full deliverance from sin's power – are tied together in a way that relates all solely to the sovereign and gracious will of God.'

1. The 'different' gospel the Galatians preached, 1:6–10

[6]*I marvel that you are so quickly turning away from him who called you in Christ's grace for a different gospel* [7]*which is not another, only there are some who trouble you and will to pervert the gospel of the Christ.* [8]*But even if we or an angel from heaven should preach to you a gospel contrary to that which we preached to you, let him be accursed.* [9]*As we said before, so also now I say again, let him be accursed; if anyone preaches to you a gospel other than the one you received, let him be accursed.*

[10]*Am I now trying to appeal to men, or God? Or am I seeking to please men? If it were men I were seeking to please I would not be Christ's slave.*

6. At this point in a letter Paul normally has something like a thanksgiving for his readers or an expression of pleasure at their progress in the faith. This is the one letter which lacks such a thanksgiving. This is in sharp contrast to what we see in other epistles. For example, though he castigates the Corinthian believers in strong terms, Paul begins his letter to them by paying his tribute to the manifestation of the grace of God in their lives (1 Cor. 1:4ff.). But here Paul has what Duncan calls 'an abrupt and passionate outburst, not softened in the Greek even by an introductory particle'. The apostle cannot wait to begin his denunciation of those who were trying to cause the Galatians to depart from the heart of the gospel. For Paul, what God had done in Christ was absolutely central. The cross meant that the death of the Saviour brought life to all who put their trust in him. Salvation comes by God's free grace, and anything that obscures this is to be opposed vigorously. What troubled him about the Galatians was that they were obscuring this truth.[20]

Here Paul writes *I marvel*, where his verb indicates amazement.[21] He had not anticipated that the Galatians who had so cheerfully accepted the gospel would so quickly be found turning away from its essential meaning into a form of religion that rejected the heart of the gospel. *I*

---

[20]*Cf.* Allan, 'Here Paul states abruptly his fundamental contention, that to make salvation depend on anything but the sheer grace of God in Christ is to replace the Gospel by a religion which is a perversion of the Gospel.'

[21]Meyer comments that the word is 'often used by Greek orators in the sense of surprise at something *blameworthy*.' See Betz, p. 47, n. 39, for references to this usage in Greek literature.

marvel, he says, *that you are so quickly[22] turning away . . . for a different gospel*. As Stott puts it, 'They are religious turncoats, spiritual deserters.' Plainly the apostle was deeply perturbed at what his correspondents were doing and which he characterizes as removing to a different gospel.[23] But we should notice his use of the present tense in the verb *are . . . turning away*. He is not referring to a process that had been completed, but to one that was in the course of taking place.[24] In place of the gospel of God's free grace (the message that God in Christ has done everything necessary for our salvation so that we receive it as a free gift) they were beginning to pervert the message they had earlier accepted.

Paul says that they are turning away *from him who called you*. Some have understood this to mean that they were turning away from Paul, but in this letter the call is from God (*cf.* 1:15; 5:8; *cf.* Rom. 8:30), and that is surely the sense of it here. This allegation would have seemed surprising to the Galatians as it has been ever since to others who have added their own requirements to the gospel message. But as Cousar succinctly puts it. 'To abandon the gospel is to forsake God', and he draws attention to 5:4. The Galatians were now coming to understand Christianity as a force of divine demand for merit (*i.e.* we must add something to what Christ has done). When we see 'religion' as basically a demand for keeping the law of God we are denying the great truth at the heart of the gospel, namely that God saves us by sheer grace. For Paul it was astonishing that people he had evangelized should make such a mistake.

Barclay brings out the point in this way: 'But look what Paul is saying – he is holding up the Cross and he is saying, "God loved you like that." And so religion becomes a matter, not of satisfying the claims of *law*, but of trying to meet the obligations of *love* . . . But all that Paul's Jewish opponents could see was that Paul had declared that circumcision was no longer necessary, and that the law was no longer relevant.'

He speaks of their conversion in terms of a call *in Christ's grace*. We

---

[22]Schmoller remarks that this might mean 'so soon . . . 1) after conversion, or 2) after his visit, or 3) after the false teachers came; all three may be included, and are true'.

[23]*Euangelion* and the corresponding verb, *euangelizein*, each occur 7 times in this letter, which is a high proportion in 6 chapters. Clearly the gospel is one of the important themes of the letter. Bruce has an article on 'The "Other" Gospel' (*BJRL*, 53, 1971, pp. 253–271).

[24]*Cf.* Burton, 'The present tense of the verb *metatithesthe* indicates clearly that when the apostle wrote the apostasy of the Galatians was as yet only in process. They were, so to speak, on the point, or more exactly in the very act, of turning.'

should probably understand the call as originating with the Father; sometimes there is the thought of a call from Christ, but mostly the call is from the Father, though, as here, it may be a call to be in Christ.[25] Paul does not see sinners as aware of their plight and strenuously seeking God. On the contrary, they are ready to carry on with their self-centred sinning, looking for nothing but the satisfaction of their personal aims. But the God who sent his Son to die for sinners is a seeking God, and when any sinner passes out of his lostness and comes into the company of the saved it is because God has first called him or her. In almost all of his letters to churches, Paul speaks of God's call, and we find it again in both letters to Timothy. Clearly the divine initiative matters to Paul.

Here we find that the calling is done *in Christ's grace.*[26] As we have already noticed (on 1:3), grace is a characteristically Pauline word and one which calls attention to the freeness and the bounty of God's call. Paul is not saying that the called were nice people before their call and that is why God called them. He is saying that they were sinners, going their own way, but that God called them out of their self-centred sinfulness and freely offered them salvation. But whatever they thought of this at first, they had now moved on to what Paul calls *a different*[27] *gospel*. The apostle also complains to the Corinthians of some who received 'a different gospel' (2 Cor. 11:4),[28] so the Galatians

---

[25]Betz says, 'Contrary to many commentaries, *en* ("in") should not be taken as the "means by which" but as a definition of the situation before God enjoyed by those who were called.'

[26]The MSS differ. Most have 'Christ's grace', but some have 'the grace of Jesus Christ' (or 'Christ Jesus'), others have 'the grace of God', and others again simply 'grace'. A strong argument could be made for simply 'grace', for there would be a great temptation for scribes to say whose grace it was. It is a confused picture, but in view of the strength of the attestation of 'Christ's grace', perhaps it is best to accept this reading.

[27]Robertson cites this passage as one of many where *heteros* means 'one of a different kind' (p. 748); he says that here 'I am bound to insist on a real difference in Gal. 1:6f. The change is made from *heteron* to *allo* for the very reason that Paul is not willing to admit that it is a gospel on the same plane (*allo*) as that preached by him' (p. 747). Elsewhere he says, *par' ho* has the idea of "beyond" and so "contrary to"' (p. 616). Whether we see a difference between *allos* and *heteros* or not, there is here the idea of otherness; the gospel of the Judaizers differs in kind from the true gospel. *Cf.* H. W. Beyer, 'There is no other Gospel; there is only the one Gospel of justification by Christ in faith. Thus the teaching of the Judaizers is not another Gospel, let alone a better. It is no Gospel at all' (*TDNT*, II, pp. 703f.).

[28]Machen points out that the difference between Paul and his opponents 'was the difference between a religion of merit and a religion of grace. The Judaizers' teaching required a man to earn at least part of his salvation by his own keeping of God's law.

were not the only ones to move away from a right faith. The word *gospel* means 'good news', and from the first the Christians used it for the good news of what God has done in Christ to bring about our salvation.[29] As God is the originator, it may be called 'the gospel of God' (1 Thes. 2:2); and as it concerns what Christ has done to bring about our salvation, it may be denoted 'the gospel of Christ' (Rom. 15:19; Mark introduces his book as 'the gospel of Jesus Christ', 1:1), or 'the gospel of [God's] Son' (Rom. 1:9). With reference to its content it may be designated 'the gospel of the kingdom' (Mt. 4:23), and with respect to the preacher Paul says that it is 'my gospel' (Rom. 2:16). Paul is constrained to preach the gospel; 'Woe to me,' he says, 'if I do not preach the gospel' (1 Cor. 9:16). This can entail suffering (2 Tim. 1:8), but Paul sees this as meaningful suffering, not as pointless pain. He tells the Corinthians that the Lord has appointed that those who preach the gospel get their living from the gospel (1 Cor. 9:14), though he adds that he has not availed himself of this privilege (*cf.* also 2 Cor. 11:7–8). The message is 'the gospel of peace' (Eph. 6:15), and Paul can speak of 'the truth of the gospel' (Col. 1:5) and 'the faith of the gospel' (Phil. 1:27). It is the birth of all Christian living, for Paul can say that he has 'begotten' the Corinthian Christians 'through the gospel' (1 Cor. 4:15). People are 'called' through the gospel (2 Thes. 2:14), and obedience to it is the way we escape from eternal destruction (2 Thes. 1:8–9). We should not think of the gospel as only a matter of words, for it comes 'with power, with the Holy Spirit, and with deep conviction' (1 Thes. 1:5); the gospel changes sinners and brings assurance. The gospel is universal in its scope, and Paul can say that just as he had the task of preaching to the Gentiles, so Peter had the task of preaching to the Jews (Gal. 2:7). He can speak of a 'brother' whose 'praise in the gospel' is through all the churches (2 Cor. 8:18). Paul is clear that there is one gospel for all; the gospel was announced to Abraham (Gal. 3:8). Paul can speak of 'the mystery of the gospel' (Eph. 6:19), where 'mystery' means something that people could never work out for themselves, but which has now been revealed by God. People are 'called' by the gospel (2 Thes. 2:14), a gospel that is 'glorious' (1 Tim. 1:11); it brings life and immortality (2 Tim. 1:10). There is more than this that Paul says about the gospel, but this is enough to make it clear

---

Paul saw clearly that to follow such teaching was to do despite to the cross of Christ' (p. 53). Dunn objects to the use of the term 'Judaizer' (*Theology*, p. 10), but it is widely used and is a convenient term for those who held to the importance of living according to the teachings of Judaism.

[29]*Euangelion* is found 60 times in Paul; next most frequent user is Mark with 8 times. It is very much a Pauline word in the New Testament.

that it is a very important concept for the apostle.

7. Paul immediately goes on to say, *which is not another*. He will not allow the conclusion to be drawn that there are various gospels and that the Galatians have passed harmlessly from one to another. There is no other gospel. There are two Greek words for 'another', and, if they are used strictly, the one in 1:6 means 'another of a different kind', and the one here, 'another of the same kind'.[30] It may well be that Paul's choice of words reflects a situation in which the apostle was saying that the new position that the Galatians were taking up was the acceptance of something essentially different from the gospel he had preached, while they were saying that there was no essential difference between the faith they were professing and what other Christian teachers proclaimed. They were apparently quite certain that what they were preaching was 'the gospel of the Messiah'; what was important for them was to insist that that gospel should be seen as including requirements such as Jewish insistence on circumcision. But Paul was very sure that they were very mistaken. To preach like this was to abandon the very heart of the Christian way. The idea of grace excludes any addition. By adding something of the law to the gospel they were destroying the very idea of grace.

Only[31] introduces an exception (*cf.* GNB, 'Actually'; REB, 'Not that it is in fact . . .'): the situation was not that the Galatians had moved to a better understanding of what the gospel means and thus attained a higher level in the Christian faith (as they apparently thought) but on the contrary – Paul does not identify those who brought this teaching, but he characterizes them as *some who trouble* (or *unsettle*) *you*.[32] They

---

[30]Lightfoot says of the two words, 'While *allos* is generally confined to a negation of identity, *heteros* sometimes implies the negation of resemblance.' REB brings this out by translating '. . . following a different gospel. Not that it is in fact another gospel . . .' Ramsay sees little difference between the two words, but he gives the meaning of the passage as 'I marvel that you are so quickly going over to another gospel, which is not a different gospel (from mine), except in so far as certain persons pervert the Gospel of Christ' (p. 265). In 2 Cor. 11:4 and in some other places Paul seems to use the two terms interchangeably, but here there is surely a difference: the teaching the Galatians were in process of accepting was not a gospel of the same kind as that preached by Paul.

[31]*Ei mē*, on which Burton remarks, 'The clause is thus a qualification of the preceding statement, intended to exclude the possible implication that that which the Galatians were urged to accept was really a gospel which might legitimately be substituted for that which Paul preached.'

[32]Ridderbos sees the present here as signifying 'who constantly busy themselves'. *Ei mē*, he thinks, may be ironic: 'Such another gospel does not exist except in the imagination of those who are bringing confusion upon you.'

aimed at taking the Galatians to a better understanding of what Christianity is, but in fact they unsettled the believers and led them away from sound teaching. It was not that they were trying to bring out the implications of the gospel and in their enthusiasm went harmlessly astray. Paul says that they willed to turn the converts away from *the gospel of the Christ*. These false teachers recognized the gospel that Paul had delivered to the new church and consciously set themselves to bring essentially new teaching. They were not trying to lead the Galatians on to new heights in the gospel they had accepted. They were trying to replace the gospel with some other teaching. It was not *the gospel of the Christ* that they proclaimed. The use of the article may be meant to bring out the truth that their teaching was not about *the* Christ, but something quite different. They were not introducing an interesting modification of the true gospel, but were perverting[33] it.

8. *But* is the strong adversative;[34] Paul is introducing something far removed from preaching[35] the authentic gospel. His *we* is emphatic;[36] it is probably a literary plural meaning Paul himself, but he may well be associating his fellow preachers with himself in this supposition. Beside this he sets *an angel from heaven* as the most authoritative preacher imaginable. Paul emphasizes that no matter how great or impressive the preacher, it is the message he proclaims that is important.[37] 'The gospel preached by Paul is not the true gospel because it is Paul who preaches it; it is the true gospel because the risen Christ gave it to Paul to preach' (Bruce). It is the message, not the messenger, that is important. If the message is not the gospel, it is to be disregarded. Paul had preached the gospel, which meant the offer of free salvation, a salvation that owed its origin and its base to God's free grace. Any other gospel was to him unthinkable; it could not be authentic. The gospel of free grace emphasizes the truth that the sinner cannot atone for his sin, but it also emphasizes that Christ's sacrifice of himself puts away all sin. All that remains now is

[33]*Metastrephō* signifies radical change, change into something 'oft. its opposite' (BAGD).

[34]Paul uses the strong adversative *alla*. Burton comments, 'This strong language shows how serious Paul considered the differences between his gospel and that which the Jewish Christian preachers were promulgating in Galatia.'

[35]*Euangelizomai* may take the accusative of the thing preached (verse 11) or of the person about whom the good news is preached (verse 16).

[36]It is preceded by *kai ean*, which, Burton says, 'introduces an extreme case, usually one which is represented as highly improbable' (Burton, *Moods*, 285b).

[37]*Par' ho* can have the meaning 'besides' or alternatively 'contrary to'. As Paul is here emphasizing the uniqueness of the gospel, 'besides' is probably the way the expression is to be understood.

for the sinner to accept by faith the gospel offer of forgiveness. Any other so-called 'gospel' requires the sinner to work for his own salvation in one way or another, and this means the rejection of grace. So Paul says of the preacher of such a gospel, *let him be accursed*.[38] Hamann makes the point that 'denunciation of error is an index of devotion to the truth. He who cannot curse cannot bless, either.' Only the person who has a firm grasp of the truth can discern what is erroneous.

9. The point is important, so Paul repeats it. What he has said before he will now say again. There are minor changers in wording, but the force of what he says is much the same as what he wrote in the previous verse. He does not appear, however, to be referring to that verse. His meaning rather seems to be 'what I said on a former occasion', in which case the reference will be to his preaching of the gospel when he founded the church in Galatia. The expression *now I say* favours this view; it can scarcely refer to a contrast with what he said in the previous sentence.[39] To add the keeping of the law to the gospel of God's free grace is to nullify grace.[40] Both cannot be true. If salvation comes by God's free grace then it is not earned by keeping the law. If it comes by keeping the law it is not of God's free grace.

10. It is clear that Paul has been accused by some of the Galatians of being a time-server;[41] he was trying to get the approval of men, they said.[42] Paul was in the business of persuading people; in the gospel he preached he was offering eternal life to all who in faith accepted God's

---

[38]BAGD point out that *anathema = anatetheimenon*, '"something placed" or "set up"', an expression which was used of something set up in a temple. This could signify what is consecrated or what is accursed. In the New Testament the meaning mostly is 'accursed', and that is the meaning in the present passage.

[39]There is a change in the Greek from *ean* + subjunctive to *ei* + indicative, which may mean that he is moving from a somewhat hypothetical supposition to something that actually happened. We should also notice the accusative *hymas*; the verb can also take an accusative of the thing proclaimed, as in Lk. 2:10.

[40]Hendriksen provides an illustration: 'A beverage may be very healthful and refreshing, but when a drop of poison is *added* to it, it becomes deadly.'

[41]Guthrie comments, 'The "now" in this statement reinforces the "now" in verse 9. It implies that Paul is answering a charge that his motives have changed since he first preached to them. His rhetorical question suggests that the charge of self-seeking was being brought against Paul.' Apparently he was accused, in short, of 'playing to the gallery'.

[42]It is easy to overlook Paul's use of *gar*, which is commonly left untranslated. The usual meaning 'for' or 'because' is unsuitable here, which probably accounts for its omission. But *gar* is sometimes found 'expressing continuation or connection' (BAGD), when it is more or less equivalent to *de*. Hendriksen renders it in this passage as 'There!' Burton has a long note on this *gar*, and he concludes that 'the

free gift. But he makes it clear that he was not trying to secure 'decisions for Christ' at any cost. The searcher for facile 'decisions' would find his 'converts' falling away in the dark days, and Paul was well aware that some such dark days necessarily awaited converts. The apostle now looks back on the strong words he has just written. There is nothing of any attempt to please people in any of those words. Instead, Paul has taken strong exception to what some of the Galatians were saying, and has even gone as far as to invoke an anathema on them ('Does anybody who is trying to please men approach them with anathemas?' Lenski, p. 43). Paul's *now* means that he is bringing his position up to date. Whatever they had thought of his teaching when he was in Galatia, *now* it was very plain that he was making no attempt to ingratiate himself with any of the Galatians. *Or God?* puts the alternative. If the preacher of the gospel is not trying to please his hearers, then whom is he trying to please? For Paul there is no other possibility than that he is trying to please God.

A supplementary question asks whether he is trying to please men.[43] There have always been preachers who have sought popular acclaim above all else, and there are some still. It is part of fallen human nature that even those charged with the responsibility of proclaiming the gospel can fall into the trap of trying to be popular rather than faithful. Paul knows that some of the Galatians held such a view of him, so he now asks whether words such as he has just written come from a time-server.

Paul concludes this part of his argument with a statement of the impossibility of trying to please[44] people, since he is *Christ's slave*. Since a slave is wholly at the disposal of his master, it is impossible for Paul, the slave of Christ, to be seeking the approval of the Galatians (*cf.* Eph. 6:6). The use of the term *slave* brings out the whole-heartedness of Paul's allegiance to Christ.[45] It also brings out

strong language of the preceding sentences suggests that this language itself is appealed to as evidence that the apostle is not now seeking to please men but God'.

[43]It is cast in the form of a contrary-to-fact condition, with the implication that the condition has not been fulfilled: 'If I were still pleasing men (as I am not) . . .' (Burton, *Moods*, 248).

[44]Betz points out that Paul's verb (*peithō*) was used of rhetoric which was seen as 'the art of persuasion'. But it came to signify the smooth speaking of the deceiver persuading men, and when it was used of persuading God it was 'a polemical definition of magic and religious quackery'. Burton cites this passage as an example of a contrary-to-fact condition (*Moods*, 248).

[45]Duncan comments, 'It is unfortunate that, except in such a phrase as "bond and (or) free," our English translations should so consistently fail to give this word its true meaning, thereby encouraging the false conception of Christian "service" (as

something of the wholeheartedness that must always characterize Christians. The Galatians had evidently charged Paul with making the Christian way too easy when he said that it was not necessary to keep the whole law.

2. Paul's experience of the gospel, 1:11–24

> [11]*But I make known to you, brothers, the gospel that was preached by me that it is not according to man;* [12]*for neither did I receive it from a man nor was I taught it, but (it came) through revelation of Jesus Christ.*
>
> [13]*For you heard of my way of life formerly in Judaism, that I persecuted the church of God exceedingly and laid it waste,* [14]*and I advanced in Judaism above many of my own age in my race, being exceedingly zealous for the traditions of my fathers.* [15]*But when God, who separated me from my mother's womb and called me through his grace, was pleased* [16]*to reveal his Son in me so that I should preach him among the Gentiles, immediately I did not confer with flesh and blood,* [17]*nor did I go up to Jerusalem to those who were apostles before me, but I went off to Arabia, and returned again to Damascus.* [18]*Then after three years I went up to Jerusalem to visit Cephas, and stayed with him fifteen days;* [19]*but I saw none other of the apostles except James the brother of the Lord.* [20]*Now the things I am writing to you, look, before God, I am not lying.* [21]*Then I came into the districts of Syria and Cilicia.* [22]*But I was not known by face to the churches of Judea that were in Christ.* [23]*Only they heard, 'He who formerly persecuted us now preaches the faith that formerly he destroyed',* [24]*and they glorified God in me.*

In this autobiographical section, which lasts until 2:14, Paul speaks first of the gospel and the importance of the fact that it came to him through no human source (specifically not from the Jerusalem believers) but directly from Jesus Christ. Then he says something about his early acquaintance with the other apostles, making it clear that they had no doubts about the gospel he preached. In the next section he will tell how on one occasion he corrected no less an authority than Peter himself. Throughout it all, Paul is emphasizing the

---

something essentially voluntary and part-time) so characteristic of modern religious idealism. The "bond-servant of Christ" is not free to offer or withhold his "service"; his life is not his own, but belongs entirely to his Lord.' In commenting on 6:17, Ramsay remarks that 'in ancient times the slave was far more closely bound by feeling and affection to his master than a hired servant – strange as that may seem to us' (p. 473), and this affection may not be out of mind in this passage.

point that the gospel he preached was of divine origin. It was revealed to him by Jesus Christ, and his contacts with Christian apostles were so few that it was impossible to think he derived his essential message from them.[46] The Galatians were to know that when they listened to Paul preaching the gospel they were hearing a message the preacher had received directly from God; he was not giving a personal interpretation or a misunderstanding of something he had heard from other apostles. Cousar draws attention to the great importance of what happened to Paul on the Damascus road: 'After the resurrection of Jesus, no single event affected the course of the church's history so much as did the call of Paul. Other individuals were converted; Constantine even baptized an empire. But the change which occurred for Paul caused reverberations, many of which are still resounding in the church.'[47] It may well be also, as Allan suggests, that Paul is reacting to a claim by his opponents that their emphasis on the law was derived from the older apostles who derived it from Christ: 'Paul, they seem to have suggested, was only a delegate of the older apostles, and a delegate who had not been true to his commission.' Whether there is anything in this or not, it is clear that Paul emphasizes his independence of the other apostles, and indeed, of the Jewish church as a whole.[48]

11. Paul evidently thought that his opponents in Galatia understood neither what the gospel he preached was, nor how he had come about receiving it. The implication of this is that they had some such view as that he had heard the Christian gospel from the older apostles and failed to understand it correctly. So Paul says, *But*[49] *I make known to you, brothers, the gospel that was preached by me.* His verb *make known* is

[46]Luther emphasizes the importance of the divine origin of Paul's message: 'Therefore neither is the Church, nor Peter, nor the Apostles, nor angels from heaven, to be heard, unless they bring and teach the pure Word of God.'

[47]Cousar, pp. 29f. He also sees Paul's treatment of the gospel as important. According to him Paul does not equate 'gospel' with 'the tradition containing the historical and interpretive statement about Christ's death and resurrection', for it is possible to 'hear the recitation of the tradition and not be gripped by the gospel'. The gospel 'is primarily a divine power whereby God changes people and situations (p. 28). Lührmann speaks of the gospel as 'the proclamation that God has created salvation in the event of Jesus' death and resurrection . . . and nowhere else' (p. 13).

[48]D. J. Verseput remarks, 'The central motif binding Gal 1.13–24 together is, curiously, not a denial of human instruction nor an insistence upon a revelatory experience, but rather an avowal of independence from the Jewish Christian community' (*NTS*, 39, 1993, p. 39).

[49]*De* is read by P46 ℵ*2 AD1 Ψ *etc.*, *gar* by ℵ1 BD*FG 33 *etc.* It is not easy to decide between the two, but on the whole *de* seems most likely. If this is read, there is contrast between what has been written and what follows.

properly used of the communication of new knowledge, not the reminder of what was already known.[50] Paul makes a play on words when he refers to 'the gospel that I gospelled to you'. This puts emphasis on the gospel and fittingly marks Paul's complaint that the Galatians did not really know what the gospel is. The Galatians knew something about it, but, from what they were saying about events after Paul had visited their cities, it was clear to the apostle that those who were criticizing him had not grasped what the authentic gospel really means. So he proceeds to make it known. He could call the gospel 'the gospel of God' (1 Thes. 2:8–9) or 'the gospel of Christ' (1 Thes. 3:2), or 'the gospel of God concerning his Son' (Rom. 1:1–3). Clearly Paul saw the gospel as originating with the Father and as accomplished by the Son whose atoning death is at the heart of the saving message. In this gospel of redemption there is no place for insisting on the keeping of the law as a necessary prerequisite of salvation. To take up such a position is to distort the message of the gospel which insists that forgiveness is freely given to those who come to the Father trusting in the Son.

We should not miss the fact that Paul does not say, 'the gospel I preach', but he uses the aorist passive, *the gospel that was preached by me*. When he expresses himself in this way he puts the emphasis on what he actually preached in Galatia. This does not mean that he preached a different gospel to the Galatians; Paul is simply drawing attention to what the Galatians had actually heard. That this was the gospel he habitually preached is indicated by the present tense, *is*.

The term *brothers* was used by Jews when referring to fellow Jews, but it is interesting that Paul uses it here of Gentiles; although they were so astray doctrinally and although they were opposing Paul so strongly, they were still *brothers*. All in the Christian church were related in this way, not only those of a common nationality. Paul's first point then is that they did not really know *the gospel* (the good news as Paul preached it), or that it was not of human origin, 'no human invention' (Phillips). Paul was not preaching some beautiful teaching that human genius had created. Indeed, a problem about the gospel Paul preached (and which others have also preached through the centuries), is that it does not conform to what human thinking holds that a gospel ought to be.

12. *For* introduces the reason for the previous statement. Paul

---

[50]Burton remarks, 'The verb *gnōrizō* suggests a somewhat formal or solemn assertion . . . The assertion that follows is in effect the proposition to the proving of which the whole argument of 1^{13}–2^{21} is directed.'

repeats that he did not *receive* the gospel *from a man* (or *from man*); whichever way we translate, Paul is denying that the gospel he preached had a human origin. His *I* is emphatic; whatever the case with other people, *Paul* did not receive the gospel from any human agency; he seems to be setting himself over against the other apostles and insisting that his commission was not inferior to theirs. There is, of course, a sense in which he did receive Christian teaching from other men (1 Cor. 15:3), but the essence of the gospel was not taught him by other people,[51] which was the way most Christians in that day would have received it. People in his time commonly received knowledge by the method of father teaching son or of teacher instructing pupil. It matters very much to Paul (notice that his *I* is emphatic) that the message he proclaimed did not come to him in the usual ways; it was not derived from any created being.[52] Thus in strong terms he makes the point that the Galatians were greatly mistaken if they thought that his essential message was one that he picked up from earlier Christians than he (and that he misunderstood what he picked up!). It matters a great deal to Paul that the gospel he preached had come to him direct from Christ. The expression *revelation of Jesus Christ* may be understood in more ways than one. It could mean that Christ was the one who taught him the gospel, or it could mean that the gospel centred on Christ or on what Christ had revealed. Whichever way we take it, Paul is saying that he did not owe the gospel he preached to human intermediaries of any sort. The pre-Christian Paul, persecutor of the church, would have known some things about Jesus as anyone would have known at that time. Jesus was born in Bethlehem, brought up in Nazareth, and died on Calvary, and other facts would have been common knowledge. But to know any number of facts about Jesus was not to know him. It was the knowledge of Christ the Saviour, Saviour in laying down his life for sinners, that was not known to Paul in those early days.

It matters immensely to Paul that he received his gospel message *through revelation of Jesus Christ* (Hamann speaks of 'a bursting into his life of divine influence'). He did not have a human teacher. As we have

[51]'His explanation might be that the essence of the gospel, "Jesus is the risen Lord", was communicated to him from heaven on the Damascus road: it was no human testimony that moved him to accept it . . . But the historical details of the teaching of Jesus, the events of Holy Week, the resurrection appearances and so forth were related to him by those who had first-hand experience of them' (F. F. Bruce, *1 and 2 Corinthians*, New Century Bible Commentary [London, 1971], p. 138).

[52]'A late catechumenate and a crash course in missionary work with Peter are thus ruled out' (G. Bornkamm, *Paul* [London, 1971], p. 28).

already noted, the expression could be taken to mean 'through revelation made by Jesus' or 'through revelation of Jesus himself'. In this context the former meaning is most likely. A little later Paul will say that after his conversion he did not go up to Jerusalem to meet the other apostles. Had he done this it might be held that he derived his gospel from them and that accordingly his teaching now should be examined to see whether it conformed to that taught by the real apostles, those who had lived with Jesus throughout his earthly ministry. Paul combats any such view when he says that he derived his message from the risen Christ, not from any human source, however eminent. From the very beginning he was independent of the believers in Jerusalem. It could not be argued that he had seen something in a vision that had to be explained to him by some human teacher. He uses the strong adversative for *but*;[53] contrary to all that might have been expected, his knowledge came from no human source. On the contrary, it came *through revelation of Jesus Christ*. The word *through* may signify that it took its origin in the heavenly Father, but we should probably not press this. For Paul it mattered that the revelation was of divine origin, and that was true no matter which Person of the Godhead was involved. 'He is affirming that his message is not his message but God's message, that his gospel is not his gospel but God's gospel, that his words are not his words but God's words' (Stott, p. 30). He insisted that on the Damascus road there was a genuine revelation, not a subjective vision.[54] There the risen Christ called him to his work as an apostle.[55]

13. Paul reminds the Galatians that before his conversion he had been a practising Jew. He makes it clear that there was nothing in his pre-Christian life that would have led anyone to expect that he would become a Christian. He had shown no sympathy with the Christians, but on the contrary had given himself over to a vigorous endeavour to

---

[53] *Alla.*

[54] Günther Bornkamm in his article in my *Festschrift* insists on the objectivity of what happened on the Damascus road (*Reconciliation and Hope*, ed. R. J. Banks [Exeter and Grand Rapids, 1974], pp. 90ff.). He points out that verse 12 'combines the noun of action, *apokalypsis*, with the objective genitive *Iēsou Christou* . . . the sentence describes a divine action of which Paul is the recipient' (p. 94). *Cf.* also Guthrie (on verse 8): 'The only authentic gospel is that originally preached by him. Neither Paul himself nor an angel could change it. It was not Paul's gospel, it was Christ's. This made it immutable.'

[55] 'Paul's claim, then, is this. His gospel, which was being called in question by the Judaizers and deserted by the Galatians, was neither an invention (as if his own brain had fabricated it), nor a tradition (as if the church had handed it down to him), but a revelation (for God had made it known to him)' (Stott).

stamp this little sect out. Duncan points out that unlike Augustine Paul does not see his pre-Christian days as associated with 'moral turpitude and degradation'. No. 'The thought from which he could never get away was rather that that career of his, into the prosecution of which he had flung himself with so much earnestness and zeal, had been running, until it was arrested, along lines directly contrary to the purposes of God.' His 'earnestness and zeal' had been real, but they could not make what he was doing right. *You heard* indicates that what Paul is about to say does not come to them as something new. They had been told what kind of person he had been before he met the risen Christ (*cf.* Eph. 4:22 for the use of a similar expression for the pre-Christian lives of the Ephesian believers). They had known that he was then totally committed to the Jewish way.[56] Now he reminds them of that way of life: he had *persecuted the church of God exceedingly.*[57] Paul leaves no doubt as to the vigour with which he had carried out his persecution of the Christians. When this is characterized as Paul's *way of life* it signifies that hunting Christians was not a sideline when he had nothing else to occupy him. For Paul in those days to be alive was to be hunting Christians (*cf.* Acts 9:1–2). The imperfect tense of the verb rendered *persecuted* indicates that the activity went on for some time. The verb I have translated as 'laid . . . waste' denotes a thoroughgoing and successful activity; the lexicon gives its meaning as 'pillage, make havoc of, destroy, annihilate' (BAGD).[58] Paul was both thoroughgoing and successful in his persecution of the Christians. He was '*actually engaged in the work of destruction* . . . Paul wished to be not a mere devastator, not a mere *disturber* . . . but a *destroyer* of the church' (Meyer).

We should notice also his use of 'the church' with reference to the whole church. The term was employed by people in general for any duly constituted assembly, and sometimes for an assembly not duly constituted, such as the rioting Ephesians (Acts 19:40). It seems to have been used by the Christians at first for the local assembly of

---

[56]*Ioudaïsmos* is found in the New Testament only here and in verse 14. It points to the Jewish way of thinking and living.

[57]Bruce points out that *portheō* is a strong term, being used for such things as the sacking of cities. *Hyperbolē* means 'excess, extraordinary quality' (BAGD). Preceded by *kath'* it then signifies 'to an extraordinary degree, beyond measure'. Paul did more than might reasonably have been expected as he persecuted the Christians. The expression is used only by Paul in the New Testament. The use of the imperfect tense indicates a continuing activity; it was Paul's habit.

[58]Ridderbos comments, 'The imperfect tenses here stress the continuing and the intensive character of the persecution and the making havoc . . .'

believers (*e.g.* 1 Cor. 11:18), or for the local church when it was not assembled (1:22; 1 Cor. 1:2). But in time it came to denote the universal church, believers wherever they might be (Eph. 5:23). It is this usage that we have here.

14. One result of his persecuting actions was that Paul *advanced*[59] *in Judaism* (the word denotes all the traditions of his race, more particularly traditional religion),[60] more so than most of his contemporaries[61] did. This probably does not mean that he became more pious than they, but rather that he was more highly esteemed by those in positions of influence, which would have resulted in his being entrusted with more important assignments, such as the trip to Damascus during which he was converted. He gives as the reason for his advancement that he was *exceedingly zealous for the traditions of my fathers*. The comparative of the adverb (*exceedingly zealous*) makes the claim that he had had a greater degree of zeal than his contemporaries had, and he locates the object of this zeal in *the traditions*[62] *of my fathers*. The law was, of course, at the heart of Jewish religion, but the interpretation of what it said could take more than one direction. Orthodox Jews insisted that the only right way was the way of their fathers: pious men of old had the right of it when there were different ways of understanding holy writ. We should perhaps notice that Paul speaks of advancing in the traditions *of my fathers*, which probably refers to his progress in Pharisaism; if he had the traditions shared by all Jews he would probably have said 'the fathers' or the like. *My fathers* points to the reverend elders in his personal family.[63]

15–16. Stott draws our attention to a significant contrast. In the previous two verses there is an emphasis on what Paul had done: 'I

[59]The imperfect *proekopton* indicates a continuing progress; Paul went on advancing in Jewish matters.

[60]Cf. Meyer, '*Judaism* was the sphere in which he advanced further and improved more than those of his own age by growth in Jewish culture, in Jewish zeal for the law, in Jewish energy of works, etc.' He further says that *en tō genei mou* is to be 'understood in a *national* sense, and not of the *sect of the Pharisees*'.

[61]*Synēlikiōtēs* is found here only in the New Testament. *Perissoterōs* is a comparative; Paul is claiming that he had been 'more exceedingly zealous' than his contemporaries. The word *zēlōtēs* came to denote a specific party in Judaism (*cf.* Lk. 6:13), but here 'zealous', 'enthusiastic', is clearly the meaning.

[62]'The word *paradosis*, "tradition," . . . embraces everything which is taught and handed down, either orally or in writing, or in both ways, from generation to generation' (Schmoller).

[63]G. Schrenk holds that the expression 'denotes the religious inheritance of the father's house' (*TDNT*, V, p. 1022). Betz, however, says that the expression here 'refers to the Jewish tradition of the Torah as a whole, not specific family traditions of Paul'.

persecuted the church', 'I tried to destroy it', 'I advanced in Judaism', 'so extremely zealous was I for the traditions'. Now there is an emphasis on what God has done: 'God set me apart', 'God called me', 'God was pleased to reveal his Son to me'. Having made it clear that his credentials in the Jewish establishment were impeccable, Paul moves on to emphasize that his membership of the Christian group did not take place because on reflection he decided to make the change. It was God who brought it about, God who separated him, called him, and revealed his Son in him. Paul makes it clear that becoming a Christian was not a bright idea that occurred to him. It was not that he became dissatisfied with Judaism and, looking around for a way that appealed to him more, settled on Christianity.[64] Nothing human could account for the great change that had taken place in him. It was God who brought it about. God, he says, who separated him . . . *was pleased*[65] *to reveal his Son to* him. We generally understand the verb 'to separate' of being separated 'from' something or someone, but Paul can use it positively of being separated 'to the gospel' (Rom. 1:1). The word is akin to that for 'Pharisee', and the Pharisees were in no doubt about it: they held firmly that they were 'separated' to God.[66] Paul does not see himself as performing the separation, but holds that God had 'separated' him from all else, and this *from my mother's womb*.[67] In other words he sees a divine purpose being worked out in all of his life, right from the very beginning. This was not due to any merit of Paul's, for being separated *from my mother's womb* means that the separation took place before the infant

---

[64]Betz points out that 'At the time of his conversion the two religions were still one and the same, so that the most one could say is that he was converted from one Jewish movement, the Pharisees, to another, the Christians'. But for Paul it was a significant change.

[65]G. Schrenk says, 'There is a sovereign ring about *eukodein'* in this passage, 'the apostle being set in a dependence on God which makes him independent of men' (*TDNT*, II, p. 741). He also says, 'Of all the terms for election . . . *eudokein* brings out most strongly the emotional side of the love of Him who elects' (*ibid.*, pp. 740–741).

[66]It is not certain that this was the origin of the name, and some scholars hold that it was derived from 'Persian' (see Matthew Black in *IDB*, III, p. 776). Another view is that 'the separated ones' had separated themselves from uncleanness. Whatever the truth about the origin of the name, first-century Pharisees delighted to see themselves as 'separated to God'.

[67]The expression is reminiscent of the call of Old Testament prophets. The expression could be taken to mean 'at birth' or 'even before birth'. It is probably better to recognize the ambiguity than to come down rigorously on one of these meanings. It is salutary to reflect that God can be at work in the life of an individual even before he or she is born.

Paul could do anything, right or wrong.[68] His separation meant that even before Paul was born God had destined him for some important work. This being so, there could be no question of his deriving his essential message from the other apostles. It was God who gave him his work, the God who had willed that Paul should do this work before ever he was born.

God not only set Paul apart to do important work, but he *called* him. A call from God is a significant divine activity. God called the infant Samuel (1 Sa. 5:4), the prophet Amos (Am. 7:14–15) and others. Paul sees his call as coming *through his grace*. He had no merit to plead but as he looked back on his life he found evidences of divine activity. There was no meritorious work that was deserving of a divine call, but God freely gave him a call to service (see on 1:3).[69]

God *was pleased* to grant Paul his special call. Paul has this verb[70] 11 times, whereas no other New Testament writer has it more than 3 times. That God called Paul means that he had a particular piece of service to render. There is a sense in which God calls everyone; we are all called to repent and believe and we are all called to live lives of service. But over and above this general requirement Paul discerned a particular call, a call directed to him personally, namely that he was to have a special function in calling Gentiles into the salvation that some in the early church thought was confined to Jews. This call was *through his grace* (for this term see on 1:3), an expression that brings out the freeness of God's revelation. There was no compulsion imposed on God; it was out of his unforced charity that he called Paul to be a missionary and an apostle.[71]

It was God's good pleasure *to reveal his Son* (cf. 1 Cor. 9:1; 15:8). Paul does not speak of some great abstract truth that was conveyed to him. No. What was revealed to Paul was a person, the Son of God. Earlier he had seen Jesus as a blasphemous imposter, but the vision on the Damascus road meant a radical change in his whole life. He saw then that Jesus was the very Son of God and he devoted the rest of his life to serving that Son of God. We might have expected Paul to say that God revealed his Son *to* Paul, but he says that the revelation was made *in*

---

[68] *Cf.* Luther, 'As if he said, "Which had sanctified, ordained, and prepared me".'

[69]Machen remarks, 'It refers to the majestic divine act by which at a definite moment of time the divine purpose becomes effective in those who are saved. Such a "call" is more than a mere invitation; it is, rather, a call which brings its answer with it' (Machen, p. 63).

[70]*Eudokein*.

[71]This is an unusual use of *dia*; the expression signifies 'by virtue of the grace' (BAGD, III.1.e).

him.[72] Cole comments, 'What begins by being a revelation of Christ to Paul becomes a revelation of Christ in Paul as the Spirit produces his fruits in unaccustomed soil.' That he became an apostle by revelation is another indication that his apostleship was not brought about by human means. The revelation was not an end in itself; it was made *so that* Paul might be a preacher of the gospel and specifically so that he should preach Christ among the Gentiles. With centuries of preaching to the Gentiles behind us, we are inclined to take this for granted. But for a first-century Jew, and specifically for one who was prepared to go far afield in persecuting the new little band of Christians, this was a tremendous step. All his previous training would have been motivated by the conviction that there is only one God and that that God had revealed himself to the Jews alone. Occasionally Jews converted others to their religion, but they had no burden to bring good news to people of every nation. Paul did.

The purpose of God's revelation of the Son to Paul was *so that*[73] *I should preach him among the Gentiles.* We should notice the accusative 'him', for it is more usual to find references to preaching the gospel or the like. But Christ was central to Paul's preaching and this passage agrees with his thoughts on preaching. We do not have a full account of how the preaching of the gospel was accomplished in the first days of the emerging church, but it seems that Paul's preaching among the Gentiles was epoch-making. Philip had evangelized the Samaritans (Acts 8:5ff.) and Peter had preached to Gentiles in the house of Cornelius (though only in obedience to a vision from heaven). But Peter's action was so unusual that he had to give to Jewish Christians an account of his eating in the house of uncircumcised men (Acts 11:3). Unnamed believers also preached to Hellenists in Antioch (Acts 11:20). Thus, while we cannot say that Paul pioneered evangelism among the Gentiles, we can say that on the information available to us his work among the Gentiles was outstanding and very significant.

The apostle also tells us that he acted straight away: *immediately I did*

---

[72]This is usually taken as the ethical dative, meaning 'to me' or 'in my case'; '"in me" i.e. "in my spirit" would be unnatural' (BDF, p. 220 [1]). But passages which speak of Christ as dwelling in Paul (2:20) and as being formed in the Galatians (4:19) lead Hendriksen to the conclusion that the meaning 'in or within me' is correct. Duncan rejects 'through me' and insists that 'to me' is the meaning here; Paul is referring to his own call, not to what he preached. Turner thinks the meaning may be 'through me' (MIII, p. 264). Lightfoot says, 'It does not speak of a revelation made *inwardly to himself,* but of a revelation made *through him to others.*' Cf. 'they glorified God in me' (verse 24).

[73]*Hina* introduces the purpose.

not confer with flesh and blood, he says. This does not mean that he had
no conversation with Ananias. Obviously he would have talked with
the man at whose prayer his sight had been restored to him, and with
other Christians at Damascus. What he is saying now is that he did not
confer with any of them.[74] He had undergone a shattering experience
on the Damascus road and evidently did not care to discuss its
implications with Ananias and his friends. The divine imperative was
clear enough and that is what mattered. There is a question whether
we should take *immediately* with the negatives that follow or couple it
with the reference to going into Arabia. It is unlikely that Paul should
couple *immediately* with what he did not do and thus we should take it
to refer to his going to Arabia as well as to the negatives. We should
not miss the apostle's further use of 'then' in verses 18, 21; 2:1. Paul is
giving us a complete list of his contacts with the Jerusalem church,
which makes it clear that he was omitting nothing. He stresses that
from the first he was quite independent of the Christians in Jerusalem.

17. It might have been expected that Paul would want to talk about
his conversion experience with other Christians, and especially we
would expect that he would confer with the apostles. After all, they
had been with Jesus throughout his earthly ministry and they were
the recognized leaders in the infant church. A new convert, especially
one who had been foremost in persecuting the believers, would
surely touch base with the leaders of the movement he was now
espousing, if only to make sure that he now had a correct understanding of what the Christian movement was teaching. But Paul did
not do this. He did not go to Jerusalem, the place where the little
church evidently had its headquarters. Nor did he arrange a meeting
with the apostles, the leaders of the church, people who had been
apostles before him.[75] This emphatic disclaimer of any contact with
earlier believers and their leaders makes it clear that Paul did not
derive his understanding of the Christian message from any who
were Christians before him. Specifically, he did not learn from, nor
was he commissioned by, those who had been apostles before him. It
could not be said that he had had instruction and had misunderstood
what earlier teachers were trying to convey to him. It is of primary
importance for Paul that he had been directly commissioned by Jesus.
Burton points out that it would have been simpler if Paul had

---

[74]LSJ gives the meaning of *prosanatithēmi* in this passage as 'take counsel with'.

[75]'With personal encounter with the risen Lord, personal commissioning by Him
seems to have been the only basis of the apostolate' (K. H. Rengstorf in *TDNT*, I,
p. 431).

retained Judaism with the addition of teaching that Jesus was the Messiah (as some of his Jewish converts seem to have thought), or if he had rejected Judaism and at the same time all other religions (as some of his Gentile converts seem to have held that he was doing). Retaining the Old Testament as God's Word, and teaching that Jesus was God's Son, meant that neither Jew nor Gentile could easily identify with him. And this, of course, may explain the reason for Paul's long stay in seclusion.

But is the strong adversative, meaning 'on the contrary'. Paul says that he went away to *Arabia*. Unfortunately we do not know exactly what this means. The *Westminster Historical Atlas to the Bible* says it was 'a vast desert area which reached almost to Damascus itself' (p. 87). Its borders seem to have varied from time to time. The term was used for territory to the east and south of Palestine, but we can scarcely be more definite that that.[76] Some suggest that we should take into account what Paul says in 4:25, and they see Paul as pondering on the new covenant in the place where the old covenant was given. But this seems fanciful, and it is questionable whether Paul would so soon have worked out his position on the old and new covenants. It is better to think of the new apostle's withdrawal as being to a place not far from Damascus. Sometimes Damascus was in the kingdom of Arabia (*cf.* 2 Cor. 11:32), sometimes not; there were fluctuations in the political and military situations. Paul need not have gone far from Damascus. It may be that after his sudden conversion Paul went off into a deserted place to pray and to think. He had to work out what this change meant in his living out of the service of God to which he had always been committed. Or it may be that Paul engaged in missionary activity in Arabia. It could be argued that this is more in keeping with the Paul who is revealed to us in his writings and in Acts. Either way, he tells us that when this period was over he went back to Damascus. It may well be that his escape from Damascus, being let down through a window in a basket (Acts 9:25; 2 Cor. 11:32f.), marks the conclusion of this visit.

[76]W. W. Wessel says, 'This territory was occupied by an Arab tribe or tribes called the Nabataeans, who had settled in the area during the 3rd century BC. By the 1st century they had established their control over an area which stretched from Damascus to the N to Gaza to the S and far into the desert to the E' (*IBD*, I, p. 86). Damascus had a large Jewish population: Josephus tells us that on one occasion 10,500 Jews were slain there (*War*, II.561): he also speaks of 18,000 (*War*, VII.368). Even allowing for an element of exaggeration it is clear that there was a considerable Jewish population in the city.

18. *Then after three years* Paul *went up to Jerusalem.*[77] It is not clear whether this means three years from the time of his conversion or three years after his return to Damascus, but most agree that Paul is taking his date from his conversion,[78] because at this stage he is concerned to make the point that he did not owe his apostleship to any human source. He is saying that he had no contact with the Christian apostles until three years after his spectacular conversion on the Damascus road. He tells us that the object of his journey to Jerusalem was *to visit*[79] *Cephas.*[80] It is Paul's custom to refer to this disciple as Cephas (he uses the name 'Peter' only in 2:7–8), but, except for John 1:42, nobody else in the New Testament employs this name. He does not say why he wanted to have a meeting with this man, but clearly Peter was seen as the chief of the apostles. It is not unlikely that Paul wanted to get acquainted with Peter and to assure him that he was now a believer and that his persecuting days were over. His future lay with the Christians and it was important that they should know that he was a changed man; important too that Peter knew this and accepted him. The stay of *fifteen days* (which, of course, may have been fourteen days and part of another, or thirteen days and parts of two more) would have been long enough for Peter to see that Paul was indeed a changed man and that his views on Christianity were acceptable. But it was short enough to make it clear that Paul's basic understanding of the Christian way was not derived from Peter. Calvin comments, 'His meaning is that he was never an alien from the other apostles and that in fact he agreed with them very well. He mentions the short time he stayed there to show that he went, not to learn, but only for mutual fellowship.'

19. Paul makes it clear that his contact with the other apostles was

---

[77]'Going up' is used in the New Testament of going up to Jerusalem.

[78]It is also possible that we should take the expression to mean 'in the third year' (*cf.* Mk. 8:31, with the possibility of taking the expression to mean 'after three days' or 'on the third day'). The term 'year' could denote a part of a year, which leaves us with three possibilities: three years as we count years, two full years and part of a third, or one full year and parts of two others.

[79]On the verb, Chrysostom says, 'He does not say to see, (*idein,*) but to visit and survey, (*istorēsai,*) a word which those, who seek to become acquainted with great and splendid cities, apply to themselves.'

[80]The name 'Peter' (in Greek *Petros*) means 'a stone', as against *petra*, 'rock', which denotes the main body of rock (Abbott-Smith). Strictly *Kēphas*, the Aramaic form of the name, is the main body of rock. But in this context we should not put too much emphasis on the fact that Greek has two words for 'rock'. The name points to rock and that is what matters. Paul is not commenting on the difference between the two.

meagre. During the visit to which he is referring he saw none of them except *James the brother of the Lord*.[81] This expression may be understood as in Lightfoot's rendering: 'I saw no other Apostle save James', or 'I saw no other Apostle but only James' (*i.e.* he saw no other apostle, but he did see James who was not an apostle). Lightfoot is probably correct in seeing the expression to mean that James was an apostle. As he is mentioned more or less as an afterthought it is likely that Paul did not see much of him. His business was with Peter. But it seems that the brother of the Lord was a significant figure in the Christian church at Jerusalem, and to omit the contact in a list like this would be to invite disbelief. Why would a person as well known as Saul claim to be a Christian, yet be in Jerusalem for a fortnight and never make contact with James?

20. Paul realized that what he has been saying was not easy to believe. This man, who had been foremost in persecuting believers, now a Christian? It must have seemed almost incredible to church people. And as he writes to the Galatians Paul realizes that it would be hard for the churches in that area to accept that he had been in Jerusalem for a fortnight and yet have only the slightest of contacts with Christian leaders. So now he says solemnly, *before God*, and thus emphasizes that he is not telling lies.

21. Paul moves to the next phase of his spiritual pilgrimage. He came to *the districts of Syria and Cilicia*. *Syria* was 'the part of Western Asia that is bounded on the north by the Taurus Mts., on the east by the lands of the Euphrates, on the south by Palestine, on the west by the Mediterranean Sea' (BAGD). Cilicia was in south-eastern Asia Minor. Its capital was Tarsus, which was Paul's native city (Acts 9:11; 21:39). *The districts* is not specific but a general term for the country round these two cities.[82]

22. We might have expected that Saul, the persecutor of Christians,

---

[81]The name of this man in Greek is *Iakōbos*. This is also the name of the brother of John (Mt. 10:2) and of the son of Alphaeus (Mt. 10:3). But the addition *the brother of the Lord* makes it clear which James is in mind here. Some early Christian writings understand this to mean a son of Joseph by a previous marriage. Another view put forward is that the Lord's brothers were first cousins of Jesus. But it is more straightforward to see the expression here as meaning a son of Joseph and Mary (as Tertullian does, *Adv. Marcion*, iv.19).

[82]Some argue that the expression used here is not to be taken as limiting Paul's activity, and suggest that we should include Macedonia and Achaia in the area Paul reached. Longenecker, however, objects, saying, 'But to include evangelistic missions to Macedonia and Achaia within the statements of 1:21–24 makes a mockery of language and discredits Paul's claim to truthfulness so fervently stated just above in v 20.' For Paul's argument it was important not to omit any place where he worked and

would be well known to them. But he says he *was not known*[83] *by face*, which will signify that, although they knew that Saul was a persecutor, they did not know him personally. In any case the director of a persecution would not necessarily be known personally to the victims. He would organize the whole process, but subordinate officials would do the actual arresting and punishing. That he was not known personally to these churches is important for the point Paul is making. If he was not known by face he could not have been taught by the people in these churches. Betz points out that this is one of the oldest references to these churches 'which must have been the oldest in Christendom'. The periphrastic tense indicates that the activity was continuing: 'they kept hearing'. He speaks of *the churches of Judea*, which appears to mean that at that time the infant church had not progressed significantly outside Judea. The plural may indicate that the term 'church' was used of a local assembly. In time, and it would seem in no small degree because of Paul himself, the word was used to designate the church universal. The term was in use for a meeting of almost any sort and, for example, it was used of the rioting assembly of the Ephesians (Acts 19:32, 40). It was used also of the congregation of the Israelites in the wilderness (Acts 7:38). The Christians made a good deal of use of this term and it stands as the typical designation of believers, either in their local groups or as the church universal. Here, of course, it is the local assemblies that are in mind. Paul makes it clear that he is not speaking of every local assembly but of those that were *in Christ*. He uses this expression 7 times in this letter.[84]

23. *Only*[85] *they heard* introduces a report that was evidently widely circulated among the churches. The periphrastic tense indicates a continuing activity: 'they kept hearing'. This seems to imply that during his years in Syria and Cilicia (1:21) he continued to preach the gospel. Paul is not mentioned by name at this point, but is

---

where he might have been under apostolic supervision. Macedonia and Achaia were far enough away from Jerusalem to make such supervision impossible.

[83] "Unknown"! It is a striking word to use of the man who, after Jesus himself, has probably influenced the world more than any other who has ever lived. No doubt, Paul could have been an instant celebrity. Instead, he worked for long years in relative obscurity' (Boice). Moulton sees the significance of the periphrastic tense here as 'I was *entirely* unknown' (MI, p. 227).

[84] For a discussion of this term *cf.* my *New Testament Theology* (Grand Rapids, 1986), pp. 51–55).

[85] *Monon* is the neuter of the adjective *monos*, 'limiting the action or state to the one designated by the verb' (BAGD).

characterized by his deeds. Formerly he was a persecutor,[86] but now he is a preacher. The verb means 'preaches the gospel',[87] so Paul is combining the thoughts of 'good news' and 'faith'. He is bringing good news to those who hear him preach, and the content of his sermons makes it clear that they must have faith, that is, they must put their trust in Jesus. But we should not overlook the definite article: 'the' faith. Paul in those days was not so much persecuting individual believers as trying to destroy 'the faith', *i.e.* the church. This use of 'the faith' shows the emphasis placed on faith from the earliest times.[88]

24. The result of his preaching was that the hearers *glorified God in Paul*. The use of the imperfect tense seems to imply that the preaching and the glorifying went on continually. The miraculous change from persecutor to preacher was more effective than many sermons. Paul demonstrated in his life the power of the gospel. As Lenski puts it, 'By a simple recounting of the historical facts Paul sets before the Galatians what they should never have allowed anyone to make them doubt: he had his gospel directly from God and Christ, by revelation and not at secondhand, the identical gospel of all the other apostles, of all the churches in Judea.'[89]

---

[86]Paul uses the verb *diōkō* 21 times out of its 44 New Testament occurrences. Galatians has it 5 times, which is striking in so short an epistle. The only New Testament books with more are Matthew, where the verb is found 6 times, and Acts, which has it 9 times.

[87]The present tense indicates a continuing activity.

[88]G. E. Ladd objects to calling Paul's experience a conversion: ' "Conversion" is not the best word to describe Paul's experience, since this term in our idiom carries a load of psychological baggage. Furthermore, Saul was not converted from disbelief to faith, from sinfulness to righteousness, from irreligion to religion, nor even from one religion to another, since he considered Christianity to be the true Judaism. He was converted from one understanding of righteousness to another – from his own righteousness of works to God's righteousness by faith (Rom. 9:30ff.)' (*A Theology of the New Testament* [Grand Rapids, 1974], p. 368).

[89]*Cf.* Guthrie: 'The real object of his mentioning it here is to demonstrate that even churches as Jewish Christian as the Judean churches could praise God for Paul, and yet the Judaizers at Galatia were critical of him.'

GALATIANS 2

3. Paul's agreement with the Jerusalem church, 2:1–10

¹Then after fourteen years I went up again to Jerusalem with Barnabas, taking with me Titus also; ²and I went up in accordance with a revelation and I set before them the gospel I preach among the Gentiles, but privately to those who were recognized as leaders, lest by any chance I was running or had run in vain. ³But not even Titus, who was with me, and was a Greek, was compelled to be circumcised ⁴on account of the false brothers brought in secretly who sneaked in to spy out our freedom which we have in Christ Jesus in order that they might enslave us, ⁵to whom we did not submit even for an hour, so that the truth of the gospel might remain with you. ⁶But from those who seemed to be important – whatever they were makes no difference; God does not accept anyone's person – those who seemed to be important added nothing to me. ⁷But on the contrary, when they saw that I had been entrusted with the gospel of the uncircumcision, just as Peter with that of the circumcision – ⁸for he who was at work with Peter for the apostolate of the circumcision was at work also in me for the Gentiles – ⁹and when they knew the grace that was given to me, James and Cephas and John, who seemed to be pillars, gave to me and Barnabas the right hands of fellowship, so that we should go to the Gentiles and they to the circumcision. ¹⁰Only they wanted us to remember the poor, which very thing I was diligent to do.

Having shown quite clearly that his first contact with the apostles at Jerusalem could not be the source of the gospel he preached, Paul now moves on to this next contact. He points out that his next visit was fourteen years later, and it seems clear that he had had no contact with the Jerusalem apostles during that period. Nor when he did go up to Jerusalem was it in response to a summons from the leaders of the church there. He went up in response to a divine revelation. He brought with him Titus, an uncircumcised man, but the Jerusalem leaders did not require this Greek travelling companion to be circumcised. Paul makes it clear that the leaders of the church in Jerusalem approved of his message and his mission to Gentiles, and that they did not require his converts to keep the law in the Jewish fashion.

Cousar points out that 'it must have crossed Paul's mind that he

could do without Jerusalem'. He was establishing churches in regions
where the church in Jerusalem had no influence whatever, and where
it could not have given financial assistance. In fact, financial assistance
went the other way – Paul took up collections in the Gentile churches
to assist the poor saints in Jerusalem. He could keep on with his
mission indefinitely whatever view the apostles in Jerusalem took of
him. But, as Cousar says further, 'One cannot be an empire-builder or
a separatist and at the same time be a passionate advocate of God's
free grace.' Paul was quite sure of the unity that bound together all
those who had experienced that free grace, and he made it his concern
to ensure that that unity was preserved.

1. *Then*[1] takes us along to the next significant time (NEB renders
'next', and Fung comments that the word 'implies that Paul is giving
a strictly chronological narrative of events and omitting nothing of
significance for his present apologetic purpose'), namely Paul's
second visit to the Jerusalem apostles. This took place *after fourteen
years*, which may mean fourteen years after the apostle's conversion
or fourteen years after the events narrated at the end of the previous
chapter, probably the former. Either way, by this time Paul had had a
significant missionary career, so there was no question of his
receiving his essential message on this visit. It is sometimes argued
that Paul is speaking here of the visit narrated in Acts 15.[2] Both here
and there Barnabas was with Paul, and in both passages the question
of circumcision was to the fore. But there are some strong arguments
against the view that identifies the two visits. Thus here Paul speaks
of setting the gospel he preached before the Jerusalem leaders
privately, whereas Luke seems to be describing an open discussion
in which Christian Pharisees argued that Gentile converts must be
circumcised and required to obey the law of Moses (Acts 15:5). Luke
speaks of 'the apostles and the elders' as discussing the question at
length, and of Peter as well as Barnabas and Paul as arguing that
Gentile converts should not be required to be circumcised and to keep
the law. He says that James gave the verdict at the end of
proceedings, namely that Gentiles should not be required to keep
the Jewish law. It is incredible that if this council had already taken
place, Paul should omit all reference to it here, where it would have

---

[1]*Epeita* continues the sequence after the same expression in 1:18, 21. *Dia* here has the
meaning 'after' rather than 'through' (see LSJ, A.II.2; BDF, p. 223 [1]).

[2]W. Gutbrod finds 'a substantial measure of agreement' between Gal. 2 and Acts 15
(*TDNT*, IV, p. 1065). For a useful summary of the evidence for this view see
Hendriksen, pp. 70–73.

been so relevant.[3] Paul tells us that he went up to Jerusalem with Barnabas and Titus. Barnabas had been his colleague in important missionary activities and could testify to what God had done through Paul, while Titus was a Greek convert, converted by Paul (Tit. 1:4). Barnabas would have been able to tell the Jerusalemites about the wonderful things God had done as he and Paul had journeyed among the Gentiles, while Titus was a splendid example of what it meant to bring the gospel to Gentiles; indeed Paul may have taken him along as a test case.

2. Paul went to Jerusalem *in accordance with a revelation*, that is to say, God revealed to him that he should make this journey. It has been suggested that the revelation in question was that which came through Agabus (Acts 11:28). Whether this was the case or not, Paul is making it clear that his Galatian opponents should not think that he had belatedly realized that he needed apostolic authorization, so had gone up to Jerusalem to get it. Nor was he going up to Jerusalem in response to a summons from some apostolic leader. Nor yet was he asking the Jerusalem leaders whether the gospel he preached was authentic. Paul is leaving no room for such false suppositions. He is telling us plainly that it was in response to a revelation that he went to Jerusalem. He is saying that God told him to go there, and that is why he went.

Paul had exercised a Christian ministry for fourteen years before this contact with Jerusalem, so his message was not a novelty. And when he went up it was with Barnabas and Titus – Barnabas his coadjutor on his first great missionary journey, and Titus part of the fruit of his mission. Osiek sees these men as 'his two witnesses', and there may be something in this, for Paul here is speaking not of what happened in open session but of private discussions between himself and the Christian leaders in Jerusalem. It was natural that when a man who had done as much church-planting as Paul had done came to Jerusalem, there would be quiet discussions with the leaders of the church there.

It might be objected that it was provocative on Paul's part to bring an uncircumcised Gentile to Jerusalem, the Jewish capital and the place from which the Christian gospel had emanated. But Paul was not trying to provoke anyone. He was letting people see by a practical example what the preaching of the gospel could do. It is important that Titus was not required to be circumcised (1:3).

---

[3]*Cf.* Calvin, 'While his opponents were falsely claiming the support of the apostles and doing their utmost to harass Paul, how careless he would have been to pass over the decree circulated among them all which undermined their position.'

Paul *set before*[4] the Jerusalem leaders *the gospel* he preached *among*[5] *the Gentiles*; the present tense, *I preach*, shows that he was still preaching the same gospel and that he is not contrasting what he does now with what he did then. He tells us that he set this gospel before those leaders *privately* ('only in a private meeting', NRSV), which may mean that he did not think it a matter to be discussed before the whole church. But that he set it before the leaders shows that he wanted those leaders to be clear that the message he preached was the authentic gospel.[6] Bruce comments, 'It is most unlikely that Paul would have modified his gospel had the Jerusalem leaders *not* approved of it – he had higher authority than theirs for maintaining it unchanged . . . But the approval of those leaders made his task less difficult . . .' He speaks of *those who were recognized as leaders*,[7] which makes us wonder why he uses the term 'recognized'. Perhaps in a church of brothers there were none who had titles of leadership. Or Paul may have simply selected those he himself saw as significant leaders and laid his case before them. But the use of this expression again in verses 6 and 9 perhaps indicates that he had James, Cephas and John primarily in mind.

He says he did this *lest by any chance I was running or had run in vain*. This too is puzzling, for it is difficult to hold that the Paul who founded so many churches and wrote so many of our New Testament epistles had any doubts whether his gospel was being preached in vain. Perhaps in those early days he had been ready for others to examine his message and certify that he was on the right track, but there is no suggestion that he was prepared to modify his message in the light of the opinions of other people. Paul uses the metaphor of running in vain elsewhere (Phil. 2:16; that of running is more frequent). The metaphor, probably taken from the Games, brings out something of the effort put into Christian service and also some idea of progress. O. Bauernfeind points out that Paul's fear of

[4]The verb *anatithēmi* is used here in the sense, 'lay someth. *before* someone *for consideration*' (BAGD, II).

[5]*En* does not limit his preaching to Gentiles. He preached in Gentile lands, but his practice of going to the Jewish synagogues where they existed is covered by this way of putting it.

[6]Duncan holds that there is a further thought: 'Paul saw that those whose work of evangelization had hitherto lain among fellow-Jews had not exhausted the meaning of the gospel until they had considered what the gospel might mean for non-Jews.'

[7]D. Müller speaks of *hoi dokountes* as 'those who matter, the recognized authorities' (*NIDNTT*, III, p. 822). G. Kittel cites the use of the expression 'for a reputation which is not merely imaginary but has some substance to it' (*TDNT*, II, p. 233).

running in vain was not that he himself might fall away: 'He is rather contemplating the situation which would arise if on the Day of Judgment he were not accompanied by the host of believers whom it was his task to win and who are to be his *kauchēma'* (*TDNT*, VIII, p. 231.)

3. Paul moves to the question of circumcision. This was of fundamental importance to loyal Jews (*cf.* those who taught that 'except you are circumcised according to the custom of Moses, you cannot be saved', Acts 15:1). And, of course, if any man was going to live a life in obedience to the law he must start by being circumcised. Paul starts with the strong adversative:[8] there is to be no doubt that he is not running in vain. He can take that for granted and proceed with his argument. He speaks of Titus, who was with him in Jerusalem, and points out that he *was a Greek*, and thus a prime case for circumcision if that was to be regarded as a necessity for all male converts. Why *not even*[9] *Titus*? Perhaps because he worked so closely with Paul and would thus be brought into frequent contact with Jews; perhaps because special pressure was brought to have him circumcised. Or the reasoning may be that 'not even this Gentile who was in the heartland of the circumcised was constrained to undergo this operation'. Paul says plainly that Titus was not *compelled to be circumcised*. Some understand this to mean, 'Titus was under no compulsion to be circumcised, but he accepted circumcision voluntarily, not as the result of pressure from the Jewish Christians' (Duncan, for example, holds this view). But, despite the learning with which this position is argued, this would have conceded the very point at issue and Paul is unlikely to have agreed to it.[10] As Boice says, 'It is hard to see how Paul could admit that he yielded to the demands to have Titus circumcised and still maintain that he had defended the "truth of the gospel"'. We should also bear in mind that Paul speaks of his opponents as 'false brothers', and 'infiltrating our ranks', as spying on our freedom in

[8]*Alla*, which BAGD classify here as 'before independent clauses, to indicate that the preceding is to be regarded as a settled matter, thus forming a transition to someth. new' (3).

[9]This use of *alla* '= "not only this, but also", used to introduce an additional point in an emphatic way' (BDF, p. 448 [6]). *Ellēn ōn* may mean 'because he was a Greek' or 'although he was a Greek'. No compelling reason is given for adopting either translation.

[10]'It would have been completely out of character for Paul to yield to the pressure of men whose nature and actions he describes so scathingly' (Hamann). Horsley points out that 'the custom was repugnant to Greeks and Romans', and holds that this passage should 'be taken to mean that Titus was *not* now obliged to be circumcised' (*New Documents*, 3, p. 81).

Christ, and trying 'to make us slaves' (*cf.* verse 4). How could he give in to the demands of people like this and still maintain his commitment to the gospel? The meaning surely is that despite pressure brought to bear by some, Titus remained uncircumcised. The passage is grammatically difficult (Lightfoot can speak of 'this shipwreck of grammar'), and this lends itself to a variety of interpretations. Clearly Paul was deeply moved when he wrote this and was not greatly concerned with the niceties of grammar. But if the leaders of the Jerusalem church were in no doubt that circumcision should not be demanded of Gentile converts, the Galatians should not find it necessary to insist on it.[11]

4. Paul moves to 'the false brothers'[12] who had caused him so much trouble. It is uncertain whether Paul is continuing to refer to the incident in Jerusalem or whether he is moving on to later experiences in Galatia. If we take it in the former sense, there was opposition in Jerusalem even at the time of Paul's visit there; if in the latter, there were similar opponents at a later time in Galatia. As both are true, perhaps we should not be greatly concerned which hypothesis is to be preferred.[13] The opponents had evidently been accepted into the fellowship of one of the Christian churches and were thus in a position to speak about Paul in Christian gatherings. These people *sneaked in,*[14] Paul says, *to spy out our freedom.* That they *sneaked in* may mean that they were new converts, but more probably that they had become Christians elsewhere and after that came into the churches where Paul was ministering. This may mean

---

[11]Luther reasons from Paul's refusal to circumcise Titus to the centrality of the truth that Christ 'suffered and died to deliver me from sin and death'. He further says, 'Most necessary it is therefore, that we should know this article well, teach it unto others, and beat it into their heads continually' (p. 101).

[12]*Pseudadelphos* signifies 'one who pretends to be a Christian brother, but whose claim is belied by his unbrotherly conduct' (BAGD). REB renders 'sham Christians'.

[13]Betz can say, 'There can be no doubt that Paul refers here to his Jewish Christian opponents in Jerusalem' (n. 302), but he also says, 'It should be clear that whatever Paul says about his opponents in Jerusalem applies also to his present opposition in Galatia.'

[14]*Pareisaktos,* here only in the New Testament, signifies 'secretly brought in, smuggled in, sneaked in' (BAGD, who add, 'of Judaizers who, as Paul felt, had come into Gentile Christian congregations in a dishonorable fashion, in order to spy on them'). Robertson thinks that here *para* 'suggests a notion of stealth' (p. 613). MM, however, say that the word 'need not necessarily have a sinister reference, but may simply mean that the brethren are "alien" to the body into which they have introduced themselves'. Either way, they were not true Christians. Ridderbos has a long note on this verse. NRSV has 'slipped in'.

that they entered the Christian church with a view to discrediting the apostle ('Paul is vehement that their whole purpose was only *to spy out*, to peep and pry into Gentile Christian freedom and bring converts back again into a new slavery, this time to the law of Moses', Cole). Alternatively, they may have come into the church in the normal manner. Either way, their subsequent conduct showed that they were no true disciples. Their brotherhood was false. They became vigorous enemies of people like Paul, and their spying out of the freedom of the apostle and his converts was part of a determined attempt to discredit him and those who thought like him.[15] That the *freedom* of Paul and his converts was to be 'spied out' may mean that this freedom was unusual in churches anywhere, but more likely it was practised everywhere in the churches Paul had founded, but was not so widespread in other churches. The object of their spying was the *freedom . . . in Christ Jesus* that Paul and his friends enjoyed, a liberty that mattered very greatly to the apostle.[16] This is not freedom in the abstract, but a freedom *in Christ Jesus*. Paul prefers the order *Christ Jesus*, which he uses 73 times whereas he has 'Jesus Christ' 18 times (there are 24 cases where the MSS are divided). Here he contrasts the liberty in Christ with enslavement; he says that the false teachers did what they did *in order that*[17] *they might enslave us*. Paul saw the life to which the false teachers were trying to lead the believers not as a praiseworthy form of service to God but as a form of slavery. There is a vast difference between living a life with few rules, but with faith in Christ Jesus as controlling everything, and a life that majors in keeping all the commandments in the law of Moses.

5. Paul dismissed the contentions of the opposing group. *Not even*[18]

---

[15]To bring out some of the distinctiveness of Christian freedom and its impact on non-Christians, Betz draws attention to a passage in the *Gospel of Philip* from the Nag Hammadi documents: 'If you say: "I am a Jew," nobody will be moved. If you say: "I am a Roman," nobody will be upset. If you say: "I am a Greek, a barbarian, a slave, [a free man]," nobody will be disturbed. If you say: "I am a Christian," [the whole heaven] will shake' (p. 3). He speculates that the Galatians' experience of freedom may have brought about some such reaction.

[16]Paul makes more use of the freedom words than anyone else in the New Testament. He has *eleutheria* 7 times out of 11, *eleutheros* 16 times out of 23, and *eleutheroun* 5 times out of 7. Clearly freedom mattered a great deal to this apostle.

[17]*Hina* indicates purpose.

[18]*Oude* is not found in D*, and its equivalent is lacking in a number of Latin MSS, but there is no doubt that it should be read. Betz thinks that the variant expresses 'the view that Paul did in fact yield for a moment – by consenting to the circumcision of Titus'. That may be the origin of the reading, but there is no real reason for accepting

for an hour[19] did he yield to them (literally, 'did we have in the subjection'; the article seems to point to the subjection demanded, *i.e.* circumcision; Moule takes the dative to mean '*in subjection*, i.e. *submissively*' [Moule, p. 45]). For Paul it was not a minor matter concerned with which piece of ceremonial he and his readers would prefer; the acceptance of circumcision meant entering into an undertaking to keep the whole law. The truth at the heart of the gospel was at stake. Paul's purpose was *that the truth of the gospel* might remain with the converts. The multiplicity of the rules involved in keeping the whole law would place new believers in a veritable slavery, whereas Christ had died to make them free. Paul might have alluded to a multitude of aspects of the gospel and it is interesting that here he chooses to speak of *the truth* of the gospel. In a situation where the false teachers were claiming to lead the Galatians further into the truth, Paul is saying that in fact the truth lies with the gospel. It is that that shows up people for what they are, sinners, and God for what he is, the Saviour of sinners, the One who sent his Son to die for believers so that they may be delivered from sin and brought into everlasting life. It is interesting that he says his purpose was that the truth of the gospel *might remain*[20] *with you*. As far as we know, the specific case of the Galatians was not brought up at the discussions Paul had in Jerusalem, but the question whether circumcision was necessary for converts to the Christian way probably was, and this had its application to the Galatian converts. So Paul can say that what was at stake was the truth of the gospel as remaining *with you*. Certainly the deliberations of those Christian leaders in Jerusalem were relevant to the circumstances in Galatia. Elsewhere Paul can speak of the essentials of the gospel as being widely accepted (*cf.* 1 Cor. 15:10–11).

6. Paul does not name the leaders with whom he conferred in Jerusalem, contenting himself with saying that they *seemed to be important*.[21] He does not even say that they were important,[22] only that they *seemed* to have that quality. His Galatian opponents might belittle

---

it. And, as we have seen, there is no good reason for holding that Titus was circumcised.

[19]The hour was the smallest unit of time, which may give the justification for Phillips' 'We did not give those men an inch', though he has exchanged time for length.

[20]The verb is *diamenō*, which puts some emphasis on remaining *continually*.

[21]*Hopoios* signifies 'what sort'; 'whatever kind of people they might be' made no difference to Paul.

[22]'Something special' (BDF, p. 301 [1]). Robertson sees *ti* here as 'emphatic = "somebody in particular"' . . . note difference between *ti* and *tines*' (p. 743).

Paul, but he was sure of his position before God, and that mattered to him more than anything that they or anyone else might think of him. He was an apostle, and in the church there is no more significant figure than an apostle. So he goes on to say that *whatever they were makes no difference*. He was concerned with the truth of the gospel, and anything the leaders of the Jerusalem church might say could in no way modify that. The facts constrained him to refer to those Jerusalem leaders, but he did not rest his case on what they (or for that matter any other leaders) might say.

Distinctions that seem very important in this earth's societies have no relevance to God's dealings. God *does not accept anyone's person* ('does not receive man's face'); divisions that matter so much to many of us here on earth make no difference to the omnipotent God (*cf.* Dt. 10:17). So to Paul, the servant of God, it did not matter that some members of the church were regarded as important by the Galatians; they only 'seemed' to be important.[23] As it concerned Paul, they *added nothing*. The NIV adds 'to my message'; this is true, but it is not quite what Paul is saying. He is making it clear that they accepted him just as he was. There was no need to add anything to his message, or to his whole ministry. This is an emphatic repudiation both of the false teachers and of the message they brought. Barclay translates, 'those men of reputation imparted no fresh knowledge to me', but this is a trifle more definite than Paul's words. He is speaking not only of knowledge, but of status, position in the church and the like. In no way did they improve Paul's lot; in no way did they add anything to him.[24] There may be a glance at the false teachers' aim to add circumcision and other demands to the requirements laid on Paul's converts. Machen thinks that there is a glance at the advantages those believers had who had known Jesus during his time on earth: 'Paul does not mean that the long association of the original apostles with Jesus was a matter of no importance; on the contrary, he regarded it no doubt as a blessed privilege. But what he does mean is that the Judaizers were wrong in thinking that such privileges of the original apostles set limits to the divine grace. "God's ways are not man's

[23]Paul repeats the participle of the verb *dokeō* which he used earlier in this verse. Then he had added *einai ti*, but here the participle carries the meaning of itself. Both times the participle is in the present tense: whatever their status was, it was continuing.

[24]Barclay also comments, 'It is a great and neglected law of life that however right we may happen to be there is nothing to be gained by rudeness.' It should also be pointed out that *emoi* is in an emphatic position – whatever be the case with others, *to me* they added nothing.

ways"' (p. 112). God could work as mightily through Paul as through any of the original apostles.

7. *But* is the strong adversative,[25] and the following adverb emphasizes the thought of what is the opposite of the truth.[26] Paul is leaving no doubts as to the depths of his certainty on the matter. This is one of his long and convoluted sentences (it does not finish until the end of verse 10). Paul says that the men who seemed to be important in the Jerusalem church *saw* that he *had been entrusted*[27] *with the gospel of the uncircumcision.* It is important that these Jewish Christian leaders came to see that God had entrusted Paul with a task that was different from their own but equally of divine origin. They acknowledged that Paul had been truly called of God to do a work that was very different from their own. We should not understand the expression to mean that there were two gospels, a gospel for the circumcision and another for the uncircumcision. The New Testament makes it clear in all its writings that there is only one gospel (*cf.* 1 Cor. 15:11). What Paul means here is that it is presented in one way to those who were circumcised and in another to those who were not. His opponents included the necessity of circumcision as part of the gospel message, but Paul emphatically repudiates that position.

One difficulty that Paul faced was the fact that he could not claim that Jesus had denied the necessity of circumcision. We may well agree that Paul's emphatic assertion of the gospel of free grace was a valid interpretation of the teaching of Jesus. But part of his difficulty when he confronted the Judaizers was that he could not quote any words of our Lord to support his position. That he was giving a true and valid interpretation of Jesus' teaching is clear enough, but we should not minimize the difficulty he must have had in commending his teaching in conservative Jewish circles.

He says that Peter[28] had a position *vis-à-vis* the Jewish converts like

---

[25] *Alla.*

[26] *Tounantion* occurs 3 times only in the New Testament, 2 of them being in Paul. The expression has the article prefixed to the adverb to bring out the idea of contrariety.

[27] The perfect tense points to a permanent entrusting.

[28] Paul uses the name 'Peter' here and in verse 8, but elsewhere he calls this man 'Cephas' (1:18; 2:9, 11, 14; and several times in 1 Cor.). Bruce cites O. Cullmann and E. Dinkler for the view 'that the passage containing the name "Peter" is an extract from a more or less official record of the conference, the reference to Paul being changed to the first person singular so as to integrate the quotation into the contextual construction' (*BJRL*, Spring, 1973, p. 279; see also O. Cullmann, *Peter, Disciple, Apostle, Martyr* [London, 1962], p. 20). This cannot be proved, but why else should Paul have varied between the two names? Perhaps we should notice that this man also had the name Simeon (Acts 15:14).

that which he himself had *vis-à-vis* the Gentile converts. In no sense was Peter a rival of Paul; they simply had two different fields in which to preach the gospel. As his Galatian opponents evidently gave a large place to Peter, it was important for Paul to make it clear that there was no significant difference of opinion between the two apostles. They preached the same gospel, even though Paul recognized that the different backgrounds of their hearers meant that there were different ways in which the two groups lived out their commitment to the Christ.

8. *For* introduces an explanatory comment. Paul refers to him *who was at work with Peter for the apostolate of the circumcision.* This is a full and free acceptance of Peter's apostolate and a recognition that neither Peter nor Paul originated the message they both preached, nor did they preach it in their own power. What was important was the one *who was at work* in both these apostles. *Apostolate* is not a frequent term in the New Testament (4 times in all). It is used elsewhere of the office in itself without reference to the hearers, as in the prayer at the time Matthias was brought into the apostolate in place of Judas (Acts 1:25) and in Paul's use of the term in other letters (Rom. 1:5; 1 Cor. 9:2). It would seem that at first Paul thought his work as a Christian would be among the Jews. In a visionary experience in Jerusalem he heard the Lord telling him to go away from that city, and he countered this by referring to the way he had persecuted the Christians, which he evidently thought would make a big impression on Jews. Surely the testimony of the converted persecutor of Jewish Christians would have a powerful effect among the Jews? But the divine voice was imperative: 'Go, for I will send you far away to the Gentiles' (Acts 22:21). And the work which God did through Paul among the Gentiles was epoch-making. It meant that thereafter Christianity could never be thought of as simply a Jewish sect.

9. The Jerusalem leaders perceived[29] *the grace that was given* to Paul, which appears to mean that they recognized the hand of God in what happened when Paul preached among the Gentiles. They accordingly recognized his divine call to preach the gospel to those Gentiles. Paul does not speak of the Gentile mission as something that he had chosen: God had commanded him to go to these people. Nor does Paul say that he had accomplished a good work among the Gentiles. He speaks of *the grace* that God gave him for his work. In other words, it was due to divine enabling that he had gone to those who became

---

[29]*Cf.* Chrysostom, 'He says not when they "heard," but when they "perceived," that is, were assured by the facts themselves.'

his converts and had done the work he did among them. He goes on to speak of three outstanding leaders in the church, *James and Cephas and John*. It is usually held that this James was James the brother of the Lord; he had become a leader in the infant church by the time that Paul was converted. There was, of course, a James among the original apostles; in fact there were two, the son of Zebedee and the son of Alphaeus (Mt. 10:2–3). But Herod put James the son of Zebedee to death (Acts 12:2), and most scholars agree that the James that Paul has in mind here was the Lord's brother; as far as we know, the son of Alphaeus had no claim for inclusion in such a list as this.

Paul links with him Cephas (again the Aramaic name; see the note on 1:18) and John. He tells us these men *seemed to be pillars*,[30] which clearly means that they were seen to be leading men among the Christians. If those three supported Paul, then he could not be said to be teaching errors as disastrous as those of which the Galatian Judaizers complained. At the same time the expression is not exactly cordial, and we have similar expressions in other parts of this passage. This is sometimes ascribed to exaggerated claims made by the Galatians or the Judaizers. But Boice asks, 'How many men would be able to strike such an emotional balance in as highly charged a situation as this and at the same time make the points they need to make in writing?' He goes on, 'Paul has done the following: (1) recognized the position and authority of the Jerusalem apostles without diminishing his own authority in the slightest; (2) indicated, in opposition to exaggerated claims made about them by the legalizers, that the apostles were men after all and hence not always perfect in their initial reactions or conduct; (3) decisively separated the gospel and policies of the Twelve, for all their weaknesses, from the gospel and policies of the legalizers; and (4) taken note of the fact that he and the Twelve, rather than the legalizers and the Twelve, stood together.'

The *pillars* gave Paul and Barnabas *the right hands of fellowship*. This expression does not appear to be used elsewhere in the New Testament, but clearly the clasping of the *right hands* was a gesture of goodwill and approval.[31] Paul is telling his Galatian readers that the

---

[30]Using 1 Sa. 2:8 as the basis, the Jews could say, 'When the patriarchs came and showed themselves righteous, God said, "On these will I establish My world"; as it says: *For the pillars of the earth are the Lord's, and He hath set the world upon them'* (*Exodus Rabbah*, xv.7). Clearly for Jews 'pillars' were important. Fung has a long note on the expression. For the Christian use *cf.* Rev. 3:12.

[31]'To give the right hand' was apparently a widespread way of indicating friendship in the ancient world. Thus Josephus speaks of the giving of the right hand

gospel he preached was accepted by leading men in the Jerusalem church as the authentic gospel. Dunn points out that 'the agreement was not simply a working arrangement between diverging interpretations of the gospel, far less a cloak to conceal radical divisions; it expressed a genuine sense of a shared experience and common message, and again a degree of recognition on the part of James in particular which has been insufficiently acknowledged in modern study of the period'.

The result of this amicable agreement[32] was that Barnabas and Paul were to go to the Gentiles with the gospel, while the Jerusalem apostles would concentrate on *the circumcision*. There was obviously solid sense in this division. While there was no real conflict between them, it might have puzzled some hearers to find James and Cephas and John preaching a gospel which said nothing about circumcision, and Paul saying to his hearers that circumcision was not necessary. But this difference of approach did not mean a difference in the essential gospel. And we must bear in mind that it did not prevent Paul from preaching to Jews outside Palestine; it was his custom to go to the synagogue when he began work in a new city. Nor did it prevent 1 Peter from being addressed to a significant number of Gentiles. Paul is not speaking of a hard and fast division, but of a practical delineation of spheres of work.

10. The Jerusalem leaders made one stipulation and, introduced as it is with *only*, it indicates that they had no problem with the message Paul preached. But they did want Paul and Barnabas *to remember the poor*.[33] Paul places *the poor* before 'that we should remember', which gives it emphasis. In the ancient world poverty was to be found everywhere, and that meant widespread hardship. There was no system of poor relief and, though those in high places sometimes made gifts to the poor, this was very haphazard and did little to meet the continuing need of the poverty-stricken. From the first, the Christian church did what it could for the disadvantaged, and this addendum brings out an important feature of Christian living. And not only was care for the poor enjoined by the Jerusalem leaders, but

---

as 'the highest assurance of security' even among the barbarians (*Antiquities*, XVIII.328). See also Longenecker, p. 58.

[32]'The *hina* clause defines the content of the agreement mentioned in the preceding portion of the sentence' (Burton, *Moods*, 217).

[33]Moule sees here 'an interesting extension of the *final hina*' wherein 'it becomes practically *imperative* in sense'; he translates, 'only, we were to remember . . .' (Moule, p. 144). Robertson says that here '*hina* seems to be merely an introductory expletive with the volitive subjunctive' (p. 933).

ı'aul tells us that he *was diligent to do* this, and his use of the aorist tense may be meant to indicate that he had already been in the habit of doing it (*cf.* Acts 11:30; REB renders, 'the very thing I have always made it my business to do'). Helping the poor was not something added to the Christian gospel which people might engage in or neglect as they chose. Paul saw it as a necessary part of living out the gospel. We should also bear in mind that there are frequent references to 'the poor' in the Old Testament (*e.g.* Ps. 35:10; Is. 3:15; 25:4; *etc.*), and it may be, as many scholars think, that it is 'God's poor ones'[34] that are in mind here and not simply the economically disadvantaged. But the poor in this world's goods will not be out of mind. Paul was specially interested in the poor saints in Jerusalem and he seems to have been responsible for organizing collections for them in the Gentile churches (*cf.* Rom. 15:25ff.; 1 Cor. 16:1ff., in which passage he tells us how the collection in Galatia was organized; 2 Cor. 8:1ff.; 9.1ff.).[35]

4. Paul's clash with Peter, 2:11–14

[11]*But when Cephas came to Antioch I withstood him to his face, because he was blameworthy.* [12]*For before some men from James came he used to eat with the Gentiles, but when they came he withdrew and separated himself, fearing the circumcised men.* [13]*And the other Jews dissembled with him, so that even Barnabas was carried away with their hypocrisy.* [14]*But when I saw that they did not walk rightly with respect to the truth of the gospel, I said to Cephas before them all, 'If you being a Jew live as the Gentiles do and not in Judaic fashion, how is it that you constrain the Gentiles to conform to Jewish practices?'*

Paul launches into a biographical section in which he tells of an experience in Antioch in which some Judaizers evidently put up a strong argument, such that Peter and even Barnabas went astray.[36]

[34]Osiek speaks of them as 'symbolically God's poor, the ones for whom Yahweh has a special predilection . . . The expression thus functions not so much as an economic but rather as a theological title of spiritual privilege.'

[35]See further E. Bammel, *TDNT*, VI, pp. 908–910. D. J. Verseput says, 'The positive evidence cited in vv. 7–10 must accordingly be read as an unequivocal endorsement from the side of the Jerusalem leaders for Paul's (Law-free) mission to the uncircumcised Gentiles' (*NTS*, 39, 1993, p. 49). He further says, '"Only that we remember the poor" was the sole request made – proving by its exceptional character (*monon*) the completeness of the "pillars'" willing concession to the independent legitimacy of the Gentile mission' (*ibid.*, pp. 50–51).

[36]'Here we have one of those practical problems whose emergence provides so often a serious challenge to the missionary in the organization and development of a

The problem arose from the fact that strict Jews would not eat at the same table as the Gentiles. There were some foods that Gentiles ate which were forbidden by the law of the Old Testament. Peter's experience in the house of Cornelius (Acts 10) should have convinced him that a Christian could eat foods that the Jewish law regarded as 'unclean', and it is consistent with this that at Antioch at first he was evidently quite happy to share the table with Gentile believers. But when some Jewish believers came from James, Peter changed his custom and no longer ate with Gentiles. It may be that the observance of holy communion was involved in this, for it seems that often in the early church it was celebrated at a meal shared by all the believers.[37] If this was the case in Antioch, there would have been a division of believers at the table of the Lord. This cannot be proved, but the possibility cannot be ruled out.

Some scholars suggest that the liberal practice in Antioch was having an effect on the church in Jerusalem. Reports that the Jewish Christians in Antioch were not observing Jewish food laws may have been making things difficult for the Jewish Christians in Jerusalem. 'In effect, Peter's practice of eating with non-Jews in Antioch is making life more difficult for the Jerusalem church, which has a particular problem of coping with the increasing fervor of Jewish nationalists' (Cousar, who also thinks that Paul's 'concern is not that Peter is insincere but that he is *very* sincere and is blind to the full impact of his actions'). So, it is suggested, James sent emissaries to urge the Jewish believers in Antioch to be more careful in their relations with Gentiles. It is perhaps curious that nobody seems to have recalled that Jesus ate 'with publicans and sinners', which can scarcely mean that he conformed to strict Jewish practice. Paul insists that he refused to go along with the practice, and rebuked even Peter. This leads him into a reflection in which he emphasizes the impossibility of salvation by

---

primitive Christian church. A congregation united in doctrine will split on some question of custom or ritual' (Duncan).

[37]Barclay sees this as important: 'Part of the life of the early Church was a common meal; they called it the *Agape*, the Love Feast. At this feast the whole congregation came together to enjoy a common meal provided by a pooling of whatever resources they had. For many of the slaves it must have been the only decent meal they had all week; and in a very special way it marked the fellowship, the togetherness of the Christians.' Osiek comments, 'What is at issue here is not a question of legalism or of inconsequential regulations. The observance of food laws could split a community in two and make it impossible for Jews and Gentiles to sit down together at the same table to share a meal. Because the Eucharist was celebrated in the context of a common meal, it would then be impossible to hold this solemn remembrance together. The very unity and identity of the community as body of Christ were at stake.'

works of law and the importance of faith.

11. Paul has been talking about a time when the leaders of the church in Jerusalem agreed that he and Barnabas should evangelize the Gentiles while Peter and others concentrated on the Jews. Now he moves from Jerusalem to Antioch to a time when Peter, whom he names 'Cephas' as he usually does (see on 1:7), came to that city. Paul does not give the reason for the visit, but moves immediately to his opposition to Peter. There was nothing hidden about this, for he *withstood*[38] *him to his face.* Evidently there was a frank and open conflict. And Paul insists that Peter was in the wrong: *he was blameworthy.*[39]

12. Paul proceeds to explain. It would seem that Peter had spent some time in Antioch with Paul and the other Christians there before *some men from James came.* Paul does not explain who they were, nor does he give the reason they[40] came *from James*[41] to Antioch. We are left to conjecture that this was something in the nature of a fraternal visit. After all, Christianity had been born in Judea, and Antioch would seem to have been the first major centre outside Judaism in which the gospel gained significant numbers of adherents. James seems to have been the leader of the church in Jerusalem, and it would be quite in keeping with what we know of the early church that he should send a delegation from the church in Jerusalem to congratulate the new believers and to assure themselves that they were on the right track. But table fellowship was very important to the Jews, and evidently the members of this embassy felt that they could not eat with uncircumcised Gentiles. Even believing Gentiles might well eat food prohibited under the law that meant so much to Jews.

This posed a problem for Peter.[42] He evidently had had no scruples about eating with the Gentile believers (the imperfect tense indicates a

---

[38]*Anthistēmi* signifies 'set against' and in the New Testament the forms have the mid. sense 'set oneself against, oppose, resist, withstand' (BAGD).

[39]*Kategnōsmenos*, the perfect passive participle of *kataginōskō* which BAGD explains as 'by his own actions or by his opinions publicly expressed'. *Cf.* Lightfoot, 'The condemnation is not the verdict of the bystanders, but the verdict of the act itself.'

[40]There is impressive MS support for 'he came', P46 (*vid*) ℵ BD*G, Irenaeus, Origen, *etc.* ('they came' is read by ACD^c HK, *etc.*). But it is not easy to see what the meaning is if we read the singular.

[41]Robertson counsels us not to read too much into the expression, for *tinas apo Iakōbou* 'does not mean "with the authority of James," though they doubtless claimed it' (p. 579).

[42]Though Schmoller wonders whether he may have imagined it; he finds 'reason to doubt whether the Jewish Christians, who came from James, really made reproaches against Peter, or even whether they would have done it, and whether it was not an

continuing practice, *he used to eat with the Gentiles;* this may refer to
ordinary meals, to the Lord's Supper, or to both). But these Gentile
believers were perhaps few in number and the strength of the church
at that time may well have been in the Christian group in Jerusalem.
Peter perhaps felt that if the members of the embassy went back and
told the Jerusalem church that he was eating with Gentiles it would
compromise his position with the leading church. Perhaps it is more
likely that he was afraid of what militant Jews might do. So when the
delegation from Jerusalem arrived, *he withdrew and separated himself.*
Paul gives the reason: *fearing the circumcised men.* If we think that 'fear'
is a mite strong, we should reflect that circumcision was the mark of a
Jew, a member of the people of God, and that those admitted to this
people had some strict rules for eating. If these rules were not adhered
to, the Jews felt that the eater became ceremonially 'unclean', and the
ceremonially clean would not eat with them.[43] It had taken a vision
from heaven to convince Peter that it was in order for him to eat with
uncircumcised men, and when he did so he had had to defend himself
against an objection from circumcised believers (Acts 11:2–3). In the
light of the visions God had given him and of the approval of Jewish
believers when he explained his reasons, it is curious that Peter did not
take up the same position in Antioch, all the more so since he was on
the home ground of Gentile believers, so to speak. But Paul is clear
about what Peter did and the fear[44] that made him do it. We should
also bear in mind that Peter was not the most consistent of men. Hard
on the heels of his acclamation of Jesus as 'the Messiah, the Son of the
living God', he had refused to accept Jesus' teaching about his coming
death and drew down the Master's rebuke, 'Go away behind me,
Satan' (Mt. 16:16–23).[45]

13. *The other Jews* will mean other converted Jews in Antioch. We have

---

empty fear on Peter's part . . .' But we must hold that Peter knew better what was
going on than later commentators.

[43]*Cf.* Cole, '. . . this withdrawal from fellowship with Gentile Christians was
tantamount to saying that they were not as good as Jewish Christians, and that in
some way they lacked something of the fullness of the gospel. Otherwise, why
separate from them?'

[44]'The same Peter who had denied his Lord for fear of a maidservant now denied
Him again for fear of the circumcision party' (Stott). Luther emphasizes Peter's
culpability: 'If Peter dissembled, then did he certainly know what was the truth, and
what was not. He that dissembleth, sinneth not of ignorance, but deceiveth by a
colour which he knoweth himself to be false' (p. 120).

[45]'The Peter of Acts 2:22–36; 4:19, 20; 5:12–16, 29 shows far more courage than the
one of Matt. 27:69–75; Mark 14:66–72; Luke 22:54–62; and John 18:15–18, 25–27'
(Hendriksen). This apostle was a man of strange contradictions.

no way of knowing how many of them there were, but clearly there were enough to create a problem for people like Paul. That they *dissembled* means that they were acting hypocritically.[46] Paul doubtless expected strong support from Barnabas, who had been with him on that notable first missionary journey when so many Gentiles had been brought into the church without any suggestion that they ought to be circumcised. But *even Barnabas* was caught up in the movement that urged that Jews be Jews even if they were Christians. He does not think of Barnabas as doing this out of conviction and willingly, but as one *carried away*[47] *with their hypocrisy*. Until now Barnabas had gone along with Paul, but evidently he felt that he could not oppose Peter. Paul and Barnabas had been through a lot together. Barnabas had brought Paul into the fellowship of believers in Jerusalem when those believers were all afraid of him, doubting the reality of his conversion (Acts 9:26–28). And it was Barnabas who brought Paul into the church at Antioch (Acts 11:25–26), Barnabas who accompanied Paul to Jerusalem with gifts to the poor saints there (Acts 11:30), and Barnabas who worked with Paul on that first missionary journey (Acts 13:2ff.). So it is not surprising that Paul evidently took this man's defection very hard. He of all men would have been expected to stand with Paul. Paul does not speak of his colleague as taking the initiative; he was *carried away*.

The *hypocrisy* would have been on the part of the Jews like Peter rather than of the men from James, for with them it would have been a matter of principle. But it was hypocritical for Peter and Barnabas to join James's associates in refusing to eat with Gentiles whereas their previous practice showed that they saw nothing wrong with it. To behave as though they did was hypocritical.

14. Not so Paul. He saw that Peter, Barnabas and the others who were putting their Gentile Christian friends into a subordinate place were not acting in accordance with their deep convictions. They knew what the gospel was and they had lived according to the gospel. Their change when James's men came meant that *they did not*

---

[46]Burton points out that the verb *hypokrinesthai* means 'to answer from under, *i.e.*, from under a mask as the actor did'. Clearly it points to those who were not speaking or acting sincerely. Perhaps Paul is implying that Peter's basic convictions had not altered.

[47]Betz says, 'The verb *synapagomai tini* ("be carried away with someone"), has a strong connotation of irrationality, implying that Barnabas was carried away by emotions.' *Hōste* usually takes the infinitive after it, but the indicative may be used as here to express 'actual result' (Burton, *Moods*, 236). Robertson notes that the indicative is used after *hōste* only twice in the whole New Testament, and says, 'Here the actual result is distinctly accented' (p. 1000).

walk rightly[48] *with respect to the truth of the gospel* (Moffatt, 'they were swerving from the true line of the gospel'). *Walk* is, of course, used here for the whole manner of life, and *not . . . rightly* means that they were on the wrong road. Their conforming to the practice of James and his associates was something that Christians should not do. It made second-class Christians of Gentile believers who until then had every reason for thinking that they had the same standing in the church as any Jewish believer. The *gospel* says nothing about conforming to Jewish food laws. This would not have been serious for Jewish Christians. It would simply mean that they kept on with the dietary habits they had formed in living according to the food laws that had always been part of their whole way of life and that they saw nothing in the gospel that meant they should renounce their lifetime practice. But for Gentiles it was different. They had never kept the Jewish food laws. If they did so now, this could mean only that they saw the keeping of those laws as part of the gospel. This it was not, and they should not obscure the teachings of the gospel by introducing them. We should not miss the point that what Paul is saying had importance also for Jewish Christians who had continued to observe Jewish food laws. Such observances could not be seen as binding on Jewish Christians any more than on Gentile Christians. The use of foods as well as the practice of circumcision must be re-evaluated in the light of the salvation Christ had died to bring.

Paul does not speak of what they were doing as simply a matter of human opinion. He speaks of failing to live according to *the truth of the gospel*. They had all accepted the gospel as conveying the truth of God, and the attitude of Peter and the others denied this fundamental principle. Perhaps it is worth pointing out that this denial has been all too frequent in the history of the church and that it still exists. We can see it in any case when professing Christians refuse fellowship with others, not because they have departed from the faith, but because those other Christians differ in matters like the way we regard baptism or admittance to the Lord's table. Paul's words are a continuing reminder that nothing should be allowed to obscure the centrality of the truth of the gospel.[49]

[48]The verb is *orthopodeō*, of which MM say, 'This verb used metaphorically "make a straight course" is found only in Gal 2[14] and in later eccles. writers, who have borrowed its use from that passage.' Moule sees two possibilities: 'their conduct does not square with the truth' and 'they do not advance towards the truth' (p. 53).

[49]'If God has accepted them, how can we reject them? If He receives them to *His* fellowship, shall we deny them *ours*?' (Stott, p. 55; his whole discussion of the passage is very valuable).

So Paul confronted Peter *before them all,* evidently before the whole church in full session. There is a sense, of course, in which it did not matter where Peter and any of the others had their meals or who their companions were as they ate. But it did matter when anyone said that Jewish Christians must not eat with Gentile believers. That was to obscure the truth that in Christ all believers are one. So Paul drew everybody's attention to the fact that Peter had been living[50] *as the Gentiles do and not in Judaic fashion.* The vision Peter had had long since had led him to a manner of life in which he did not differentiate between Jews and Gentiles. He was now going back on what had been his way of life, and in doing so was denying the truth of the gospel in what he did, even if he still preserved the right form of words. But now he was contradicting his previous preaching and way of life in constraining Gentile converts *to conform to Jewish practices.*[51] Paul does not say how far Peter went, but it is probable that he was concerned with separating the uncircumcised from the circumcised when they ate. He could surely not have demanded that Gentile believers be circumcised. It is table fellowship that is in mind at this point. And the important point is that Peter was constraining Gentile converts to live as Jews: his refusal to eat with Gentile converts 'amounted not simply to maintaining the validity of the Jewish law for Jewish Christians, but involved the forcing of Jewish practices upon the Gentile Christians' (Burton). That amounted to a denial of the freedom that lay at the very heart of the Christian way.[52]

5. Justification by faith alone, 2:15–21

[15]*We, Jews by birth and not Gentile sinners,* [16]*knowing that a man is not justified by works of law but through faith in Jesus Christ, we also believed in Christ Jesus so that we might be justified by faith in Christ and not by works of law, because by works of law shall no flesh be*

[50]'The *zēn* is not the *moral* living according to the Gentile or the Jewish fashion, but the shaping of the life *with reference to the category of external social observances . . .*' (Meyer).

[51]The verb is *ioudaizō,* 'live as a Jew, acc. to Jewish customs' (BAGD). Longenecker points out that the verb is used 'in roughly contemporary Greek writings' in the sense, 'to embrace the Jewish faith', 'to become a Jew'. He argues that the meaning here is '"to become a Jew" rather than just "to live like a Jew"'.

[52]*Cf.* Luther, 'For if that compulsion or necessity be admitted, then is faith abolished; and where faith perisheth, all the promises of God are made void, all the gifts of the Holy Ghost trodden under foot, and all men must of necessity simply perish and be damned' (p. 126).

justified. [17]*But if when we were seeking to be justified in Christ we also were found to be sinners, then is Christ a minister of sin? By no means.* [18]*For if I build again the things I destroyed I show myself to be a transgressor.* [19]*For I through law died to law in order that I might live for God. I have been crucified with Christ.* [20]*I live, but no longer I, but Christ lives in me; and what I now live in the flesh I live in faith in the Son of God who loved me and gave himself up for me.* [21]*I do not nullify the grace of God; for if righteousness were through law then Christ died needlessly.*

From Peter's vacillation Paul turns to the great Christian doctrine that underlay his own attitude throughout the dispute. For him there was not the slightest doubt but that justification by faith is all important, and he proceeds to bring this out.

15. There is a problem in that the ancients did not have anything equivalent to our quotation marks to show exactly where quoted matter began and ended. The NIV sees all the rest of the chapter as part of what Paul said to Peter, but NRSV, GNB, REB and others, in my opinion rightly, end the quotation at the end of verse 14 (though it may well be that Paul was 'mentally addressing Peter, if not quoting from what he said to him', Burton). The rest of the chapter does not read like part of a conversation with Peter. Rather, Paul is carrying on with an important part of his message to the Galatians.[53] As Bruce puts it, 'He probably summarizes his rebuke to Peter and then develops its implications, thus passing smoothly from the personal occasion to the universal principle.'

His *we* is emphatic; he sets the Jews in strong contrast to the Gentiles. *By birth* marks a contrast with Gentiles who may have become Jews by conversion, but who had not been born into the people of God. The Greek term[54] means 'by nature' and points to the life into which Jews had been born. Paul contrasts this with *Gentile*

[53]*Cf.* Longenecker, 'Rather than 2:15–17 being simply a continuation of Paul's rebuke of Peter that has in some way universal application, the passage should be viewed as the propositional statement of Galatians that then is unpacked in the arguments that follow. While often largely ignored in the exposition of Galatians, this passage in reality is not only the hinge between what has gone before and what follows but actually the central affirmation of the letter.' Duncan says, 'It looks as if in the end Peter is forgotten, and what began as an account of a remonstrance with a brother-apostle changes imperceptibly into a passionate address to the readers.'

[54]*Physei.* We should also notice that *ethnōn* has no article, so that it is 'people who have the quality of being Gentiles' rather than 'the Gentiles' as a group that are in mind.

sinners (or 'sinners from the Gentiles'). It was fundamental to strict Jewish thinking that only those who kept the law of God were righteous – all others were sinners. This could apply to Jews and, for example, in the gospels we read of 'publicans and sinners', Jews who did not keep the law. Jews could have a right relationship to God, but all the Gentiles were seen as necessarily sinners in his sight; how could they be anything else when they did not have the law? 'What made the Gentiles sinners in the estimation of the Jews was not only that they did not observe the law but also that they did not even possess it and consequently lacked the possibility of obtaining righteousness through it' (Fung).

16. *Knowing* points to something more than a personal opinion: Paul is talking about basic knowledge. Interestingly, the knowledge of which he speaks is not knowledge shared by all Jews, but only by those who have come to salvation through Christ. Such people know that *a man is not justified*[55] *by works of law*, but this knowledge was not shared by those Jews who so consistently opposed the apostle, or indeed by any Jews who had not come to faith in Christ. *Works of law* is a New Testament expression (not found in the Old Testament), seen by some modern commentators to point us to what they call 'covenantal nomism'. The thought is that God had long ago made a covenant with his people and had given them 'the law' (contained in the books Genesis to Deuteronomy) to guide them into the right way of living. Jews saw the law as so important that keeping the law was what God expected of all his people. 'Covenantal nomism' means that God has made a covenant with his people and that that covenant is permanently valid. It binds the covenant people to obey the law given in the Old Testament. While every detail of the law could not, of course, be literally fulfilled in the first century in every country, it was held by pious Jews in general that they must do all the works laid down in the law that they possibly could. Circumcision and the food laws in particular must be strictly observed (something like this may have been behind Peter's separating himself from eating with the Gentiles, verse 12). These two requirements were seen as specially important. Dunn can say, 'Evidently these two in particular had been

---

[55]Lenski remarks, 'A *dikaios* is "righteous" because God so declares in his judicial verdict. *Dikaiosynē* is the quality of "righteousness" possessed by him whom the heavenly Judge pronounces righteous. The passive is to be understood in the same sense: "to be pronounced righteous," and is never converted into the middle "to become righteous."' Machen comments on Goodspeed's translation of 'the word that means "justify" by "make upright"'! It would be difficult to imagine a rendering which more completely fails to get the meaning of the Pauline word' (p. 145).

"make or break" issues for Jewish identity and covenant faithfulness since the Maccabean crisis' (p. 136). Perhaps we should notice that Dunn speaks of 'works of the law' whereas Paul uses the expression without the definite article, 'works of law' (he has this expression 6 times in Galatians).

The Christians, of course, saw themselves as God's covenant people, but that did not mean that in their view they or their converts were under the obligation to keep the law. The Council of Jerusalem explicitly rejected the demand that Gentile believers be required to be circumcised and to keep the law (Acts 15). And Paul sees the saving work of Christ as central, which means that Christians cannot be expected to be circumcised or to uphold the food laws. He teaches that *works of law* are not a condition of salvation. People are justified before God, this apostle says, only on the grounds of Christ's sacrificial death. Salvation is appropriated by faith alone, not by any 'works of law', understand the expression how you will. For all those who had put their trust in Christ for salvation it was crystal clear that people are *not justified by works of law*.[56] Perhaps not all saw this quite as clearly as Paul did , but for him it was basic that no-one is justified by keeping the law or, for that matter, good works of any kind. It is *through faith in Jesus Christ* that anyone is justified, not through good works.[57] It is possible to understand this expression as meaning 'through the faithfulness of Jesus Christ' (as Longenecker has strongly argued; see also his contribution to my *Festschrift,* R. Banks, ed., *Reconciliation and Hope* [Grand Rapids and Exeter, 1974], pp. 142–152; AV has 'by the faith of Jesus Christ'). But while this points us to an important truth, I am not convinced that that is what Paul is saying here; he goes on to say *we also believed in Christ Jesus,* which clearly points to faith in Christ rather than the faithfulness of Christ.[58] But in any case this way of

---

[56]Paul uses the preposition *ek* (*ex ergōn nomou*); it is not 'out of' works of law that anyone is justified. Howard notes the following *ei mē* (for *alla*) as due to an underlying Aramaic idiom (MII, p. 468).

[57]Lührmann points out that 'the antithesis of his proclamation of justification is, strictly speaking, not faith versus law, but faith in Jesus Christ versus the law, because the mediation sought in faith no longer lies in the law, but rather in Christ.' Dunn sees a reference to covenantal nomism rather than to 'self-achieved righteousness' (*Theology,* p. 77). But this scarcely gives sufficient weight to the Pauline contention that it is believers in Christ who are within the covenant.

[58]Betz says of the expression 'we have come to believe in Christ Jesus' that it 'rules out the often-proposed but false idea that the genitive refers to the faith which Jesus himself had'. In a footnote he draws attention to writers who adopt that idea and says, 'Because of the grammatical ambiguity the problem must be decided by context analysis, a methodical principle which these authors violate.'

taking the expression still roots our salvation in what Christ has done for us, not in what we can do for ourselves. Paul is pointing to the truth that sinners can do nothing for their salvation but must put their trust in Christ. This is basic to Paul's theology and nowhere is it clearer than in this passage. This is the first time Paul uses the concept in this epistle. Justification signifies a reckoning as just or righteous. It is a legal* concept; the person who is 'justified' is the one who gets the verdict in a court of law. Used in a religious sense it means the getting of a favourable verdict before God on judgment day. To many it seemed that this was done by doing good deeds; to Paul it was crystal clear that no-one can do this, for we are all sinners.

So he now says, *we also believed in Christ Jesus.* His *we* is emphatic: the apostle is not separating himself and his associates from the lowly members of the church in Galatia. He and those associates *also believed.* Paul not only wrote about faith, but practised it. He knew what it was to put his trust in Jesus, as did his associates, and he lets the Galatians know this. Such knowledge would encourage them in their faith. For the order *Christ Jesus* see the note on 1:4. It places something of an emphasis on Jesus' messiahship, and the frequency with which Paul used this construction shows that it mattered a great deal to him. The one who was his Saviour was the anointed Messiah of God. *So that* emphasizes the purpose; they believed in order that they might be justified. And Paul repeats that this is *by faith in Christ*[59] and *not by works of law.* It was common to the religions of the day, as it has been common to other religions throughout history, that they put their emphasis on what people did. People must offer sacrifice; they must honour their deity, and so on. But Christians had the revolutionary idea that nothing the worshipper could do could bring salvation. That came as a free gift from God or it did not come at all. All the sinner can do is to trust Christ for this world and the next. Paul concludes this part of his argument with the emphatic *by works of law shall no flesh be justified,* a quotation of Psalm 143:2.

[59]Luther emphasizes this: 'Wherefore Christ apprehended by faith, and dwelling in the heart, is the true Christian righteousness, for the which God counteth us righteous and giveth us eternal life' (p. 135). Perhaps we should notice that here we have *ek pisteōs* where faith is the origin, whereas earlier in the verse Paul used *dia pisteōs,* where faith is the means. D. A. Campbell finds little difference between Paul's uses of *dia* and *ek* with *pisteōs,* saying 'they are stylistic variations of the same basic idea' (*JBL,* 111, 1992, p. 96). He points out that, while Paul uses *ek pisteōs* 21 times, he never uses it outside Romans and Galatians, a fact he connects with the apostle's use of Hab. 2:4 only in these two letters (p. 101). Faith, not law, is important in both letters.

17. The conditional construction implies nothing as to the fulfilment or otherwise of the condition. Paul usually refers to justification as being by faith or by faith in Christ; here the thought is that it is only by being *in Christ*[60] that sinners are justified. Being *in Christ* points to the closest possible unity, a unity that comes from trusting Christ completely. *We also* is an emphatic expression and we should probably understand its primary reference to Peter and Paul. Paul's firm rejection of salvation by works of any kind must have been a problem to many, especially to faithful adherents of any religion that emphasized the importance of upright living. If no-one will be saved by the good works they do, if everyone who is saved is saved by Christ, then, such people may have asked, does that mean that Christ is a *minister*[61] *of sin*? They may have remembered that Jesus said that he did not come to destroy the law but to fulfil it (Mt. 5:17). Surely, some of Paul's opponents would have argued, Jesus called on Jews to fulfil their calling as the people of God to the full, not to renounce the importance of keeping the law.[62] If Paul's view were accepted, questions arise. Since Christ does not insist on good works as a condition of salvation, does that not mean that he encourages sin?

Paul had a difficult time in proclaiming the gospel to a world that had never known anything like it. On the one hand he insisted that people can do nothing at all to merit salvation, and on the other that in the power of the Holy Spirit they must forsake all evil. It is not surprising that he encountered the problem of which he writes here, that his teaching implies that Christ is a *a minister of sin*. If sinners can do nothing to bring about their salvation, if they simply trust Christ to put away their sin, then, some apparently reasoned, does it not follow that sin does not matter? Will not Christ do what is necessary? May not Christ's people then live sinful lives? But no sooner does Paul raise this possibility than he dismisses it emphatically, *By no*

---

[60]Paul uses the expression 'in Christ' frequently; the problem of how many times is complicated by the use of 'in him' and the like. A. Deissmann says there are 164 such passages, and A. M. Hunter about 200. See the discussion in Richard R. Longenecker, *Paul: Apostle of Liberty* [New York, 1964], pp. 160–170.

[61]The word is *diakonos*, the usual word for 'deacon' in the New Testament. It signifies a servant or a helper (*cf.* Mt. 20:26). Is Christ a helper of sin, Paul is asking, in leading people not to see that they must forsake sin if they are to be saved?

[62]Duncan suggests that these teachers would argue that the work of Christ 'was to enable the Jews to rise to the height of their calling, not to make them sink to the level of Gentile sinners. He was an agent of righteousness; but Paul was making Him out to be an agent of sin!'

means.[63] It is of central importance to the apostle that believers must turn away from evil of every kind. The idea that Christ is to be seen helping people sin is an idea that is to be decisively repudiated. There is no basis for it.

18. The impossibility of Paul's seeing Christ as ' a minister of sin' is brought out when the apostle points to his own activities. If he were to do this he would be building again *the things I destroyed*. This will refer to his renunciation, when he became a believer, of things that were very important to him in his pre-Christian life. To become a Christian means to undergo a revolution. Things that were highly prized before cease to have value. For Paul the persecutor it was service to God that led to the persecution, whereas for Paul the believer service to God meant living out the implications of the gospel and proclaiming it far and wide. To go back to the things that mattered so much before his conversion and which he now saw to be wrong would be completely erroneous. It would show him to be a *transgressor*.[64] The gospel is God's greatest gift to sinful people. To profess it and then to go back to pre-Christian ways is to deny God's goodness and to place oneself among the transgressors.

19. Paul explains. His *I* is emphatic both from his use of the pronoun and by his placing of it first in the sentence. Paul is writing out of his own experience, writing of things he knows.[65] It was *through law* that he *died to law* (*cf.* 16). The demands the law made on him were such that he could never meet them all. No matter how hard he tried he failed (*cf.* the divine rebuke, 'it is hard for you to kick against the pricks', Acts 26:14; even what he had understood to be the service of God proved to be no more than a kicking against the pricks). *Through law* he *died to law*.[66] As long as he remained a faithful and loyal Jew, with the divine law as the way he was meant to live, he was 'kicking against the pricks' for he could never keep the law fully. 'With the mind' he might be a slave to the law of God, but 'with the flesh' he was a slave to sin's law (Rom. 7:25). So it was that he had to die *to law*

---

[63]*Mē genoito,* 'May it not be.' The expression is found once in Luke (20:16), but all its other 14 occurrences in the New Testament are in Paul. Burton points out that in 12 of them 'it expresses the apostle's abhorrence of an inference which he fears may be (falsely) drawn from his argument' (*Moods,* 177). That is its significance here.

[64]BDF cites this use as signifying 'To prove to be' (p. 157 [4]).

[65]'From 19 on a genuine 1st person is used, but in such a way that the words are meant to be universally valid for all true Christians' (BDF, p. 281).

[66]'The expression really stands for the idea of the law dying as the controlling principle of Paul's life, but it is much more vivid when Paul speaks as if it was he himself who had died to the law' (Guthrie).

in order that he might *live for God*. It had always been Paul's aim to *live for God*, but as long as he tried to do this by the way of the law he was on the wrong track. The vice of legalism is that 'it comes between the soul and God, interposing law in place of God' (Burton). Now Paul knew that he had had to die to law in order to live for God.[67] He says, *I have been crucified with Christ*,[68] which is a strong affirmation of the certainty of the cross for Christian understanding and Christian living. The verb is in the perfect tense, which means not simply that at some time in the past Paul was crucified with Christ, but that he continues in the capacity of one crucified with Christ. What happened in the past is powerful in the present. To understand intellectually that Jesus died on the cross to save sinful people is not enough. Paul identified himself with the crucified Christ. He knew that a crucifixion had taken place within himself as he wholeheartedly believed in the crucified Saviour. He had died to a whole way of life.[69]

20. That does not mean that he is no longer living. The apostle can say, *I live*, though he immediately adds, *but no longer I*. His death to the old way of life meant an entry into a new way of life, a way of life in which Paul was in some way identified with his Saviour.[70] And that meant that it was not the old Paul that lived (*no longer I*). The old Paul is dead; the apostle goes as far as to say, *but Christ lives in me* (*cf.* Phil. 1:21). This is a forceful way of making the point that his conversion to Christianity meant a complete change in his way of life. He saw now that upright living could never merit salvation, for we are sinners all. But at the same time Paul saw that Christ is the Saviour of all who believe. He says that Christ lives in him. His faith in the crucified Saviour has brought about a Copernican revolution (if I may be permitted an anachronism) in his whole way of life.[71] So the life he

[67]Lightfoot sees three stages: '(1) Prior to the law – sinful, but ignorant of sin; (2) Under the law – sinful, and conscious of sin, yearning after better things; (3) Free from the law – free and justified in Christ.'

[68]In most editions of the Greek text these words are found in verse 19, but in translations into English they are often taken with the opening words of verse 20. If we follow the Greek, being crucified with Christ is connected with living for God.

[69]Turner points out that the verb *synstauroō* is used of the robbers who were crucified with Jesus, and from this and other passages he wonders whether Paul had in fact been physically crucified (Turner, pp. 93–94).

[70]Cole sees it as important to realize that this verse 'is not so much an exhortation to personal sanctification as a powerful argument for the total sufficiency and efficacy of the work of Christ'.

[71]'The most horrible and shameful means of criminal execution has been transformed into a positive image for spiritual growth' (Osiek). 'I have been put to death with Him, and now His life is lived *in me*' (Loane, p. 10).

now lives *in the flesh*[72] is a life lived in faith. Faith is not simply a topic about which Paul preached from time to time. Nor is it a virtue which he practised occasionally. It is central in all that he does. It is that which gave meaning to his whole way of life now that he had entered into the meaning of the death of Christ for sinful people.[73]

And in what is for me personally the most moving text in the whole of Scripture, he speaks of *faith in the Son of God who loved me and gave himself up for me*. It is true that the Son of God loved the world and that this is rightfully the burden of much that the church teaches. It is true that Christ died on the cross for the salvation of those who trust him throughout the world and throughout the centuries. But it is also true that *the Son of God . . . loved*[74] *me and gave himself up for me*. On the Damascus road, Saul the persecutor met the Son of God who had been crucified for him, and the discovery transformed his whole life. And it is only as each of us makes the same discovery that we enter into what the Christian faith means. It is one thing to know intellectually that the Son of God died for the whole world, and quite another to be able to say with Paul, *the Son of God . . . loved me and gave himself up for me*. And that is what counts.

21. Continuing with the thought that salvation comes only through the death of Jesus, Paul now says that he does not *nullify the grace of God*. As we have seen, *grace* for him is central; here he particularizes by adding *of God*. There is never any real doubt that divine grace is meant when Paul refers to grace, but the addition *of God* means that there cannot be the slightest uncertainty about it. To nullify grace would be to put one's trust, not in salvation as God's free gift, but in one's own efforts. To do this is to reject grace altogether, and relying on one's own puny effort means that one nullifies that grace.

Paul is clear that the way of grace and the way of law are mutually exclusive. The way to salvation is the way of relying on God,

---

[72]Paul adds 'in the flesh', according to Meyer, 'simply with a view to indicate that after his conversion the material form of his life remained the same, although its ethical nature had become something entirely different'.

[73]Luther brings out the bearing of this on the good works Christians do. Good works 'ought to be done, not as the cause, but as the fruits of righteousness . . . The tree maketh the apple, but not the apple the tree' (p. 171).

[74]We should not miss the force of the aorist tense. Paul could have used the present or the perfect, but the aorist places the love at a point of time. It might not be misleading to say, 'who made an act of love for me'; it concentrates our contemplation of the love of the Son of God on what he did on the cross. Calvin comments, '*For me* is very emphatic. It is not enough to regard Christ as having died for the salvation of the world; each man must claim the effect and possession of this grace for himself personally.'

JUSTIFICATION BY FAITH ALONE

specifically in the atonement that was wrought out on Calvary. Those who opposed Paul evidently held that it was by the keeping of the law of God that people obtained the salvation of God. Paul now says bluntly that if they were right, then *Christ died needlessly*. If salvation can come by our own human efforts, then there is no need and no place for the cross. Salvation by Christ's atoning death and salvation by human effort are mutually exclusive. Probably no-one in the early church thought that Christ's death accomplished nothing. The people who were in error would have held that the cross is important, even if they saw their keeping of the law as what brought about their salvation. Paul will have none of this muddled thinking. The cross is at the heart of the Christian way and the cross means salvation by grace. Anything other than this is not Christian.[75]

---

[75]Longenecker sees Paul as dealing with both 'legalism' ('the attempt to gain favor with God by means of Torah observance') and 'nomism' ('the response of faith to a God who has acted on one's behalf by living a life governed by Torah'). The whole of the Christian's life from beginning to end is due to the grace of God, not human merit or achievement.

GALATIANS 3

III. A Christian view of the law, 3:1 – 4:31

For the next two chapters Paul is concerned with the law set forth in the Old Testament, but in the way the Christians regarded it, not the way the Jews understood it. It was evidently a matter of great concern among the Galatians, and the apostle sets himself to demolish false teaching that he could see was causing great trouble to the church. The law was an important part of the Old Testament. There was no doubting that it was the word of God to his people. But, as Paul saw it, that did not mean that the law had to be observed in precisely the way the Judaizers insisted. He takes time to make it clear that the law gave important teaching, but that in the light of Christ's sacrificial death it must be seen as something quite different from the rule of life that the Jews so easily accepted. To take the Jewish view was to cut the heart out of the Christian system.

1. The experience of the Galatian Christians, 3:1–5

> [1]O foolish Galatians, who bewitched you before whose eyes Jesus Christ was placarded as crucified? [2]This only I wish to learn from you; did you receive the Spirit from works of law or from the hearing of faith? [3]Are you so foolish? Having made a beginning in the Spirit, are you now being perfected in the flesh? [4]Did you experience so many things in vain? – if indeed it is in vain. [5]Does therefore he who provides you with the Spirit and works miracles among you do this by works of law or by the hearing of faith?

Until now Paul has been showing the truth of the gospel from his own experience. That was important. But so was the experience of the Galatians, and he now turns to the topic of what the gospel had meant in the lives of his correspondents. With a series of indignant questions, the apostle reminds the Galatians of the wonders they have experienced since they became Christians, and challenges them with the alternatives: did all this happen because of something that they did, the keeping of the law? Or was it the result of the working of God's Spirit within and among them? Their own experience should have taught them that God grants wonderful gifts to believers and does it out of sheer grace, not as a reward for merit. There is a strong emotional element here, and Martin Dibelius can say that 3:1 – 5:12 'contains a powerful differentiation between the old and the new faith. In spite of several proofs from scripture, it is full of passion heightened with frequent personal appeals to the readers – we might almost say hearers.'[1]

1. With greater forcefulness than tact Paul addresses his readers as *O[2] foolish[3] Galatians.[4]* It is not simply that, confronted with alternatives, they have taken the one that is slightly less valuable than the other. It is that they have been mindless, they have acted without thinking. This can scarcely be the result of the normal processes of reasoning, so Paul wonders whether his converts have been *bewitched* (GNB, 'Who put a spell on you?').[5] What other reasons can there be for his converts to come to such a wild conclusion as to hold that adherence to the law was more important than salvation by grace? He reminds them of the preaching that had led to their becoming Christians in the first place. This centred on *Jesus Christ*, not on human achievement. Christ was *placarded* before their eyes, which is an emphatic way of saying that Paul's preaching had been forceful and clear.[6] There should have been no way of misunderstanding. And the point of the placarding was to make it plain that at the heart of the

---

[1]*A Fresh Approach to the New Testament and Early Christian Literature* (London, 1936), p. 159.

[2]'In exclamations . . . expressing very strong emotion, the force of ō is not confined to the following vocative but dominates and colors the whole sentence' (BDF, p. 146). Turner points out that the O is mostly omitted apart from classical Greek and that there is only one certain use of it in pre-Christian papyri. He sees its use here as expressing anger (MIII, p. 33).

[3]*Anoētos*, 'mindless', points to what is not understood or what is not thought about. It is used of the two who met Christ on the walk to Emmaus (Lk. 24:25). In both places it is lack of spiritual perception that is meant. 'The reference is not so much to a lack of intelligence as to a mistaken use of it' (Ridderbos). Phillips translates, 'O you dear idiots of Galatia' and REB, 'You stupid Galatians!'

[4]Willi Marxsen comments, 'It seems unlikely that Paul would address the inhabitants of Pisidia and Lycaonia as "Galatians" (iii.1: "O foolish Galatians"). This can only be a racial term and cannot · refer to the inhabitants of a Roman administrative district' (*Introduction to the New Testament* [Oxford, 1974], p. 46). But this overlooks the important point that 'Galatians' was the only term that could be used to cover all the inhabitants of the Roman province.

[5]G. Delling points out that *baskainō* signifies 'witchcraft "exercised through hostile looks or words"'. He further says, 'The characteristic point of the *baskania* is that it exerts its influence without extraordinary means' (*TDNT*, I, pp. 594–595). BAGD gives the meaning of the verb as 'bewitch', while MM cite several examples of its use in the papyri in the sense 'employ the evil eye'. Horsley also thinks that Paul 'is entirely alert to its association with the evil eye' (*New Documents*, 4, p. 31).

[6]The verb 'is the common word to describe all public notices or proclamations'

message was the fact of the crucifixion. The perfect tense conveys the idea not so much of the act of crucifying Jesus as 'the *state* of being crucified. In other words, what is announced is not the historical fact of the crucifixion but rather the eternal truth which that fact embodies' (Duncan). It was by his death on the cross that Christ put away our sins.[7] To understand that was to understand that no keeping of the law was necessary for salvation. Alongside the cross it becomes clear that no human activity can achieve merit in God's sight. When the cross is accorded its rightful place, the idea of the Judaizers that the keeping of the law was an advance on the gospel is shown up for the heresy it is. For the Judaizers the death of Jesus on the cross was reduced to an unfortunate tragedy, a useless death. For Paul it was the heart of the Christian faith. Curiously, Luther takes the words to mean that the Galatians are re-crucifying Christ: 'Now he addeth moreover, that they do even crucify Christ . . . As if he should say: "Ye have now not only rejected the grace of God, not only to you Christ died in vain, but also he is most shamefully crucified among you"' (p. 196).

2. Paul moves from the atonement at the heart of the gospel to the gift of the Spirit which is central to the living out of the implications of the gospel. 'God's Spirit had worked to bring about changes in the lives of individuals and to create a community of faith and support. He had become an energizing reality in their midst' (Cousar). *This only* indicates the one thing necessary for the making of his point ('The only thing I want to learn from you is this', NRSV). By asking his question of the Galatians Paul is forcing them to think about the central importance of the Holy Spirit in their lives and of their attempts to keep the law.

Paul is not introducing some novel teaching that would come as a complete surprise to them. His case would be made conclusively if the Galatians would only give proper attention to the work the Spirit had done in their lives when they were first converted and before they had been told by the Judaizers that they should keep the law.[8] The verb *receive* points to the truth that the Spirit is given to believers, not

---

(Lightfoot). MM cite a papyrus: 'In announcing that he will no longer be responsible for his son's debts a father directs that a public proclamation to that effect be set up.'

[7]'The story of Jesus is clearly a fundamental presupposition for Paul's theology in Galatians, particularly in its focus on Jesus' death and resurrection. And not just for Paul, but also for both his Galatian converts and the other missionaries' (Dunn, *Theology*, p. 46).

[8]'Before, he had convinced them by what he said to Peter; now, he encounters them entirely with arguments, drawn not from what had occurred elsewhere, but from what had happened among themselves' (Chrysostom).

acquired as the result of some merit they possessed. Paul contrasts two theoretical ways whereby the Spirit may be received: *works of law* and *the hearing of faith*. It is plain enough that the Holy Spirit of God is not given to people who perform acts of obedience to the law as a reward for that obedience. And in the case of the Galatians it had to be borne in mind that the gift of the Spirit preceded their knowledge of the law. That gift came when they accepted the gospel, and they came to know of the law only at a later time, when the Judaizers came to them.

We should also bear in mind that those who stressed the law put no emphasis on the Holy Spirit. But from the day of Pentecost on, the Christians emphasized the importance of the Holy Spirit for Christian living. It was necessary to have the guidance of the Spirit to know the right way to live, and it was necessary to have the indwelling of the Spirit to have the power needed to defeat the forces of evil and to do the service of God. Presently Paul will go on to point out that miracles have been done among the Galatians (3:5), and this is clearly evidence of the work of the Spirit, not the keeping of the law.

The hearing of faith is an unusual expression, and it is not made any easier by the fact that both nouns can be understood in more ways than one. The first may signify the act of hearing, or that by which one hears (the ear), or what is heard (a report, a message); and the second may mean either the act of believing or what is believed. It is not surprising accordingly that we are confronted with a variety of translations, as 'the hearing of faith' (AV), 'hearing with faith' (RSV), 'believing the gospel message' (REB), 'believing what you heard' (NIV, NRSV), 'hearing the gospel and believing it' (GNB), and there are other translations (Moule gives the meaning as 'a sort of hearing which issues in belief', p. 175). Clearly the expression points to that hearing of the gospel message that is the accompaniment of faith. Trust in God is at the heart of Christian living, and when believers trust God they receive the divine empowerment that only the divine Spirit can give. The response of faith to the preaching of the gospel is of overwhelming importance.

3. In asking, *Are you so foolish*? Paul repeats the adjective he has used in verse 1: 'Are you mindless?' 'Are you senseless?' (REB has 'Can you really be so stupid?').[9] The implication is that they have given no real thought to the position they are taking up. That they had *made a*

---

[9] 'It is sheer folly for men who have entered on the Christian life on the level of high spiritual experience to descend to the level on which the main emphasis is on codes of behaviour and regulations governing ritual acts' (Allan).

beginning in the Spirit[10] points to the truth that from their first embracing of the gospel they had accepted the truth that they could not serve God acceptably in their own strength. They had come to see that they must look to the Holy Spirit for the wisdom and the strength they needed to live out their Christian faith. We should not miss the point that the gift of the Holy Spirit is not reserved for those who have made great progress in the Christian faith, but is a gift conferred on every true beginner. Having made such an excellent beginning, it would be expected that they would go on, looking for the Spirit to guide and strengthen them continually. But, Paul asks, *are you now being perfected in the flesh?* Throughout the New Testament, but more particularly in Paul's writings, *the flesh* is used 'of the flesh as the seat and vehicle of sinful desires' (Abbott-Smith). To ask the question is to show the inherent impossibility of the course to which the Galatians had given themselves over.

4. *Did you experience so many things . . .?* is often understood in the sense 'Have you suffered so much . . .?' (NIV), and of course the verb Paul uses often conveys the meaning 'to suffer'.[11] But this is not invariable, though BAGD says that this passage is the only one in the New Testament where it is employed 'of pleasant experiences'. Taken in the way I have translated it, Paul is reminding the Galatian converts of the experiences, pleasant or painful or both, that they had had as they started out on the Christian life. We have no way of knowing what those experiences were, and it is, of course, possible that there were persecutions that befell the infant Galatian church (though we have no information about any such troubles). And in any case a religion of grace, a religion with the cross at its heart and with the gift of the Holy Spirit to every believer, demanded that people live in a very different way from that which was usual in the Roman world in which they lived and moved and had their being. To undergo that transforming experience, with or without persecution, certainly meant that the Galatian believers had experienced *so many things*. But Paul complains that they had experienced them *in vain*. If they were to add the keeping of the Jewish law to what they had been told about the Christian way, they would be nullifying what they had learned. Paul is clear that salvation by grace and salvation by law are two very different things, and that each of them excludes the other.

[10]Lenski sees a reference to the human spirit rather than the Holy Spirit, but this seems improbable.

[11]Meyer takes it this way: he says that Paul means 'everything with which the false apostles in their Judaistic zeal had molested and burdened the Galatians'.

But he adds, *if indeed it is in vain*. Despite all that he has heard about the situation in Galatia, and despite the evidence that many of his converts had embraced the legalistic error, Paul cannot believe that it has all been in vain. He leaves open the possibility that what he has written may be a trifle too strong, as he has striven to make clear the danger inherent in legalism. Perhaps we should notice also that it is possible to understand the addition as an intensification, with a meaning like 'if indeed *in vain* is strong enough to suggest what it is' (Ridderbos).

5. *He who provides you with the Spirit* clearly refers to God (and some translations, such as NIV and REB, insert the word 'God' to make this clear). Paul speaks of two things God does in believers – he gives the Spirit to his people and he works miracles among them (or 'in' them; the Greek could mean either). The word I have translated 'provides' conveys the thought of liberal supply.[12] The implication is that the Spirit is given to all God's people, and further that miracles of some sort are to be found among all the people of God. This does not mean that they all perform miracles, but it does mean that there are miracles done among them. Conversion is, of course, always a miracle, but it would seem that Paul means miraculous happenings other than this. We learn of some miracles from the narratives in Acts and it is clear that Paul expected such unusual happenings to be part of the life of the church.

Paul rounds off this section of his argument by asking whether God does these things *by works of law or by the hearing of faith*. Clearly obedience to the law never brings about miraculous happenings, and the only other possibility that Paul leaves open is *the hearing of faith*. The way the Galatian believers should be walking is the way of faith, not the way of conformity to the Jewish law.

2. Abraham, 3:6–9

> [6]*Even as Abraham believed God and it was reckoned to him as righteousness;* [7]*know then that they who are of faith, these are Abraham's sons.* [8]*And the Scripture, foreseeing that God would*

[12]The verb is *epichorēgeō*. MM cite its use in a papyrus where a man says, 'I for my part provided for my wife in a manner that exceeded my resources.' Barclay points out that the word group is used for providing the chorus at a Greek play, contributions patriotic citizens made to the state and the support a husband gives his wife. 'The word underlines the generosity of God, a generosity which is born of love . . .'

*justify the Gentiles from faith, preached the gospel to Abraham
beforehand: 'In you all the nations will be blessed.'* [9]*So then those who
are of faith are blessed with faithful Abraham.*

Paul is fond of appealing to the example of Abraham: 9 times he
mentions him in this short letter. It mattered a great deal to the
apostle that God saves people by grace, not on the grounds of their
human achievement, and he found Abraham an excellent illustration
of that truth.[13] Scripture makes it clear that Abraham trusted God and
that he was accepted by God on the grounds of that trust and not
because of any merit that the patriarch might have. If the great and
highly revered Abraham was accepted by God on the grounds of
faith, then that should be good enough for people like the first-
century Galatians.

We should notice that Jews often had a very different picture of
Abraham. They revered him very highly, but not for the same reasons
as Paul. Thus ben-Sirach wrote, 'Abraham was the great father of a
multitude of nations, and no one has been found like him in glory; he
kept the law of the Most High' (Ecclus. 44:19–20, RSV). The law was
not given for centuries after his time, but ben-Sirach sees the greatness
of Abraham in that he complied with the provisions that later would
be laid down in the law. Others stressed Abraham's obedience when
he was instructed to take his son Isaac and offer him in sacrifice (Gn.
22). What endeared Abraham to many Jewish thinkers were his
virtues and his deeds. They understood him to have kept the law
before it was written.

Paul's emphasis on Abraham's faith must have come as a
complete surprise to the Galatians. But there was no gainsaying the
fact that when God called Abraham, no store of good deeds is
recorded of him. He simply heard the call of God and responded to
it in faith. And Genesis 15:6 expressly says that it was his faith that
mattered. For the Jews, it seems that it was the deed that counted:
Abraham obeyed God in going out. For Paul it was the faith that
was the reason for the deed that mattered; Abraham believed in
God, trusted him, and acted in accordance with that faith. He sees
the great doctrine of justification by faith as taught in the law so

---

[13]Warren comments, 'We shall not understand Paul and the dynamic behind his
view of faith unless we can see how for him Jesus Christ his Lord filled out all those
intimations of faith which are seen in Abraham, and filled them with a fuller meaning.
For Paul the Christ was far more than the object of faith, He was in fact its complete
embodiment' (p. 19).

highly esteemed by the Jews and as exemplified in the example of no less than Abraham, the great patriarch and the father of the nation. As Cousar puts it, Paul is making the point that 'the law, the Pentateuch, does not offer two ways of salvation – one based on human performance in keeping the commandments and another based on a divine activity to which humans respond by faith. The law from the beginning has indicated only one way of salvation, and that is something done by God and not by humans. The person who *really* keeps the law realizes that the law can never justify and so puts his trust in the faithfulness of God.'

6. *Even as* is a perhaps unexpected way of introducing a quotation from Scripture, but it has the merit of putting those of Paul's day on the same level as Abraham when it came to acceptance before God.[14] The apostle cites from Genesis 15:6 the classic statement of justification by faith, *Abraham believed God and it was reckoned to him as righteousness* (he cited these words for much the same purpose in Rom. 4:3). *Believed*, of course, means more than that he accepted what God said as true (though, of course, he did that); it means that he trusted God. The command to go out from his home was all that he needed; he did not know his destination (Heb. 11:8), but he knew that God had told him to leave his country, his people and his father's household (Gn. 12:1). Obediently he went.

This, Paul says, was *reckoned*[15] to *him as righteousness*. It is easy to take this in the wrong way, seeing it as a reference to the ethical quality. But in the Bible righteousness is basically legal; the righteous are those who get the verdict when they stand before God. This is clearly what is in mind in the present passage.[16] Abraham is not said to have achieved righteousness or to have performed a righteous act. He had righteousness *reckoned* to him.[17]

[14]It is, of course, possible to understand the passage in the sense 'Consider Abraham: "He believed . . ."' (NIV). It is unusual to have the adverb *kathōs* without *gegraptai* in such a passage.

[15]The verb *logizomai* is a Pauline characteristic. It occurs 34 times in his writings and only 6 times in all the rest of the New Testament. No non-Pauline writing has it more than once. It has a meaning like 'reckon, calculate', and may be used of placing something to someone's account, here of placing righteousness to Abraham's account. It was not something he earned or merited; it was something that God credited him with.

[16]*Cf.* Lenski, 'God's accounting did not *make* him righteous, it did not change Abraham's *person*, it changed his *status* with God.'

[17]For 'righteousness' see further my *The Apostolic Preaching of the Cross* (London and Grand Rapids, 3rd edn. 1965), chs. 8 and 9, and the note in my *The Epistle to the Romans* (Grand Rapids and Leicester, 1988), pp. 100–103.

7. *Know* is imperative; Paul commands the Galatians to acquire this piece of knowledge. The form is, of course, identical with the indicative, but Paul is not saying that this is something that the Galatians know.[18] On the contrary, it is precisely because they did not know what this means that they were acting in the way they were. *Then* is an inferential particle; it means 'so, then' and the like; BAGD see the meaning of this passage as 'you may be sure, then' (BAGD, 1). *They who are of faith* are those whose characteristic is faith;[19] it is not that they sometimes have an impulse to believe, but rather that believing is their constant attitude; faith is characteristic of them. The expression is unusual (but *cf.* 3:9; Rom. 3:26). Paul's opponents were taking the line that the law was the supreme characteristic of the people of God. Paul counters by pointing out that they do not realize that faith is supremely important in the Old Testament Scriptures. Abraham, the father of the people of God, was a man of faith, and right from the beginning of his dealings with God it is faith that is his characteristic. The Jews were alone the descendants of Abraham in the physical line, but Paul makes the important point that the true sons of Abraham are those who believe, those whose characteristic is faith. Evidently Paul's opponents were telling the Galatians that they would become the sons of Abraham if they were circumcised. 'So Paul counters by saying that the Galatians were *already* the sons of Abraham, not by circumcision, but by faith' (Stott).

8. Paul personifies Scripture, maintaining that it 'foresaw' what would happen in later days. He speaks of *the Scripture*, which may mean Scripture as a whole or a particular passage in Scripture. It would not be beyond Paul to say that the whole thrust of Scripture is its call for faith, but in this place it is more likely that he has in mind the one passage which he proceeds to quote. He first gives the sense of it, *foreseeing that God would justify the Gentiles from faith*, goes on to speak of Scripture as preaching the gospel, and then cites Genesis 12:3. To cite the inspired Scripture is to draw attention to what God wills, and to the fact that Scripture looks through the years and foresees what God will do. Paul is maintaining that it was always God's plan

[18]Though some fine exegetes take it in this way (*e.g.* Longenecker, who sees it as 'a typical disclosure formula in ancient Hellenistic letters that serves more to remind readers of what is known than to exhort'). Betz, Fung and others maintain that it is imperative.

[19]This use of *ek* is 'to denote origin, cause, motive, reason' (BAGD, 3). It points to faith as fundamentally important. *Cf.* Lightfoot, 'they whose starting-point, whose fundamental principle is faith'.

to *justify the Gentiles from faith.*[20] This does not mean that faith is to be regarded as a virtue, meriting justification. Rather it is no more than the means by which sinners receive God's gracious gift. It is God who justifies the Gentiles, not faith. But he justifies them in the same way that Abraham was justified, *i.e.* by faith; faith is the means God uses to bring about justification.

In this, Paul sees a pre-preaching of the gospel[21] to Abraham. The unusual compound indicates that what God did to Abraham amounted to a preaching of the gospel before the gospel was formerly enunciated. In other words, when Abraham believed God and it was reckoned to him as righteousness, what was happening was essentially what happened in Paul's own day when evangelists called on sinners to trust Christ crucified for salvation. It was the heart of the gospel that sinners put their trust in God for their salvation, and that was what Abraham did.[22] His faith was very real, for in response to God's leading he went out to go to a land that God said he would show him (Gn. 12:1). Abraham did not know what land this would be. But he did know that God is gracious. And he obeyed him. Guthrie draws attention to Jesus' words that Abraham saw his day (Jn. 8:56) and comments, 'Both our Lord and his apostle recognize that there is continuity between Abraham's faith and the Christian era.'

The words Paul chooses to cite from Scripture look beyond Abraham to *all the nations*, and these, the quotation says, *will be blessed.* The Genesis passage does not specify in what the blessing consisted, but clearly Paul sees it as being concerned with the gospel message. What God was doing in saving sinners by Christ crucified he had foreshadowed centuries before when he called Abraham.

9. Paul draws a conclusion from the Scripture he has cited. *So then* indicates that this is logical: because Scripture spoke thus, therefore certain blessings follow. *Those who are of faith* is an unusual expression (but see the note on 3:17). Paul is taking Abraham as the exemplar of

---

[20]*Ek pisteōs*, a construction that recurs in verses 9, 11, 12, 22, 24. Clearly it means a great deal for the argument of this chapter. Meyer comments, '*of faith*, not of the works of the law as the causal condition on the side of man'.

[21]The verb *proseuangelomai* is not found elsewhere in the New Testament; it is a very rare word. Luther saw this argument as 'very strong. The promise of blessing is given unto Abraham four hundred and thirty years before the people of Israel received the law' (p. 234).

[22]'While Abraham is the forefather of the Jews, when he received this promise he was as much a Gentile as the Gentile Galatians themselves. He was still uncircumcised . . .' (Lenski). This was important for the apostle; his Gentile converts were just as surely accepted by God as was Abraham.

faith, so he can say that *those who are of faith* are blessed along with *faithful Abraham.*[23] It is their faith in Jesus that he commends. It is basic to the present argument and to Paul's theology in general that sinners must put their trust in Jesus if they are to enter life eternal. For all those who accepted the Old Testament as Scripture, Abraham was the exemplar of the blessed person. Paul points out that that was due to the fact that the great patriarch put his trust in God. He was a man of faith.[24] Christians who seek the blessing of God must come in the same way, the way of faith.

3. No-one is justified by the law, 3:10–14

[10]*For as many as are law-workers are under a curse, for it stands written, 'Cursed is everyone who does not continue in all the things that are written in the book of the law to do them.'* [11]*But that no-one is justified with God by the law is obvious, for 'He that is just by faith will live';* [12]*but the law is not of faith, but 'He who does them will live in them'.* [13]*Christ redeemed us from the law's curse, having become a curse for us, for it is written, 'Cursed is everyone who hangs on a tree',* [14]*so that the blessing of Abraham might come to the Gentiles in Christ Jesus, so that we should receive the promise of the Spirit through faith.*

From the thought that the great patriarch Abraham was accepted by God because of his faith, Paul goes on to emphasize the importance of faith in the lives of all God's people. Specifically it is faith rather than any keeping of the law that brings about justification. He argues strongly that justification by keeping the law is impossible. To concentrate on law-keeping means to bring oneself under the curse that falls on failure to keep the law, for such failure is certain. Stott points out that, while these verses 'may seem difficult in both concept and vocabulary, yet they are fundamental to an understanding of biblical Christianity. For they concern the central issue of religion, which is how to come into a right relationship with God.' Boice draws attention to an important point when he says, 'The law is not a

[23]The expression *tō ek pisteōs Abraam* occurs in Rom. 4:16, but it is not faith in Abraham that is meant, but faith like that of Abraham. For Paul faith is always faith in Jesus.

[24]'The word *faithful* is very emphatic. For it is as if he had said that they are blessed, not with Abraham as circumcised, nor as endowed with the works of the law, nor as a Hebrew, nor as relying on his own worth, but with Abraham who by faith alone obtained the blessing. No personal quality is taken into account here, only faith' (Calvin).

collection of stray and miscellaneous parts, some of which may conveniently be disregarded. It is a whole, and must be kept in all its parts if it is to be considered kept at all.' Those who see salvation as 'living a good life' overlook the fact that from time to time they do things that are not good. No-one can keep the whole law of God.

10. *For* ties this to the preceding: it is precisely because of what we learn from Abraham that it follows that we are all under the law's curse. If even the great patriarch was accepted by God only because of his faith, then it follows that lesser mortals will not succeed in producing the good deeds that would allow them to be accepted before God. To rely on keeping the law[25] is to sentence ourselves to being accursed.[26] 'He takes it as indisputable that no one actually does all the things demanded by the law' (Hamann). There will be a contrast with the blessing mentioned in 3:8–9. Paul proves his point by quoting Deuteronomy 27:26, which numbers people who do not carry out the words of the law among those who are 'cursed'. Their devotion to the law and their profession that they keep it are immaterial. Jewish keepers of the law would overlook small transgressions. Paul would not. For him it was plain enough that nobody keeps all the regulations in the law, and because of this everybody comes under the curse that Deuteronomy makes so clear. *Continue*[27] makes it clear that small lapses now and then are not to be overlooked, as does the specification *all the things*. The GNB brings this out by translating, 'Whoever does not always obey everything that is written in the book of the Law is under God's curse!' Paul is reminding his hearers that for the law-keeper, the one who saw salvation as depending on keeping the law, every provision of the law was important. And it was important that every provision be observed continually.[28] The Galatians who had embraced circumcision had not reflected on the full obligations that their commitment

[25]Paul does not say exactly 'law-workers' but 'as many as are *ex ergōn nomou*'. The preposition denotes origin and here will mean those whose essential position originates in the law, those who see law-keeping as the essence of our approach to God. It is not simply that they see the law as important: they see it as all-important. Their whole position depends on the keeping of the law. There is a contrast with *hoi ek pisteōs* in verse 7.

[26]BAGD see this use of *hypo* as that for 'power, rule, sovereignty, command' (2b); those who rely on their keeping of the law are in fact making a great mistake. They are not achieving merit in God's sight but subjecting themselves to the rule of curse.

[27]*Emmenei* points to a 'remaining in'. Any Jew would keep some of the law's regulations, but remaining in them all at all times was quite another matter.

[28]Burton remarks, 'The principle of legalism ... leads logically to universal condemnation, by bringing all under the condemnation of the law.' Curiously E. P.

involved. They should be in no doubt that if they failed to keep all the law's provisions then the law itself pronounced them accursed.[29]

11. Not only does the law pronounce its curse on all those who fail to keep its provisions, but Paul sees Old Testament Scripture as pointing plainly to the truth of justification by faith. He says that it is *obvious* that *no-one is justified with God by the law*: the Bible itself makes it clear that law-keeping is not the way to salvation. He has made much of this point in 2:16, but it is important and he repeats it. The apostle cites the words of Habbakuk: *He that is just by faith will live* (Hab. 2:4; the words could also be understood in the sense, 'He that is just will live by faith', but this is not as likely; Paul is writing about the way the sinner receives salvation, not the way he lives out the implications of his salvation).[30] This places salvation squarely in the hands of God. The sinner cannot merit his salvation, but he can trust God and when he does he receives salvation as a free gift. *Cf.* Goodspeed, 'the upright will have life because of his faith'.

It is sometimes urged that Paul's 'proof' of justification by faith by his citation of Habakkuk 2:4 is flawed, but as Cole remarks, 'Paul does not even try to prove his doctrine of "justification by faith" from this verse; he only illustrates it. He actually proves it from God's ways of dealing with Abraham.' Cole also doubts whether Paul is in fact misrepresenting Habbakuk. It may be that Paul's method of exegesis differs from ours, but we must reckon with the fact that he is giving an important exegesis of some critical texts.

Sanders holds that 'the thrust of Gal. 3:10 is borne by the words *nomos* and "cursed," not by the word "all," which happens to appear' (*Paul, the Law, and the Jewish People* [Philadelphia, 1985], p. 21). That the word 'all' just 'happens' to appear is contradicted by its threefold occurrence in the very next chapter after that from which the quotation is taken (Dt. 28:1, 15, 58). It is an important word. *Cf.* W. Grundmann, 'In no case can there be dispensation from even the smallest commands' (*TDNT*, IV, p. 536).

[29]'Paul is speaking here of the law as a *life-principle*. As such it stands diametrically opposed to faith' (Ridderbos, p. 125, n. 7). Fung has a thoughtful discussion of this passage and concludes, 'Because Scripture says that it is he who is righteous (that is justified) *by faith* that will live, it follows that no one is justified by works of the law (irrespective of one's success or failure in keeping it).' Bruce cites M. Noth, who points out that 'on the basis of the Deuteronomic (Dt. 12 – 26) and Holiness (Lv. 17 – 26) codes alike, "there is no place for the idea of good, meritorious works and a reward which may be earned thereby; the blessing is not earned, but freely promised. On the basis of this law there is only one possibility for man of having his own independent activity: that is transgression, defection, followed by curse and judgment. And so, indeed, 'all those who rely on the works of the law are under a curse'."'

[30]Betz reminds us that in LXX Hab. 2:4 reads *ek pisteōs mou zēsetai*, which yields the sense 'will live by my [God's] faithfulness'. But this is not the sense of the Hebrew and should not be accepted.

12. This is markedly different from putting law in the first place. Nobody receives the keeping of law as a free gift; it comes only as one strives against evil and puts forth a strong effort to do good (*cf.* Rom. 9:32). Conformity to the law is not a matter of trust, of belief; it is a matter of achievement. Paul goes on to cite Leviticus 18:5, an exhortation to the Israelites to keep the Lord's decrees and laws because *he who does them will live in them.* The primary thrust of this may well signify the way to live this present life to the full,[31] but Paul sees as more important the eternal life that comes through faith. He insists that justification before God is the result of trusting God, not of achieving merit by one's own efforts. Duncan reminds us that 'in every age the profession of evangelical religion may go hand in hand with a punctilious attention to religious observances'. But Paul is not objecting to any 'punctilious attention to religious observances'; what he is insisting 'is that faith and the observance of Law are incompatible as grounds of *justification'.* The law is concerned with doing things; it prescribes conduct. But faith is not concerned with doing things; it means trusting someone. And because Scripture speaks of faith as the way to God, salvation cannot be by works. Faith and works may well exist together in the one life; indeed, they should exist together. But faith and works cannot both be the way to salvation. Doing something to merit salvation is one thing; trusting God to do what is needed is quite another.

13. The apostle moves to the atonement Christ wrought for sinners. Christ, he says, *redeemed us from the law's curse.* There are various ways of looking at the atonement: it may be seen as bringing forgiveness, as putting sinners into a right covenant relationship to God, or as a process of justification, and there are other ways of looking at it. Redemption points to the payment of a price that sets sinners free.[32] It referred to the practices of warfare. After a battle the victors would not uncommonly capture some of the vanquished. The poorer ones would

---

[31]G. J. Wenham comments on Lv. 18:5, 'What is envisaged is a happy life in which a man enjoys God's bounty of health, children, friends, and prosperity. Keeping the law is the path to divine blessing' (*The Book of Leviticus* [Grand Rapids, 1979], p. 253). A little later he says, 'it is Jesus and Paul who insist that the full meaning of life is eternal life.' *Cf.* Calvin, 'And yet it does not follow that faith is idle or that believers are not free from good works. For the present question is not whether believers ought to keep the law as far as they can (which is beyond all doubt), but whether they obtain righteousness by works; and this is impossible.'

[32]Paul's verb is *exagorazein* (4 times in the New Testament, all in Paul). BAGD say that it means literally 'buy back', but that it may be used in the sense 'deliver', while 'The thing from which deliverance is obtained is added with *ek.*' I have discussed the meaning of this verb in *The Apostolic Preaching of the Cross,* pp. 55–59.

almost certainly finish up as slaves, but the men of rank, men who mattered in their own country, would be held to ransom. When the people in the homeland had raised the necessary sum of money they would pay it to the victors and the captives would be set free. The process was called redemption, the price was called the ransom.

The terminology in time was extended to other areas of life. Thus a slave might be set free on payment of a price (which he himself might painfully acquire and in due course pay to his owner). This could take place in a temple and the record could be carved in the wall so that all might know that this slave was now a free man (Osiek finds this imagery 'attractive'). A man under sentence of death might on occasion be set free on payment of a price, and this too was seen as a process of ransoming the condemned.

There are other ways of looking at what Christ has done for us, but this one is used on a number of occasions. It brings out the truth that sinners are not able to break free from their sin; they are slaves. It also emphasizes that a great price has been paid for their freedom. Christ has done all that is necessary and his death is the means of making sinners free. Luther insists on the importance of the words *for us*: 'For he saith not that Christ was made a curse for himself, but "for us". Therefore all the weight of the matter standeth in this word "for us"' (p. 269).

Here Paul relates the slavery of sinners to their being under a curse, a truth he demonstrates by quoting Deuteronomy 21:23. This passage did not refer to crucifixion (which the Jews did not practise), but to the hanging on a tree or a wooden post of the corpse of a criminal who had been executed. But in New Testament times a cross was often called a tree and there is no doubting that that is what Paul has in mind here. The curse meant a death sentence and sinners are ransomed from this by the death of Jesus. Paul does not let his readers escape from the truth that sin is serious, for it brings God's curse on the sinner. But he insists just as firmly on the truth that those who put their trust in Christ have nothing to fear.[33] They are redeemed, bought

---

[33]Paul says that Christ became a curse 'for us', *hyper hēmōn*, which, as Ridderbos points out, 'is the thought of *substitution*'. He reminds us that in the papyri *hyper* is used in signatures where a scribe wrote in the place of an illiterate person. Robertson argues that one who acts on behalf of another mostly takes his place. 'Whether he does or not depends on the nature of the action, not on *anti* or *hyper*' (p. 630). Here, 'we were *under* the curse; Christ took the curse on himself . . . We went free while he was considered accursed' (p. 631). George Carey writes, 'The curse from which Christ redeemed us was *our* curse . . . He stood where we should have stood and died a death we should have died. If that is not *substitution*, I don't know what is' (*The Gate of*

out of the effect of the curse that rested on them, and brought into the glorious liberty of the people of God.[34]

14. Paul brings out the purpose[35] of God in Christ's atoning death. He speaks of *the blessing of Abraham*, another reference to Genesis 12:3 with its assurance that God will bless everyone who blesses Abraham and that all the nations will be blessed through Abraham. Paul goes on to specify *the Gentiles* as the recipients of the blessing, but we should notice that the blessing is on these people only as they are *in Christ Jesus* (for this expression see the note on 1:22). The apostle rounds off this part of his argument with four important words. The first is *receive* (he is speaking of a gift), the second is *the promise* (this is not to be seen as an unexpected novelty, but as the fulfilment of God's purpose from of old), the third is *the Spirit* (for believers are not left to their own efforts as they try to serve God; the very Spirit of God is given to them;[36] *cf.* Lk. 24:49; Acts 1:4–5), and the fourth is *faith*, another reminder of the truth that Christians do not earn their salvation by hard work, but receive it by faith as God's good gift.

4. Covenant, 3:15–22

> [15]*Brothers, I am speaking as a man; even a human covenant, duly ratified, no-one nullifies or alters.* [16]*Now the promises were spoken to Abraham and to his seed. It does not say 'and to the seeds', as in the case of many, but as of one, 'to your seed', which is Christ.* [17]*Now this I say: a covenant ratified beforehand by God, the law, 430 years later, does not void so as to nullify the promise.* [18]*For if the inheritance were of law it would no longer be of promise; but to Abraham God gave it through a promise.*
>
> [19]*Why then the law? It was added on account of transgressions,*

Glory [London, 1992], p. 143). Hendriksen lists about 40 passages in which he finds Christ's substitutionary atonement taught in Scripture. It is an important part of our understanding of the atonement.

[34]Longenecker comments, 'All of this, it seems, suggests that what we have here is a pre-Pauline, Jewish Christian confessional statement regarding Jesus' death as a redeeming and atoning self-sacrifice.' If this is so, the words are a very early Christian understanding of the cross. Chrysostom comments, 'As by dying He rescued from death those who were dying, so by taking upon Himself the curse, He delivered them from it.'

[35]The clause is introduced with *hina*.

[36]Meyer points out that the expression could mean 'that which is promised by the Spirit' or 'the promised Spirit' and argues that the second is meant. Moule sees the expression as 'equivalent to an English phrase such as *the promised Spirit*' (p. 176).

until the seed to whom it was promised should come, being appointed through angels in the hand of a mediator. ²⁰But the mediator is not of one (party), but God is one. ²¹Is the law then contrary to the promises of God? By no means. For if a law had been given that could give life, surely righteousness would have been by law. ²²But the Scripture has shut up all things under sin so that what was promised, being through faith in Jesus Christ, might be given to those who believe.

Paul has made it clear that it was Abraham's faith that mattered, and that following the law, as the Judaizers advocated, led only to the curse (3:10). What then are we to make of the purpose of that law and of the covenant into which Moses led all the nation? Do they not nullify all previous arrangements? Paul argues strongly that they do not. They must be understood in the light of the covenant God made with Abraham, not as effectively nullifying it. Allan points out that God made promises to Abraham 'of his own free and gracious will'. The subsequent giving of the law does not alter this, for 'once gracious, he is always gracious'.

15. *Brothers* is the warm personal address. Paul is taking up a position radically different from that of the Judaizers in Galatia. But, although he might scold some of his converts who were impressed by this new teaching and were wavering in their attachment to him, he still sees them as brothers in Christ. He qualifies what he is about to say by telling his readers that he is *speaking as a man*, speaking on a purely human level.[37]

There are problems about the following words. First, there is the meaning of the word rendered *even*.[38] Whichever way we take it, Paul is pointing to human practice, and reasoning that this gives us a clue to what has happened with the divine establishment of a covenant with Abraham.

Then there is the question how we should understand the word I

---

[37]The exact expression *kata anthrōpon legō* is found again in the New Testament only in Rom. 3:5, though similar words occur in Rom. 6:10; 1 Cor. 9:8; 2 Cor. 11:17. D. Daube remarks, 'The phrase is an apology for a bold statement which, without such an apology, might be considered near-blasphemous – be it because it is too anthropomorphic or be it because it sounds otherwise lacking in reverence for God or an established religious idea' (*The New Testament and Rabbinic Judaism* [London, 1956], p. 394).

[38]*Homōs.* It usually has a meaning like 'nevertheless' (LSJ) and most scholars take it in this sense, reasoning that the word has been misplaced and that we should take it after *diathēkē*. BDF, however, suggest that 'we have to do rather with the earlier *homōs* "equally", and it is therefore to be translated "also, likewise"' (BDF, p. 450 [2]).

have translated *covenant* (and which recurs in 3:17). In Greek generally it is commonly used in the sense of a last will and testament, but in the Greek Old Testament it is the regular translation of the Hebrew word for 'a covenant'. The experts are divided as to which sense we should understand here. The AV and NIV have 'covenant' in both places, JB has 'will' in both places, and Phillips has 'contract' both times. The NRSV has 'will' in verse 15 and 'covenant' in verse 17, GNB chooses 'agreement' and 'covenant', and REB has 'will and testament' in 3:15 with 'a testament, or covenant' in 3:17.[39]

With the experts so divided, it is not easy to come to a decision (and Boice suggests that we should understand both meanings here). But it is surely unlikely that Paul is using the word in two different senses in these two places, so close together and with no indication of a shift in meaning.[40] We should understand him to be following the biblical meaning both times. Accordingly I take the word throughout this passage to mean 'covenant' rather than 'testament' (though the impossibility of changing a testament may well lurk in the background). Paul is pointing out that a covenant is a binding engagement. A duly ratified covenant means that the parties have come to an agreement and the covenant expresses the terms of that agreement. When that has been done *no-one nullifies or alters*[41] the terms agreed upon. If such alterations were possible, human affairs would be thrown into complete confusion. It is of the first importance that binding agreements be honoured.[42]

16. The apostle invites his readers to pay attention to what was done

[39]*Diathēkē* in Greek generally signifies *'disposition* of property by will, *testament'* (LSJ), but in LXX it translates the Hebrew word for 'covenant'. Is Paul following Greek usage generally or is he using the term as it is employed in the Old Testament? It seems likely that he is employing the word in the biblical sense in a passage like this which draws attention to the Old Testament. It is also relevant that Paul uses the word *diathēkē* in all 9 times and in every other place it is in the sense 'covenant'. See further my *The Apostolic Preaching of the Cross,* ch. 2. For the view that the term should be understood in the sense 'will, testament' see the discussion in Ramsay. Another suggestion is that it was a 'Jewish deed of gift' (*New Documents,* 6, pp. 46f.).

[40]Cf. Betz, 'Schlier . . . is correct in saying that one should not render *diathēkē* in 3:17 differently from 3:15'. Burton sees this meaning as required by 'the usage of N.T. in general and of Paul in particular and the context here'.

[41]*Epidiatassomai* occurs here only in the New Testament. It is a technical legal term with the meaning 'add a codicil' to a will (BAGD).

[42]Though he argues for the meaning 'will' for the word in this place, Bruce can yet point out that 'when a deed of settlement is properly signed, sealed and delivered and the property legally conveyed, not even the original owner can revoke it or alter its terms'. Longenecker draws attention to evidence that alterations to wills could be made, but he concludes, 'the point of Paul's example in its application is clear: that

when God made his covenant with Abraham. This involved promises made *to Abraham and to his seed*. Paul is particularly concerned with what happened after the time of Abraham and he draws attention to the singular *seed*. It was, of course, true that the singular could be used in a collective sense, referring to all the descendants (as with us). But there is no denying that the word *seed* is in the singular and Paul insists that this is important. He points out that the word for *seed* is singular in Genesis 13:15–16 (this is the case also in Gn. 17:8; 24:7); it is not 'seeds' but *seed*. While his method may have rabbinic justification,[43] his interpretation of the passage he quotes is most unusual even if he is drawing attention to an important scriptural truth.[44] The term *seed* not uncommonly denotes all the descendants of some great ancestor, but it is not normally used of one person. Used in this way it points to the person as in some way outstanding; the *seed* is not simply one descendant among many but THE descendant. Paul adds *which is Christ* to make it quite clear who *the seed* is. The absence of the definite article shows that he is using *Christ* as a proper name, and not as a title. His argument is not concerned with the fact that Abraham's descendants became a nation, a nation that persisted through the centuries. It is concerned with the fact that God's chosen one, the Christ, appeared in due course and that the covenant God made centres on him.[45]

17. Paul is about to make an important statement. He prefaces it with *Now this I say*, which underlines what follows as significant. He goes on to speak of *a covenant ratified beforehand*[46] *by God*; such a covenant duly established by God is not something that can be altered. *The law*, Paul points out, came *430 years later*,[47] which means

---

God established his covenant with Abraham in an irrevocable manner, so it can never be annulled or added to'.

[43]There is evidence that some Rabbis based arguments on the use of the singular or plural of nouns in Scripture (SBk, III, p. 553). Paul is employing a method that would have been familiar to his fellow countrymen.

[44]Osiek points out that 'of Abraham's two sons, only Isaac and not Ishmael, was to transmit the promise' (and we might add, Jacob and not Esau). Osiek further holds that 'Paul is faithfully representing the intention of the author and carrying it forward to show that the divine selectivity rests ultimately on Christ'.

[45]*Cf.* Cole, 'Paul is saying, in typically Jewish fashion, that there is an appropriateness in the use of the singular form here, in that the true fulfilment came only in connection with one person, Christ.'

[46]The verb *prokyroō*, '*make valid or ratify previously*' (BAGD) is found here only in the New Testament. It makes it clear that the covenant had been legally established long before the law made its appearance.

[47]Luther suggests that the Jews might have reasoned that when the law 'as a better successor, was come, not the idle, but the doers of the law might be made righteous

that many generations had lived and died secure in the knowledge that God's covenant with Abraham had been established. People had lived their whole lives in reliance on what God had done and in the certainty that the promises made in the covenant would be fulfilled. There is a problem with the specification of *430 years*, for this is the time the Israelites lived in Egypt (Ex. 12:40). It may be that Paul is simply giving good measure – the Israelites were in Egypt for this period of time and the patriarchs lived before it began. Another suggestion is that we should bear in mind that the promise to Abraham was confirmed to Jacob (Gn. 28:14), and date Paul's words from this, for it was in Jacob's time that the people went into Egypt. A further suggestion is that we should remember that Abram was told that his descendants would be enslaved for 400 years (Gn. 15:13). Some of the rabbis seem to have reasoned that 400 years was the time spent in Egypt, while 430 years was the period between God's covenant with Abram and the giving of the law to Moses (SBk, II, p. 670). Whichever view we adopt, it is plain that a lengthy period elapsed between God's making his covenant with Abraham and his giving of the law to Israel, and it is this that is important.

The law was something quite different from the promises of God and it did not make its appearance until 430 years later. This time lapse meant that it *does not void*[48] the covenant; a law subsequent to the covenant cannot make it *void*. The Jews were putting their emphasis on the law as of divine origin and insisting that believers must be circumcised in accordance with the provisions of the law. Paul's counter is that the law is too late. God had made his covenant with Abraham and that covenant had stood for 430 years before the law was given. A duly ratified covenant cannot be annulled by a novel provision made hundreds of years later.[49]

Paul makes this point by drawing attention to the fact that the law is not able *to nullify the promise*. God's promise to Abraham was a serious undertaking. It is not to be set aside by the fact that hundreds of years later God gave Israel a law which would be their guide as they sought to serve him. Paul is not denying the validity of the law. He is not saying that Jews ought not to take it as their guide and seek to keep its many provisions. Those God-given provisions showed them the way

---

thereby'. But 'that which God once hath promised and confirmed, he calleth not back again, but it remaineth ratified with him for ever' (p. 288).

[48]MM cite examples of the use of the word group in the papyri to denote actions 'voided by illegality', and they add that this is 'a classical use'.

[49]The Jews dealt with this problem by holding that Abraham kept the law before it was given (see SBk, III, pp. 204–206).

they ought to live. But he is saying quite firmly that those provisions did not provide a path by which they could merit salvation. The promise of God given in the covenant was not lightly given and must not be overlooked by those who try to worship God and to serve him. They must not think that the law can void the provisions of the covenant, or, as Paul puts it, *nullify the promise*.

18. Paul sets out the alternatives: *law* and *promise* are mutually exclusive. The apostle's opponents were insisting on the importance of God's law. Let them realize then that God has made a promise and that this does not depend on people keeping the law. Paul reminds them that God promised the inheritance to Abraham and did not put before the patriarch a legal system. The relationship between God and the great patriarch was not that of two contrasting parties who had come to an agreement. It was that of a great God making a promise to one of his people. The law was a much later phenomenon.[50] The concluding words of the verse are forceful: *to Abraham* comes first, for the example of the patriarch was specially important. *Through a promise*: the preposition indicates the means through which God conveyed his good gift; 'promise' is very much in Paul's mind at this section of his argument; he uses the word 8 times in this chapter. He is emphasizing the fact that the gift God made to Abraham was far from being the result of law-keeping. It came to the great patriarch only by promise (*cf.* Schmoller, 'not put him in actual possession, but assured it to him'). The verb that follows is in the perfect tense, which indicates that the gift was complete and permanent.[51] And the subject of the verb, *God*, comes last for emphasis. It was none less than God who made this gift.

19. All this raises the question of the nature and place of the law. There was no doubting that for most Jews of that day the essence of religion was law: God had given the law through Moses and the duty of the people of God was to obey it. But there was no doubting either,

---

[50]Lenski stresses that the Judaizers were not taking seriously what God had done: 'Abraham had the inheritance of the confirmed testament by faith in the testamentary promise alone without any law or works of law, and these Judaizers are now telling the Galatians that they can have it only by obeying the Mosaic law that was given hundreds of years later. This is not even modification, it is utter cancellation of God's testament.' Stott points out that 'God said that in Abraham's seed all the families of the earth would be blessed', and proceeds to ask, 'How could the whole world be blessed through Jews living in the land of Canaan?'

[51]'The perfect *kecharistai* implies that God not only granted the inheritance to Abraham in the past but continues to make it good to his descendants' (Bruce). It 'emphasizes the gracious, uncommercial, character of the grant, and the perfect tense marks the grant as one still in force' (Burton).

as Paul here points out, that Abraham was given a promise by God and that that patriarch could not follow a divine law that would not be given for hundreds of years. So the question arises, *Why*[52] *then the law?* If God always intended to give the blessing by grace, as he had done with Abraham and as he had promised to do with Abraham's descendants, then why did he later give *the law* to his people? Paul says it was *added*; it was something extra, something in addition to the covenant made with the patriarch; it was an addition, not a substitute. The expression indicates that the promise was the primary thing; the law was simply a supplement to the promise. Duncan can say that 'it was designed, not to reveal fully His will, but to deal with a special necessity, viz. the necessity of bringing home to His chosen people their sinfulness'.

And it was added *on account of transgressions*. The apostle does not explain this, and it may mean that the law gave directions which steered people away from transgressions (JB, 'to specify crimes'). Or it may signify that it made provision for sinners to make offerings to God to 'make atonement' when they had done wrong; or that it enabled sinners to see sin for what it is (REB, 'It was added to make wrongdoing a legal offence'); without the law sinners would not recognize that they were sinners in God's sight (*cf.* Rom. 3:20; 4:15). The law was given not so much to take away sin as to show us how greatly we need salvation.[53] The addition did not indicate a permanent change. Paul says it was there only *until the seed . . . should come.* He has already used the term *seed* to denote Christ (verse 16), and now *should come* points to the time of the incarnation. The function of the law was to point people to Christ, not to provide for all time the way the people of God should live. *To whom it was promised* indicates that the central function of the law was that it pointed to Christ, to who he was and what he would do. The Galatians who set such great store by the law, Paul is saying, were missing its central function. The law was never meant to be a permanent guide to the people of God showing them the way of salvation. It was there to point people to the Son of God. That it *was promised* shows that this was the divine intention from the first.

Paul does not want the Galatians to miss the great dignity of the law. It was *appointed through angels* (*cf.* Acts 7:53; Heb. 2:2), which means that it had heavenly significance and was not to be denigrated

---

[52]See BAGD, *tis, ti,* 3a; BDF, p. 480 (5).
[53]Stott quotes Andrew Jukes, 'Satan would have us to prove ourselves holy by the law, which God gave to prove us sinners.'

by anyone. There are several references to angelic activity at the time of Moses. An angel appeared to him in flames of fire at Horeb, and there are several references to an angel as going before the Israelites as they went out of Egypt through the wilderness to the land of Canaan (Ex. 14:19; 23:20, 23; 32:34; 33:2). But there do not appear to be references to angels in the plural (except perhaps in Dt. 33:2).

In the hand of a mediator points to the way the law was given to Israel. We should probably understand that Moses is the mediator[54] in question, for it was through him that the law was given on Mount Sinai, though we should notice that some have seen the meaning as an angel or angels. It is perhaps curious that Paul speaks of *the hand* of the mediator,[55] but there is no real difficulty in seeing the meaning. Both angelic and human efforts are to be seen in the way the law came to the people of God.

20. There have been many ways of interpreting this verse (Lightfoot says the number 'is said to mount up to 250 or 300'; Meyer examines 16 views apart from the one he accepts). We should accordingly maintain a reverent reserve in our exposition of its meaning. But Paul appears to be saying that when there is mediation going on, *the mediator is not of one*: there must be two parties in dispute before there can be a place for mediation. Human sin had made a gap between sinners and God, thus bringing about a situation where mediation was needed. Paul, however, does not follow this up; he goes on immediately to say, *but God is one*. There is to be no doubt but that God is not divided. There is only one God and in all Israel's relationship to God that is clear. There is no second god to whom sinners may go when confronted with the demands deity makes on them. There is one God and his demands are unchanging.

21. The Judaizers had emphasized the significance of the law; in their eyes it was of central importance that converts should see the law as of divine origin and therefore as binding on all believers. Paul has denied that Christians are under any obligation to seek salvation by keeping the law. It is central to his whole argument that believers are saved by what Christ has done for them, not by any effort of their own. All that they can do is to believe, to trust God, to retain a firm hold on the promises God has given them. He has argued that God

---

[54]The term *mesitēs* is applied to Moses by Philo (*Moses*, II.166; *Somn.* 143). Ridderbos sees 'the lesser glory of the law' in that it 'unlike the promise, had not come directly from God to the people, but by way of angels, and even these again proclaimed it through the service of a human mediator, namely Moses'.

[55]Meyer takes this literally, '*With the tables in his hand*, he was God's envoy to Israel, acting between the two parties.' *Cf.* Ex. 32:19.

accepted Abraham without requiring anything from him other than trust, and he has further argued that nothing more than trust is required of Christians for salvation.

Now he turns to the question whether there is an opposition between *the law* on the one hand and *the promises of God* on the other. Are we to say that at one time God accepted Abraham on the basis of that patriarch's faith, but that later he led Moses to teach a changed position, namely that people must earn their place with God by keeping the law? It might be argued by some that the law is *contrary to the promises of God*. Whereas promises had been made to Abraham and extended to his descendants after him, are we now to say that the coming of the law altered the whole position so that believers can no longer rely solely on God's promises?

The apostle's answer is an emphatic *By no means*.[56] The idea that there should be contradictions in what God does is preposterous. In Paul's thinking *the law* could not possibly be in contradiction of *the promises of God*. It is the one God who gave the law and made the promises. *The law* and *the promises* have different functions, but that does not place them in contradiction. Paul points out that it is reasonable to expect that if *a law had been given that could give life* then keeping the law would be the way righteousness would be attained.[57] The implication is that the law given in the Old Testament, like every other law, was quite unable to make people righteous. It was evidently accepted by the Galatians in general (as by most other peoples at most other times) that people become righteous by doing righteous deeds. But it was basic for Paul that nobody can do righteous deeds all the time. All people slip from their highest standards from time to time and it is the sins that they commit that form the problem. Because they commit sins they are sinners, not righteous people. The law can keep telling them to do what is right but it cannot give them the power to do this.

When Paul says, *if a law had been given that could give life*, he is drawing attention to the fact that no law, not even that divinely given in the Old Testament, can bring life to people. A law can lay down what people ought to do, but it cannot give them the power to overcome the temptations to do evil. Even the divinely given law

[56]For *mē genoito* see the note on 2:17.

[57]Righteousness would then have been *ek nomou*; *ek* indicates the source; righteousness would have sprung from the law. But to Paul it is plain that nobody keeps all the law and that accordingly righteousness is not 'from law'. The construction in the Greek sentence, *ei* with a past tense in the first clause and *an* with a past tense in the second, implies that the condition has not been fulfilled. The law cannot give life.

could do no more than direct people to the right way. It could demonstrate that people were not righteous, but it could not make them righteous people, people fit to be in the kingdom of God.

22. *But*[58] is strongly adversative; the true situation is very far from the law bringing people into a state of righteousness. Paul goes on to refer to what Scripture does. He is probably referring to Scripture as a whole, not to any one specific passage in the Bible. He points out that Scripture extends far beyond the law. Indeed what Scripture does is to *shut up all things*[59] *under sin*. That is to say, the Bible makes it clear that we are all sinners. It excludes every other possibility. As Calvin puts it, 'It shuts up all men under accusation and therefore, instead of giving, it takes away righteousness.' The singular may be a way of referring to the Old Testament as a whole, or it may refer to a specific passage (such as Dt. 27:26 or Ps. 143:2). The verb *shut up*[60] indicates imprisonment; it is not just that people sometimes do what they should not, but they are the prisoners of sin. They may on occasion do good, but they cannot break free from all evil. Scripture makes it clear that we are all sinners, a truth Paul brings out on a number of occasions. It is basic for him that the saved are saved by the grace of God, never by virtue of their own ethical achievements.

Paul sees a divine purpose in all this. We are all shut up under sin *so that*[61] God's blessing might be given to believers. Sin is personified and seen as a jailor, keeping sinners under its control so that they cannot break free. The apostle speaks of *what was promised*, which brings out the thought that salvation comes about through the exercise of God's will. It is not merited, nor is it the result of some supreme effort whereby the prisoner makes his way out of prison. Salvation comes about only because of what God has promised. We should be clear that this salvation comes to sinners who see themselves for what they are and repent.

Paul underlines the freeness of God's bounty. Having made the point that the blessing comes by way of promise, he goes on to say

---

[58]*Alla.*

[59]Nigel Turner cites this as an example of the use of the neuter where 'the emphasis is less on the individual than on some outstanding general quality' (MIII, p. 21; he notes that the masculine is used in the similar Rom. 11:32).

[60]*Synkleiō* is used in the sense 'confine, imprison' (BAGD). MM cite a papyrus containing this verb, and which is translated as 'you will be put in prison until you pay'. REB translates here, 'But scripture has declared the whole world to be prisoners in subjection to sin.'

[61]*Hina* indicates purpose. Barclay comments, 'The consequence of the law is simply to drive everyone to seek grace, because it has proved man's helplessness.'

that it is *through faith*, that it is *given* and that the recipients are *those who believe*. 'Not only is the promise grounded in faith; it is also dispensed only to those who believe. In no clearer way could Paul bring out the inseparable connection between promise and faith' (Guthrie). He leaves no room for the acquiring of merit by keeping the law that seems to have meant so much to the Judaizers who were leading his flock astray and to the converts who followed them. As we have seen before, *faith* is one of the great topics of this letter (the term occurs 22 times), and the addition *in Jesus Christ* makes it clear who is the object of the faith of which he writes.[62] That the blessing is *through* faith points to the truth that faith is not a merit which of itself brings the blessing; it is no more than the channel *through* which the blessing comes. This is reinforced when Paul goes on to speak of it as *given* (it is not in any sense merited) *to those who believe*. The Judaizers insisted on the importance of working, Paul on that of believing.

5. The law our tutor, 3:23–29

> [23]*But before faith came we were held in custody by law, shut up to the faith that was to be revealed,* [24]*so that the law was our custodian to bring us to Christ, so that we should be justified by faith.* [25]*But since faith has come we are no longer under a custodian.* [26]*For you are all sons of God through faith in Christ Jesus.* [27]*For as many of you as were baptized into Christ have clothed yourselves with Christ.* [28]*There is neither Jew nor Greek, there is neither slave nor free, there is no male and female; for you are all one in Christ Jesus.* [29]*But if you are Christ's then you are Abraham's seed, heirs according to promise.*

Paul proceeds to emphasize the primacy of faith. The law has been in vogue for centuries, but he makes it clear that this has not been in order that people should earn their salvation by complying with its commands. Rather, the law shows us up for what we are, sinners. And in this way the law points us all to Christ, the Saviour. Paul puts some emphasis on the truth that there is but one way of salvation, so that neither nationality nor social position nor sex makes any difference.

---

[62]This is the only place in his 22 uses of 'faith' in this letter where Paul explicitly connects faith to *Jesus Christ* (faith 'in Christ Jesus' occurs in 2:16; 3:26). Strictly he speaks of 'faith of Jesus Christ' but the genitive refers us to 'a Jesus Christ kind of faith' which we know from Paul's general usage to be faith 'in' Jesus Christ. Some writers take it in the sense 'the faithfulness of Jesus Christ', but this seems an unlikely meaning.

Faith in Jesus Christ is the one way to salvation, no matter what our earthly station.

23. Paul looks back to the time before Jesus came, but instead of speaking of him directly, he says *before faith came* ('Not the Christian Faith as a system of teaching, but faith as a principle of religious life', Allan; others suggest that Paul passes from the one meaning to the other in these verses). Trust in God has always been the characteristic attitude of the saved, but it was not possible to have faith in Jesus before Jesus appeared on earth. So Paul characterizes the new situation brought about by Jesus' spotless life and atoning death as the coming of faith. Prior to this, he says, *we were held in custody*[63] *by law*. The word *law* lacks the article here (it has it in the next verse), but it seems that the law given in the Old Testament is primarily in mind. The thought is that sinners cannot escape while they are confronted by the majesty of the law. They cannot avoid its condemnation. They cannot establish themselves as righteous. While the Gentiles were not subject to the law in the same sense as the Jews were, yet, as Paul puts it elsewhere, Gentiles can give evidence that the law is written in their hearts (Rom. 2:14–15). Just as surely as Jews were subject to the law of Moses, so surely were the Gentiles subject to the law they found written in their innermost being. With a change of verb (though with much the same meaning), they are *shut up*,[64] which signifies that they are quite unable to meet the law's demands. They are prevented from any advance by the way of law; the only way forward is that provided by *faith*. Far from the law being the gateway into a glorious liberty, it turns out to be a jailor, shutting people up. The result is that the only way of escape was through faith. But Paul is not speaking of faith as a virtue in itself, as though people were to be saved by a kind of 'believism'. It is *the faith that was to be revealed* of which he writes, faith in the Christ who alone can bring forgiveness of sins. Paul is making the point that there is but one way of salvation, the way of faith in the Christ who died to put away our sins. This faith is not a human discovery, but a faith *that was to be revealed*.[65] Paul is not saying that there was no way of salvation in Old Testament times (people could and did trust God through all those centuries), but simply that the

---

[63]*Phroureō* may be used in a good sense as in the peace of God guarding the hearts of believers (Phil. 4:7). But it may also signify being held in custody, which is the meaning here.

[64]*Synkleiō* is used literally, for example, of confining fish in a net, but here '(God's will as expressed in the Scripture) *has imprisoned everything under the power of sin*' (BAGD). Cole sees the idea as 'in protective custody'.

[65]This use of *mellō* is that for *'be destined, inevitable* (acc. to God's will)' (BAGD).

way salvation was brought about was not known in those times.

24. The result of this[66] was a situation in which *the law* functioned[67] as *our custodian to bring us to Christ.* The *custodian* was not a teacher, but a slave whose special task was to look after a child. He exercised a general supervision over the boy's activities, and it was his responsibility to bring him to the teacher who would give him the instruction that befitted his station.[68] The *custodian* looked after a boy from about the age of seven to seventeen. He took him to school and to other places; he watched over him to ensure that he acted in a way appropriate to his position in life. Paul is saying that the law was not the teacher that makes clear the way of salvation. It was the leader, which, properly followed, would bring those it led to Christ. This does not mean that the law leads people to Christ as from one teacher to another. Christ is the Saviour. The principal function of the law was not that of providing the way of salvation, but rather that of pointing to the Saviour. Betz rejects 'the idea of a positive educational development from Judaism to Christianity', and sees the meaning as 'until Christ'.

The purpose[69] of this was *so that we should be justified by faith.* Paul's readers should not see the law as antagonistic to the divine purpose. It was very much part of that purpose, though not in the way that the teachers who were leading some of the Galatians astray evidently thought. It did not bring people into salvation. It could do no more than show them that they had need of salvation and it pointed to the One who would bring salvation. And when that salvation came to any sinner it was because of *faith*, not on account of any keeping of the law.

---

[66]*Hōste* introduces the actual result.

[67]The perfect tense, *gegonen*, indicates the continuing function of the law.

[68]Longenecker cites several passages from ancient authors which show that 'The *paidagōgos*, though usually a slave, was an important figure in ancient patrician households'; he looked after the education of his young charge and saw to it that he was properly instructed. Ridderbos points out that a pedagogue was not a teacher and that the name 'had a stigma attached to it'. He thinks that in the present passage 'we are to understand this living under the law as under a pedagogue or tutor, not as a gradually formative education in freedom in the positive sense, but as a growing passion for freedom because of the oppressive yoke'. Hamann speaks of 'the unlovely ways of many slaves entrusted with the pedagogue's task' and sees the picture as marking the law's work 'as one of force, restraining power, strictness, severity, and harshness'. Luther takes the word in the sense 'schoolmaster', and evidently he had had some unfortunate experiences, for he writes, 'Although a schoolmaster be very profitable and necessary to instruct and to bring up children, yet show me one child or scholar which loveth his master' (p. 333).

[69]*Hina.*

The centrality of faith in the apostle's understanding of things shines through once more.

25. Paul personifies faith and speaks of what has happened since it came. There is a sense in which God has always looked for people to exercise faith, but Paul can say that now faith *has come*. This does not mean that there was a time when nobody had faith. It means rather that until the coming of Christ people did not see that they must have faith in him if they are to be saved. Now that *faith* is to be seen for the great reality it is, there is no longer any need for a *custodian*; people are no longer under the sway of any such being.[70]

26. *For* introduces the reason, and Paul goes on to point out that all the converts in Galatia are *sons of God*. He has been accusing them of a number of failings in their understanding of the Christian way, but he recognizes that despite their shortcomings in understanding they are genuine members of the family of God. Schmoller sees *all* as significant: *all* 'without distinction. This word is meant to emphasize strongly the power of faith. Whoever he be that has it, becomes a son of God and free from the schoolmaster, therefore you also are free.' That they are *sons of God* means that they are now members of the heavenly family. Lenski stresses the importance of the word *sons*: it 'suggests the idea of standing, independent standing, that is free from any mentor such as children would have (a nurse, a slave-guardian)'. And this, the apostle points out, is *through faith in Christ Jesus.*[71] The Galatians may have been extolling the place of the law and criticizing Paul despite his faithfulness to the gospel. But what mattered above all was that they genuinely had *faith in Christ Jesus* (for this word order see the note on 2:4). It is important to be clear on this. Many of God's children lack deep understanding of the Christian way, but that does not mean that they are not genuine Christians. Being a Christian is being a believer, not having an intellectual answer to all the problems we meet as we live out our Christian lives.

27. *For* introduces evidence to support what the apostle has just said. A number of scholars hold that the rest of verses 27–28 may be a quotation from the baptismal liturgy of the early church (*e.g.* Betz, Longenecker). This is, of course, possible, but as we have no information about such a liturgy, or indeed whether such a liturgy

---

[70]BAGD see *hypo* here as 'of power, rule, sovereignty, command, etc. *under*' (2.b); Moule suggests 'subject to' (p. 66). The preposition points to the truth that the law no longer controls the way people look for salvation.

[71]It is possible to take the words in the sense, 'in Christ Jesus you are all children of God through faith' (NRSV). *Cf.* Rom. 3:25.

existed, it is precarious to build anything on the possibility. *As many as*, of course, means all of those who had been baptized. Paul is not saying that baptism of itself brings salvation, but he is writing in a situation when some of the Galatians had accepted circumcision, the rite of admission into Judaism. He is affirming that those who have accepted Christian baptism with all that that means, that is to say those who have a genuine faith and whose baptism accordingly is meaningful, have done more than engage in an edifying piece of ceremonial. They *have clothed* themselves *with Christ*.[72] They have identified themselves with their Saviour. The metaphor does not point to something completely outward; rather (as I have commented on the similar expression in Rom. 13:14), 'it signifies not that which is merely external but habitual association and identification with Christ'. If they had reflected on what their baptism signified, the Galatians would not have been misled by the false teaching that led them to circumcision.

28. Paul brings out his point by referring to the unity that there is in Christ. There are many distinctions in human society, and in the first century the Jews despised the Gentiles (even proselytes were often not fully accepted), the Greeks looked down on uncultured people outside their race, the Romans felt themselves superior to those they had conquered, and so on. Probably people of every nation look down on outsiders. But in Christ all such distinctions are meaningless. Many commentators draw attention to an ancient prayer in which the Jewish man gives thanks that God has not made him a Gentile, a slave or a woman.[73] It is in rebellion against such a background that Paul affirms that *There is neither Jew nor Greek*. This means that the great divide between Jew and Gentile that meant so much to the Jews in general is meaningless.[74] If Christ has saved a person, that person is a Christian and whether he or she is Jew or Greek is irrelevant. Baptism unites

---

[72]Calvin comments, 'The sacraments present the grace of God both to the good and to the bad; nor do they deceive in promising the grace of the Holy Spirit; believers receive what is offered. By rejecting it, the ungodly render the offer unprofitable to themselves, but they cannot destroy the faithfulness of God and the true meaning of the sacrament.'

[73]The idea had a wider currency than among Jews. Thus A. Oepke speaks of 'a saying current in different forms among the Persians, Greeks and Jews in which man gives thanks that he is not an unbeliever or uncivilised, that he is not a woman and that he is not a slave' (*TDNT*, I, p. 777). Loane devotes all of his chapter 3 to the magnitude and the significance of the Christian stress on unity.

[74]'Actually, the Galatians were neither: to the Jews they were Gentiles, but to the Greeks, barbarians' (Lührmann). But the Galatians would have known accordingly what it was to be despised by both!

people across all national boundaries. Nationality was important for both Jews and Greeks. Jews divided the whole human race into Jews and Gentiles and they saw only themselves as making up the people of God. Greeks perhaps did not make such a complete division into the cultured and the uncultured, but they certainly saw themselves on a cultural level that they did not see elsewhere, and they looked down on all who lacked their cultural sensitivity.

The apostle moves on to the great social division of antiquity when he affirms that in Christ slavery makes no difference.[75] Throughout the Roman world the division between slave and free was of the greatest importance. Slaves had no rights, and the lowliest free person was infinitely more important than any slave, however gifted. To recognize that a believing slave was just as important in God's sight as the highest among the nobility was to point to a radical abolition of a distinction that was taken for granted throughout Paul's world. These words mark a revolution.

It was hardly less so with *no male and female*.[76] While occasionally women might attain importance or notoriety, it was almost universally true that the female of the species was allocated a very minor role. Women were not educated; often it was regarded as a sin to teach a woman. This meant that women had a very limited sphere in life. Their function was to be faithful wives, to bear children, to look after domestic affairs and generally to be subordinate. To affirm that *male and female* was an irrelevant distinction, indeed that there was no such distinction, was to make another revolutionary statement. Osiek sees a reference to Genesis 1:27 and speaks of 'an expression of the deep unity of humanity as it comes forth from the creating hand of God'. It is perhaps worth noticing that outside the Christian world to this day the idea of the equality of the sexes has not been widely accepted; non-Christians tend to assign women a restricted and inferior sphere (even nominal Christians do this at times, but that is not being true to Scripture). Ramsay thinks that the equality of women is very important, for 'the progress of the Christian nations is founded on the keeping alive of education and thought and conscious moral purpose among their women . . .'

[75]Stott remarks, 'Nearly every society in the history of the world has developed its class or caste system. Circumstances of birth, wealth, privilege and education have divided men and women from one another.'

[76]Both terms, *arsen kai thēly*, are neuter, which is the case also in Mt. 19:4; Mk. 10:6 and in Gn. 1:27 (LXX; this may well be a quotation). Betz remarks that this 'indicates that not only the *social* differences between man and woman ("roles") are involved but the *biological* distinctions'.

For introduces the reason for the world-shattering statements the apostle has made. He uses the personal pronoun *you* (he could have left it to the verb to show whom he was addressing, but the pronoun adds emphasis), which puts some emphasis on the Galatians to whom he is writing. His *all* is important. It makes no difference on which side of the distinctions he has made a given believer stands. It makes no difference if other distinctions are affirmed. *All* believers are one in Christ Jesus and the unity is the important thing. It does not matter whether a given believer is Jew, Greek, slave, free, male, female – all are one. It is the unity that counts, not the subdivisions into which believers may be divided.[77] This will have its application to the division between Jew and Gentile in Galatia, but Paul leaves no doubt that the principle applies much more widely.

We should not miss the point that the unity of which Paul writes is a unity *in Christ Jesus.* He is not writing about a unity that comes about as a result of human achievement. He is saying that when people are saved by Jesus Christ they are brought into a marvellous unity, a unity between the saved and the Saviour and a unity that binds together all the saved. Even the major divisions in the human race cannot do away with this unity. The Galatians should realize that the demands the Judaizers were making were irrelevant: people on both sides of the circumcision debate were already one if they were *in Christ Jesus.*[78]

29. Paul underlines his point. His *you* is emphatic: 'If *you* are Christ's'. He is not speaking only in general terms that might apply to people elsewhere but which had no relevance to Galatia. He is making a comment that had special relevance for Galatian Christians. The form of his conditional sentence points to the condition as fulfilled, 'If you are Christ's (as you are) . . .' Then it follows that they are *Abraham's seed.* All concerned in the debate that was going on were united in reverence and respect for Abraham. All the Jewish converts

[77]Bruce comments, 'No more restriction is implied in Paul's equalizing of the status of male and female in Christ than in his equalizing of the status of Jew and Gentile, or of slave and free person. If in ordinary life existence in Christ is manifested openly in church fellowship, then, if a Gentile may exercise spiritual leadership in church as freely as a Jew, or a slave as freely as a citizen, why not a woman as freely as a man?'

[78]W. Klassen remarks that 'the holy kiss' was important in the early church, as it 'helped Paul and his colleagues in the early church to keep Christianity from degenerating into an abstraction and also into a ritual and over some centuries "maintained the unity of the church". For it is difficult to ritualize a kiss. The admonitions to kiss one another serve to stress the liberty to express without inhibition to all people of whatever background, rank or gender, the ardour of *agapē* in any context. The "holy kiss" is a public declaration of the affirmation of faith', and he proceeds to quote Gal. 3:28 (*NTS*, 39, 1993, p. 135).

were physically his descendants and all the Gentile converts were spiritually his descendants. It is this second point that Paul brings out. The Gentile believers to whom he writes are no less than *Abraham's seed*. They are Abraham's spiritual descendants just as surely as the Jewish believers are Abraham's physical descendants.

Heirs is an important word in the present discussion. The Jews were very proud of the fact that they were the descendants of the great patriarch and physically his heirs. But more important than this was the fact that all who had faith, whether Jews or Gentiles, were heirs *according to promise*. God had made great promises to Abraham, and for Paul it was crystal clear that those promises were fulfilled in believers, not in those who could claim no more than physical descent.

GALATIANS 4

6. Sons of God, 4:1–7

¹But I say, for as long a time as the heir is a minor he is no different from a slave, though he is lord of all things, ²but is under guardians and managers until the time set by the father. ³So we also, when we were infants, were enslaved under the elemental principles of the world. ⁴But when the fullness of the time came, God sent his Son, born of a woman, born under law, ⁵in order that he might redeem those under law, so that we might receive adoption. ⁶But because you are sons God sent the Spirit of his Son into our hearts, crying, 'Abba, Father.' ⁷So then you are no longer a slave but a son; but if a son, also an heir, through God.

Paul proceeds to bring out something of the dignity of being members of God's household. The Judaizers might stress the importance of keeping the law in order that believers would merit a reward from God,[1] but Paul has a grander vision. He sees believers as already members of God's household, with all the rights and privileges that that involves. They are not in the position of being no more than minors, possible future full members of the divine family. They are *sons* now with all that that means.

1. *But I say* moves us to a different aspect of the topic. Paul has just called his readers 'heirs' (3:29), and he proceeds to develop an aspect of heirship by referring to a situation with which they must all have been familiar, the owner of an estate dying while his heir is still a young child. Paul does not in fact say whether the owner in his illustration is alive or dead, and some have thought that the situation he envisages is that which exists after the will has been made but before the owner has died. The more natural understanding of his

[1]Warren says that missionaries 'who go from the West, might be better expounders of the Epistle to the Galatians if they were more self-critically aware of the extent to which they consciously or unconsciously press upon the Christians of Africa and Asia ways of worship, interpretations of behaviour, and methods of community action which, albeit the treasured heritage of the West, are not of the essence of the good news of what God has done, and is willing to do, for all men everywhere' (p. 29). And not only missionaries should keep this in mind when we consider what the Judaizers were doing in Galatia. Paul's emphasis on what constitutes the essential teaching of Christianity is of permanent importance. It is all too easy to think that *my* brand of Christianity is superior to that of everyone else.

words, however, is that a man has died leaving his property to his young son with the proviso that the boy should be subject to guardians until he reaches a certain age.[2] Clearly a little boy cannot be put in the position of running an estate. He does not have the capacity, and he must be trained so that in due time he will be able to do all that is necessary. But throughout those years of training *he is no different from a slave*. Betz points out that there are some differences, but 'both, the minor and the slave, lack the capacity of self-determination'. In this respect there is no difference. The heir who is still a minor is all the time being told what to do instead of himself giving the orders. Everybody knows that *he is lord of all things*; everything in the estate is his property and in due course he will take over full control. But until that time comes he is no better than a slave. That, of course, does not alter the fact that the whole estate is his property. The way he lives day by day may reflect his real status very imperfectly. But it does not alter the fact that the truth of the matter is that he owns it all.

2. Though the heir is lord of the whole estate, during his minority he is *under guardians and managers*. The term *guardian* covers a variety of functions. It was used, for example, by Antiochus Eupator, who, when he became king, appointed Lysias to a position where he could be called 'the king's guardian' (2 Macc. 11:1). The word occurs in one of Jesus' parables, where it refers to the man who ran a vineyard for the owner (Mt. 20:8). There are other ways the term was employed, but it is clear that it points to someone who actually carried out the work of

---

[2]Ramsay points out that in Syrian law 'a child is subject to an *Epitropos* up to fourteen, thereafter he is able to make a Will and dispose of his own property, but the practical management of the property remains in the hands of a *curator* till the ward reaches the age of twenty-five'. He sees this as presupposed in what Paul says and regards it as supporting the South Galatian destination of the epistle. Duncan, however, finds this too dogmatic: 'It is probably true that Paul has here a definite situation in mind, but it may be doubted whether we have the *data* for interpreting that situation with precision.' Burton sees it as 'precarious to assume that the law found in a Syrian law book of the fifth century was in force in Phrygian cities in the first century'. Part of our problem lies in the fact that we do not know exactly what were the arrangements for guardianship and the like in first-century Galatia (or for that matter, first-century Judaism). Further, Burton points out that, unlike the Syrian book, Paul does not say 'who appoints the *epitropos* and *oikonomos* but does indicate that the father fixes the time at which the son passes from under their control' (the times were fixed in the Syrian book). We do not know of a guardianship in the ancient world in precisely the terms Paul uses (though *cf.* the guardianship Antiochus arranged for his son, whereby Lysias brought him up and in due course made him king [1 Macc. 3:32f.; 6:17]).

direction, even though it did not belong to him by right. So with respect to an inheritance, the *guardian*[3] is a person who does not own the property but who acts as though he does. He discharges all the responsibilities of management. He makes the decisions. He directs the workers. He buys and sells. The *manager*[4] signifies more or less the same functionary in this context. If there is a difference, the *guardian* is a person charged with the responsibility of bringing up the boy (with all else subordinate to this), while the *manager* is concerned with the running of the estate. The use of the two words underlines the significance of the fact that during the time of his minority the heir occupies a subordinate position. The plural in both words makes the point that there are many ways of arranging the management.

But however much authority the *guardian* or *manager* wields, he is still a subordinate. He does not own the property he administers. He occupies his position only *until the time set*[5] *by the father*. We might have expected that there would be a legal age at which the heir took over, but this expression shows that Paul envisages a situation in which the man who appointed the guardian might set any age he chose as that on the attainment of which the heir would take charge of the estate.

3. The use of the pronoun puts some emphasis on *we*; Paul is speaking not only about the coming of age of youthful heirs. He is referring to something of importance for both the Galatians and himself (and as he was a Jew the expression may be intended to place Jews in general in the same category). *Also* points to a similarity between immature heirs and Christians such as the Galatians and the apostle.[6] The expression translated *the elemental principles* is difficult.[7] The basic meaning of the word 'is apparently "standing in a row," hence "an element of a series" ' (Burton, p. 510). It is used of the letters of the alphabet, the ABC, which gives rise to the meaning (which some see here), 'rudimentary instruction', 'the elementary truths' (*cf.* its use

---

[3]*Epitropos.*

[4]*Oikonomos.* Several translations render 'trustees'.

[5]*Prothesmia.* MM give the meaning as 'the previously appointed day', and explain that this 'is a common legal term'. J. I. Packer sees a reference to 'a special guardianship operating during the father's lifetime rather than the regular guardianship of an orphaned minor' (*NIDNTT*, I, p. 477).

[6]*Nēpios* means a very young child; in Heb. 5:13 it is a child whose food is milk.

[7]*Stoicheion.* Meyer has a long note on the word, as does Burton (pp. 510–518). See also G. Delling in *TDNT*, VII, pp. 670–687. He says that Paul here is using the expression 'in a new way'; it 'denotes that whereon the existence of this world rests, that which constitutes its being', but Paul is using it 'for that whereon man's existence rested before Christ even and precisely in pre-Christian religion' (p. 685).

in that sense in Heb. 5:12). Then just as the ABC is the basis on which words and sentences are built up, so the term comes to be used of the basic elements out of which everything in the world is composed. This may give rise to the thought of the elemental spirits (*cf.* Moffatt, 'the Elemental spirits of the world'), or from another point of view, the heavenly bodies (Duncan cites Edwyn Bevan, 'The fear of these world-rulers, particularly the Sun, the Moon and the five planets, lay heavy on the old world. The Mysterious Seven held humanity in the mechanism of iron necessity', p. 135). In this passage the connection with *infants* indicates that Paul is concerned with the beginnings of knowledge, the ABC, and, of course, with religious knowledge. That we *were enslaved*[8] indicates that we were quite unable to break away from the elementary truths which were all that we could attain as infants. We are not to think of *the elemental principles* as religiously neutral, for elsewhere Paul uses the same expression in warning the Colossians to beware of false teaching which is 'according to the elemental principles of the world and not according to Christ' (Col. 2:8), and again when he says, 'If you have died with Christ from the elemental principles . . .' (Col. 2:20).

Paul then is saying that in our early life we were subject to these 'elemental principles'. Exactly what they were the apostle does not say. He may have in mind that the world in general was subject to evil influences or that the teaching given to the Galatians as well as to Paul was such as to enslave them to the things of this world or to the spirits at work in this world. Allan comments, 'Judaism and Paganism, the Law and Gentile ritual are put practically on the same level as inferior and slavish forms of religion. This is a suprisingly extreme view of the Law.' The revelation God has made in Jesus shows up the ideas of both the Jewish and the Gentile worlds for the elementary teaching they were.

4. *But* introduces a contrast. The control of the *elemental principles* was only for a limited time. In due course God sent his Son and that transformed everything. We should not miss the emphasis on the divine act. Paul is not saying that Jesus decided to start a new religious movement. He is saying that God acted in Christ. *The fullness*[9] *of the time* is an expression found only here in the New Testament (though

[8]Paul is 'classing all the non-Christian world as being in slavery to powers utterly beyond their control. The implication is that Jews are included and therefore any submission to Jewish scruples would be a return to their former slavery' (Guthrie).

[9]*Plērōma* may be used in the sense of 'that which fills' and so may signify what fills baskets (Mk. 6:43) or a patch which fills a hole (Mt. 9:16). But it also can have a meaning like 'full number' (Rom. 11:25). Here it signifies the filling up of the time, and thus 'the right time', 'the time for the fulfilling of God's purpose'. Hamann points out

Eph. 1:10 is similar). The noun *fullness* indicates here that God has been working his purpose out through history, and it was only when the right time came that he *sent his Son*. Paul is not talking about a more or less casual happening: *God*, no less, *sent*[10] *his Son*, no less. It is a divine activity of which Paul writes, not a more or less haphazard human activity. At the major point of human history God took action. Paul sees the coming of Jesus into this world as the high point. The reality of the incarnation is underlined with *born*[11] of *a woman*: Paul is not talking about an angelic visitation but about a genuinely human mother giving birth. Jesus really came where we are. Some see in the phrase a reference to the virgin birth, but this seems to be reading something into it. The words rather give expression to Jesus' true humanity (*cf.* Mt. 11:11; Lk. 7:28).

His incarnation as a Jew meant that he was *born under law*. Again we have the verb 'be, become', and again we must understand it as *born*. If he was to become incarnate it was not necessary that he should be under law. Indeed, if he had come to this earth as a member of any nation other than the Jewish nation he would not have been subject to the law revealed in the Old Testament. It is this law that is primarily in mind, of course, even though the word *law* lacks the article.[12] This was the law given to the people of God and it was to this law that the child Jesus became subject. Paul is objecting to the Galatians' becoming subject to the law, but he does not minimize its place in the divine plan. The law was important, as is seen by the fact that the Son of God became subject to it. But it did not occupy the place that the Galatians were supposing.

5. The coming of Jesus was for the purpose[13] of redeeming people. The verb[14] is used only by Paul in the New Testament and it forms part of the way he sees the atonement Christ wrought out. Atonement

---

that a number of factors may be cited for this: 'the blending and the unity of the various nations under Roman rule, the wide-spread use of the Greek language, the Jewish Dispersion, the network of Roman roads making for easy communication, the bankruptcy of paganism as seen in the multiplication of cults and the degeneracy of the old religions of Greece and Rome'. But he agrees that 'the fullness of time is the time in which God fulfils the promises given to Israel'.

[10]The verb 'comprises two thoughts: the going forth of the son from a place at which He was before; and His being invested with divine authority' (Ridderbos).

[11]The verb is *genomenon*, which, of course, has no necessary connection with birth. It signifies 'be, become', and is often used in the sense of passing from one state to another, here of the transition from the womb to the world.

[12]'Though Christ was born under the Mosaic law, the application of the principle is much wider' (Lightfoot).

[13]The clause is introduced with *hina*.

[14]*Exagorazō*. It has been used in 3:13, where see note.

is a many-sided affair. People who sin have broken God's laws and may be viewed accordingly as those deserving of penalty. They have forfeited all claim to legal standing and so have need of justification. Paul is reasoning that sinners are slaves to their sin (*cf.* Jn. 8:34). If they are to be rescued from their plight, a price should be paid, and that is what happened at Calvary. This way of looking at the cross puts some emphasis both on the price that was paid to bring sinners out of their plight and also on the freedom into which they have been introduced by Christ's atoning work.

Those under law strictly refers to the Jews, for whom the law of God was a most important category. The absence of the article here means that Paul is speaking of more than the law under which the Jews tried to live their lives (*cf.* Rom. 2:14–15). Here the apostle doubtless has in view all those who come under condemnation from whatever law they serve; they will be without any hope of saving themselves. But by Christ's death those who believe are redeemed. We should not miss the point that even those under law who are saved are *redeemed*; the law does not save them. It is not necessary for Gentiles who have been redeemed to seek to place themselves under the law. The purpose[15] of this is the admission of saved sinners into the family of God. They receive adoption.[16]

6. There is probably no adversative force in *But*; we could equally translate it as 'and'. Paul is moving to something of the meaning of adoption into the family of God. The redeemed have been adopted into that divine family, and because of their membership certain consequences follow. They are *sons of God*, full members of the divine family. That they are sons has further consequences. It is *because* they are sons that God *sent the Spirit of his Son* into their hearts.[17] We are to see the expression as referring to the Holy Spirit and not to some abstract 'spirit of sonship'. The Holy Spirit is not often linked to the Son as here, but all three members of the Trinity must be seen as

---

[15]*Hina* occurs twice in this verse: Christ came to be under law *in order that* he might redeem . . . *in order that* we might receive . . .

[16]The verb for *receive* is *apolambanō*, but it seems to be used much in the sense of the uncompounded verb. *Adoption* is *huiothesia*, a word which is used by Paul only in the New Testament (5 times). It was a technical term for the adoption of children into a family, and is here used of believers who turn to God and are adopted into the heavenly family. Following on the reference to redemption we see that God's purpose 'was that we might not only be delivered from the greatest evil but might also be crowned with the choicest blessing' (Hendriksen).

[17]Moule understands the passage in this way: 'not because *you are sons, God sent* . . . *but* [proof] that *you are sons* [*is the fact that*] *God sent* . . .' (p. 147).

closely connected. The emphasis is on the Son's saving activities. It is the Son who redeemed the readers and brought them into the divine family. The gift of the Spirit follows all this, and it is natural to link the Spirit with the Son accordingly.

The Spirit is sent by God; all three members of the Godhead are linked in the activity Paul mentions here (it was this kind of language that would eventually lead the church to formulate the doctrine of the Trinity). And God sent the Spirit *into our hearts*. We should notice that the presence of the Spirit in believers is in their *hearts*; it is something that happens in their innermost being and is not a minor disturbance on the surface of life. We might have expected Paul to say at this point 'into your hearts' (and indeed some manuscripts read 'your hearts'); both before and after this expression he has addressed the Galatians as 'you'. But it would seem that the presence of the Spirit in all believers influenced the apostle, so that he included himself with them in those who have the Spirit in their hearts.

The result of the indwelling of the Spirit is that those in whom he has come to dwell cry, *Abba, Father*. This expression is used elsewhere (Mk. 14:36; Rom. 8:15). *Abba* is the Aramaic for 'Father';[18] it is the term used by a little child to its parent (*cf.* our 'Papa'; both apparently represent the babbling of little children and thus point to familiarity within the family). Here Paul is linking the Aramaic and the Greek ways of saying 'Father', and in view of the occurrence of the expression elsewhere we are probably correct in seeing it as an accepted expression in the early church, not improbably being derived from Jesus' usage. Paul is saying here that it is the presence of the Spirit in the inmost being of believers that enables them to call God *Father* and to appreciate what that means.[19] In many religions the supreme deity is a grim and powerful figure and, even if he is thought of as well disposed to his worshippers, he is remote, a being far removed from concern for the lowly affairs of earthlings. Even if he is thought of as Father, this is in the sense of one who exercises a paternal rule over all. Boice comments, 'It is not always recognized how unusual the addressing of God as "Father" was in antiquity nor what an unforgettable impression Jesus' habitual mode of praying made on his followers.' We should not take it for granted that we can call God

---

[18]Lührmann finds it 'astonishing that with the Greek-speaking Galatians Paul can obviously presuppose this prayer address, which he himself way well have introduced to them'.

[19]'And the way He assures us of our sonship is not by some spectacular gift or sign, but by the quiet inward witness of the Spirit as we pray' (Stott).

'Our Father'. It is a wonderful privilege and one that we can understand only as the divine Spirit leads our understanding. But it is central to the Christian understanding of God.[20]

7. Paul draws a conclusion from all this with his *So then*. What he has been saying leads those who have followed his reasoning to see that the Galatians occupy a position of privilege. Paul makes this personal by using the singular instead of the plural ('thou' rather than 'you'; he is addressing each one of his readers personally, rather than the group collectively). *No longer a slave* indicates that they have been slaves, but now each has the position of *a son*. They are not people trying hard to keep the law so that they might possibly become acceptable to God. They are members of the heavenly family with all the privileges that that implies.

There are many such privileges, but Paul picks out one; he goes on, *if a son, also an heir, through God*. We tend to think of an *heir* as one who inherits possessions on the death of the owner, and it is hard to fit this into the apostle's argument. But we must bear in mind that on a large estate in antiquity the owner's heir was an important person even during the lifetime of that owner. Everybody knew that one day the estate would be his and, even though this had not yet taken place, deference was paid to him and all sorts of privileges went with his position. Paul will have all this in mind as he thinks of believers as the possessors of privileges in the heavenly realms. He may well have in mind also the fact that his readers inherit all these good gifts because of Christ's atoning death. *Through God* is a reminder that all is owing to the heavenly Father. Paul is not writing about things the Galatians have done for themselves, but about gifts from none less than God himself. And that, of course, gives a note of certainty: since God has made the gift the Galatians can be sure of it.[21]

---

[20]Mary Rose D'Angelo has written an article, '*ABBA* and Father: Imperial Theology and the Jesus Traditions' (*JBL*, 111, 1992, pp. 611–630), in which she takes issue with those who emphasize the importance of the term *abba*. She concludes that this term 'cannot be attributed to Jesus with any certainty . . . It may have originated or been of special importance in the Syrian communities . . . Second, "father" or "my father" was used as an address to God and as an epithet for God in antique Judaism . . . Third, "father" as an address to God cannot be shown to originate with Jesus' (p. 630). She makes some valid criticisms of many who have written on this term, but never comes to grips with the significance of the frequent application of *patēr* to God in the gospels (Matthew 45 times, Mark 5 times, Luke 17 times, John 118 times). If the title does not go back to Jesus, why should the writers of the gospels make such use of it?

[21]Evidently the scribes found *through God* a very difficult expression, and the manuscripts have a variety of readings, such as 'of God', 'through Christ', 'through Jesus Christ', 'of God through Christ', and there are other readings. But *dia theou* is

7. The beggarly elements, 4:8–11

> [8]*But then, not knowing God, you were slaves to those who by nature are not gods; [9]but now having come to know God, or rather having become known by God, how are you returning again to the weak and beggarly elemental principles to which you wish to enslave yourselves again? [10]You observe days and months and seasons and years. [11]I am afraid for you lest by any chance I have laboured for you in vain.*

Paul proceeds to bring out his dissatisfaction with the Galatians by contrasting their pre-Christian life with their coming to know God, and going on to make the point that they have not made progress in the faith. Rather, they have gone back to some of the things they had left. Duncan sees these verses as 'a passionate appeal': Paul's 'ultimate concern is not to establish a theological position, it is to save the souls of his converts'.

8. Having outlined something of the dignity of the position of the Galatian converts now that they have become members of the family of God with all that that means, Paul moves on to their failure to live up to what their exalted station implies. He looks back to the time before they were Christians. *But* is the strong adversative; so far from living as God's children in those pre-Christian days, they had been nothing more than slaves.[22] And their worship had been directed to beings *who by nature* (*i.e.* essentially) *are not gods.* For Paul the multiplicity of the ecclesiastical activities in which the Galatians engaged before they responded to the gospel stamped them as slaves,[23] not of the one true God, but of spirit beings that were behind the demand for such acts.

9. *But now* introduces a contrast. When the Christians came among them and preached the gospel, there was a new beginning. Those who were now in the Galatian church had responded to the preaching, with the result that they came to know the one true God. Or, as Paul goes on to say, they had *become known*[24] by God. The important thing in conversion is never what the new convert does, but what God does in

---

read by P46 אA* ABC 33, some MSS of it, vg, boh and several of the Fathers. It is the most difficult reading and should be accepted.

[22]Calvin comments, 'You were then wandering in darkness; but how disgraceful it is that now, in the midst of light, you should stray so horribly . . . the Galatians were less excusable for corrupting the Gospel than they had formerly been for idolatry.'

[23]*Edouleusate* signifies 'served as slaves'.

[24]The verb in verse 8 was *eidotes*, while here it is *gnontes*, but there seems no significant difference in meaning.

that person. It is true that the convert comes to know God, but more exactly and more importantly the person has become *known by God*.[25]

Paul proceeds to the question of how it is that they are returning to the life they had left, and specifically to the *weak and beggarly elemental principles* ('feeble and bankrupt elemental spirits', REB) they had abandoned when they became Christians. The Galatians thought they were making progress in the Christian faith when they embraced the teaching of the Judaizers. Paul saw them as essentially reverting to the lives they had led before they became Christians. The basic teaching of the gospel he preached was that Christ's death took away all the sins of those who trusted him. The lives the converted live they live as their response to what Christ had done for them and not as a way of acquiring merit in the sight of God. The Galatians had evidently lost sight of this and saw the conformity to the laws that the Judaizers taught them as a wonderful advance in the Christian way. Paul saw it as a return to *the weak*[26] *and beggarly elemental principles* from which they had made their escape when they first believed. And moreover it meant enslaving themselves once more after they have once been set free. Faith in Jesus Christ alone is one thing. Faith in Jesus Christ plus conformity to the law is quite another.[27]

You wish to enslave yourselves is a striking expression. Surely nobody wants to be a slave? Not put precisely in such terms. But Paul is referring to the fact that in their old pre-Christian religion the Galatian believers had been enslaved to their gods, and they were so used to this that now that they were free in Christ they could still feel the

---

[25]'To recognize oneself to be the centre of divine attention is one of the profounder aspects of Christian conversion. It is also one of the most humbling' (Guthrie).

[26]Barclay finds 'the religion based on law' weak 'because it is helpless. It can define sin; it can show a man when he is sinning; it can convict him of sin; but it can neither find for him forgiveness for past sin nor strength to conquer future sin. The law's basic and inherent weakness always was, and is, that it can diagnose the disease but it cannot produce a cure.' Luther comments, 'Whoever is fallen from the article of justification, is ignorant of God, and an idolater. Therefore it is all one thing, whether he afterwards turn again to the law, or to the worshipping of idols; it is all one whether he be called a monk, a Turk, a Jew, or an Anabaptist. For when this article is taken away, there remaineth nothing else but error, hypocrisy, impiety and idolatry' (p. 380).

[27]Paul puts some emphasis on the thought that the Galatians are repeating what they had done before: *returning again* is *epistrephete palin*, and *again* in the next expression is two words, *palin anōthen*. What seemed to them a wonderful advance was essentially a return to their pre-Christian state. Bruce cites G. Howard, 'For the Galatians to accept circumcision was for them to return to the concept of local deities and to be enslaved once again to the elemental spirits of the universe.'

attraction of slavery. The slave does not have to make decisions. His job is to do what he is told. Putting the Jewish law into the central place, so that all that is necessary is to obey that law, is to revert to the kind of life to which the converts had been used.[28] The life of faith is a wonderful life, but it involves living as free people with all the demands that that makes (as well as all the privileges it brings). While the Galatians doubtless did not say to themselves, 'We would like to be slaves', they were used to a religion in which they did not have to make decisions and they still felt the attraction of a religion that enslaved them.[29]

10. Paul explains. He lists their observance of *days and months and seasons and years*.[30] The Jewish law provided for a goodly number of *days* to be observed, and it is clear that the holy days prescribed in the law were an important feature of life for those under the law. *Months* are not so common, but certainly the month Abib was to be observed (Dt. 16:1). *Seasons* may well point us to such times as the ingathering of the harvest, while *years* remind us of the provision for special observance of the first five years after the people entered the land of Canaan (Lv. 19:23–25) and for the seventh year as a sabbath year (Lv. 25:4–6). And, of course, there are many regulations about the year of jubilee (Lv. 25:8ff.). Clearly the passage of time gave those who observed the Jewish law a good deal to perform. Meticulous observance of the law's provisions for holy occasions meant that much of one's life must be changed.

11. All this, Paul says, makes him *afraid*[31] for his converts. What they were doing was so far from living out the Christian life in quiet trust in Christ, that Paul feared for them. The apostle was afraid *lest*[32] he had

---

[28]Fung cites Ellicott for the view that submission to the demands of the Judaizers would be a *'relapse to* bondage and *recommencement of* its principles. The Galatians had been slaves to the *stoicheia* in the form of heathenism; now they were desiring to enslave themselves *again* to the *stoicheia*, and to *commence* them *anew* in the form of Judaism.'

[29]'This is a very bold, and even revolutionary, identification. What unites the two is the belief that religion is the way by which man makes his own way to God and brings about his own salvation' (Hamann).

[30]The present tense, *paratēreisthe*, indicates that the practice has already started. Betz argues that we should understand Paul to mean that these are the activities the Galatians would be undertaking if they 'took up Torah and circumcision'. But surely scholars like Bruce and Longenecker are right in seeing a reference to what the Galatians were already doing.

[31]The accusative *hymas* is unexpected, but the meaning must be 'I fear for you' rather than 'I fear you'.

[32]Robertson sees this as an example of *mē* 'in the sense of "perhaps"' (p. 1169).

wasted his time in evangelizing them ('I have wasted my efforts on you', NIV; 'my work for you may have been wasted', NRSV).[33] What was the point of preaching salvation by the sheer grace of God if people were going to respond by living their lives in bondage to the elemental spirits and the like? If Paul had done nothing, they would have remained in such bondage. His preaching had taken them out of this slavery, but it now appeared that that was only for a short time. The Galatians were set on going back to bondage. Chrysostom, however, reminds us of the importance of *lest*, 'which is as much as to say, the wreck has not happened, but I see the storm big with it; so I am in fear, yet not in despair' (this comment will stand even if we agree with Moulton that we should understand the term in the sense 'perhaps', MI, p. 193).

8. Paul's perplexity, 4:12–20

> [12]*Be as I am, because I also am as you are, brothers, I beg of you. You have done me no wrong;* [13]*but you know that on account of infirmity of the flesh I preached the gospel to you formerly,* [14]*and you did not despise or disdain what was a trial to you in my flesh, but you received me as an angel of God, as Christ Jesus.* [15]*Where then is your blessedness? For I testify to you that if it had been possible you would have plucked out your eyes and given them to me.* [16]*So then, have I become your enemy in telling you the truth?* [17]*They are zealous for you in no good way, but they wish to shut you out so that you may be zealous for them.* [18]*It is good to be zealous always in what is good, and not only when I am present with you.* [19]*My children, for whom I am again in pains of childbirth until Christ be formed in you,* [20]*I wish to be present with you now and to change my tone, because I am perplexed about you.*

In a highly emotional passage Paul gives expression to his deep concern for his Galatian converts and to his sorrow at the change that had occurred in them. He reminds them of their devotion to him when he had been among them in Galatia and of their readiness then to do almost anything for him. And he leaves them in no doubt about his passionate desire that they should return to their first love as

---

[33]On *kekopiaka* Lightfoot comments, 'The indicative mood, because the speaker suspects that what he fears has actually happened.' Betz holds that the word 'stresses the ongoing work, perhaps including the writing of the letter' whereas the aorist would see the work as past.

Christians and not persist in their flirtation with erroneous notions. Longenecker finds 'a major shift in Paul's argument' at this point. 'In 4:12ff. Paul is no longer so much concerned to accuse or defend as to persuade his Galatian converts to adopt a certain course of action.' There are problems about the interpretation of this passage. We do not know in detail the relationship between Paul and the Galatians, nor do we know precisely what Paul's physical condition was. Such considerations make it difficult to interpret in detail some of the things that Paul says. But his general drift is plain enough.

12. *Be as I am* is an exhortation to the Galatians to become Christians in the same sense as Paul is a Christian, one who is not bound by the Jewish law. It is a call to understand that justification by faith excludes such additions as the compliance with the law that the Judaizers were demanding. *Because* introduces the reason: Paul points out that he is *as you are*, *i.e.* one who lives free from the restrictions imposed by the law. This means that he had thrown off his Jewish shackles and come to be like a Gentile; he beseeches his converts not to try to become like Jews. *Brothers, I beg of you* is an affectionate note.[34] The apostle is taking up no superior position. He was a sinner just as the Galatians were, and he needed salvation by Christ just as they did. He argues from the similarity of their positions and reinforces his argument with *I beg of you*. He is not taking up some position of superiority but simply pleading with his converts. Paul makes it clear in more places than one that it was his practice to become like those to whom he preached (perhaps the classic expression of this habit is found in 1 Cor. 9:19–23).

You have done me no wrong is puzzling. In view of what follows, the apostle may mean that the Galatians had not despised the first preaching, but had accepted it despite anything to which they might have taken exception in the apostle. Or the point may be that it is not Paul, but Christ, who has been wronged.[35] Burton thinks that it is probably 'an allusion to an assertion of the Galatians that they had done the apostle no wrong, it being equally their right to accept his message when he came and that of the later Christian teachers when they came'.

13. Paul goes back in thought to the time when he had first come to Galatia. *On account of infirmity of the flesh* seems to indicate that it had not been his original plan to spend time in Galatia, but he had been held up by *infirmity*. The expression points to some physical limitation,

---

[34]'The language of softened and deeply moved love' (Meyer).

[35]'The emphasis does not rest on *me*, a mere enclitic in the Greek, as if implying that they had injured God and Christ' (Schmoller).

but unfortunately we do not know exactly what it was ('The difficulty
of diagnosing the case of a living patient should warn us of the futility
of attempting it for one who has been dead almost nineteen hundred
years', Stamm, *IB*). It has been suggested that Paul was taken with an
illness either when he first arrived in Galatia or just before that event,
so that he went to Galatia to recuperate.[36] Either way, the apostle is
reminding his readers that he had been very unwell when he first[37]
came to them. But he had not let his physical infirmity stop him
preaching the gospel. We should add that some take Paul's words in
the sense 'amid bodily weakness', which would point to his usual
condition, not some illness. But this is not as likely as the other
interpretation.

14. A number of commentators (*e.g.* Bruce) hold that there must
have been something repulsive in Paul's appearance when he first
came to Galatia. But despite his physical handicap Paul had been well
received. The Galatians, he says, *did not despise or disdain*[38] his illness,
which makes it seem as though the sickness had been a demeaning
one. Paul speaks of it as having been *a trial* to the Galatians, and he
specifies that it was *in my flesh*. There had been some physical
unpleasantness,[39] but the Galatians had not let that turn them away

[36]Barclay says, 'Pamphylia and the coastal plain were districts where malarial fever
raged; it is more than probable that Paul contracted this malaria, and his only remedy
was to seek the highlands of Galatia.' He further says, 'This malaria recurs and it is
accompanied by a prostrating headache which those who have experienced it liken to
"a red-hot bar thrust through the forehead" or a dentist's drill boring through the
temple.' He conjectures that this may have been Paul's thorn in the flesh (2 Cor. 12:7).
Others argue that this passage has nothing to do with that thorn. There is no real
evidence for either position. It is often suggested that Paul suffered from epilepsy or
that he had some disease of the eyes (*cf.* verse 15), but again, there is no evidence. We
simply do not know what his *infirmity of the flesh* was.

[37]*To proteron* signifies 'once, formerly'. Some have argued that it indicates that Paul
had been to Galatia twice and that this refers to the first of his visits, *e.g.* Ramsay,
pp. 414–416, Lightfoot and others. But 'fr. a lexical point of view it is not poss. to
establish the thesis that Paul wished to differentiate betw. a later visit and an earlier
one' (BAGD, 1.b.β). It may mean 'earlier, formerly existing' (BDF, p. 62). Paul is
probably contrasting the 'formerly' when he preached to the Galatians with the 'now'
of their dallying with the Judaizers. Fung sees the meaning as 'originally', 'at the first',
and cites a number of New Testament passages where it has this meaning.

[38]*Ekptuō* means literally 'spit out' and thus is a strong term for 'disdain'. Some see
this literal meaning here, and think it refers to spitting as a means of warding off the
evil spirit some of the Galatians thought had taken possession of Paul. But there seems
no good reason for taking this view; 'disdain' is surely the meaning.

[39]BAGD see a possible mixture of two ideas: 'You did not despise me in my physical
weakness' and 'You did not yield to the temptation to despise me because of my
physical weakness'. But they also see it as possible to translate: 'You neither treated

from the message Paul brought (cf. NIV, 'Even though my illness was a trial to you, you did not treat me with contempt or scorn'). Paul was not unmindful of the fact that the Galatians might well have rejected his message because of the nature of his physical complaint. It is clear that he had had some very distressing physical symptoms; we would like to know precisely what they were and what caused them, but we can do no more than speculate. Betz points out that in antiquity 'illness was likely to be interpreted by common people as demon possession, a fact which would be incompatible with the claims of an apostle'.

But they had not rejected the apostle. Indeed, far from it, he says, *you received me as an angel of God, as Christ Jesus.* Paul gives no reason for this high estimate of him, but there is no doubting his appreciation of it at a time when his physical complaint might well have turned strangers away from him. The word *angel*, of course, means 'a messenger' (and Cole prefers this meaning here),[40] but in Christian writings it is usually employed of a messenger from heaven, an angel. There can be no doubting that that is what is in mind in the present passage. But it is not enough for Paul. The Galatians had welcomed him *as Christ Jesus*: they had treated him as though he were the Saviour himself. Paul could not possibly have praised the warmth of their reception of him and his message more warmly than that.[41]

15. That made it all the more puzzling that they were now in danger of rejecting his message altogether. *Where then is your blessedness?* he asks ('What has happened to all your joy?' NIV; 'What has become of the happiness you felt then?' REB).[42] Calvin sees in the words *I testify to you* evidence of Paul's affection for his converts.[43] Paul was in no doubt about the devotion the Galatians

---

me w. contempt nor did you turn away from the temptation that my physical appearance might have become to you' (*exoutheneō*, 1, 2).

[40]Margaret M. Mitchell also prefers the idea of 'messenger' here 'since it is so clearly bound up with the assumption that the envoy should be properly received' (*JBL*, 111, 1992, p. 646, n. 17).

[41]Some suggest that this is a reminiscence of the attempt by the citizens of Lystra to worship the apostles when they came to their city (Acts 14:8–18). But in Acts the apostles rejected this decisively while here Paul approves. As Boice says, the expression used here is 'an impossible expression if he were thinking of their attempt to receive him as one of the Greek gods'.

[42]F. Hauck sees *makarismos* here as used 'for the blessedness of receiving the message of salvation' (*TDNT*, IV, p. 367). Cf. Lightfoot, 'your happiness in my teaching'.

[43]He remarks, 'It is not enough that pastors be respected, if they are not also loved. Both are necessary; otherwise their teaching will not have a sweet taste. And he

had shown him in those days, for, he says, they would have *plucked out their eyes* for him. The word *eyes* is placed in an emphatic position: 'your eyes, having plucked out, you would have given me'. Obviously, a plucked-out eye would be a gift nobody could use, but Paul's point is that his converts had been ready to do anything for him in those early days. Some commentators have argued that the words indicate that Paul had an eye ailment. This may indeed have been the case, but these words do not prove it.

16. A rhetorical question[44] brings out the point that Paul is in no sense hostile to the Galatians. What he has done has been to tell them *the truth*. When did this take place? Some have thought the words are a reference to Paul's initial preaching of the gospel in Galatia, others to the present letter. Either is possible, and the probability is that he is maintaining that he spoke the truth in his initial preaching and is repeating it. This should have been seen as a friendly gesture, but the converts had apparently not understood this.[45] So Paul asks them to face the reality of what they were doing. His frankness in telling the truth does not mean that the apostle has ceased to care for his converts and becomes their enemy (he puts emphasis on *enemy* by placing it first, 'your *enemy* did I become . . .?').

17. Paul turns his attention to the false teachers. They are *zealous for you* (*i.e.* zealous to win you to their way of thinking, 'they court you', Lenski), but zeal is not enough. Throughout history there have been many earnest people whose zeal for their cause has far exceeded their grasp of reality. This is always a recipe for strife and division and the Galatian situation was no exception. The false teachers were certainly zealous, but *in no good way*; what they were trying to do would result not in helping the Galatians but in harming them. It is not easy to see precisely what is meant by their wish *to shut you out*, but Paul may mean that these teachers aimed at isolating the Galatians from other churches, or perhaps from other teachers, who wholeheartedly agreed with Paul. Another possibility is that they distanced themselves from Paul and thus from the gospel. If they could be kept from seeing that Christians generally took much the

---

declares that both had been true of him among the Galatians. He had already spoken of their respect; he now speaks of their love.'

[44]Longenecker argues that the clause beginning with *hōste* 'must be read as an indignant exclamation' and cites Burton, Zahn and Seiffert in support. But most commentators and translators see it as a question.

[45]'The fact is that at his first visit Paul was warmly welcomed by the Galatians, but subsequently, thanks to the Galatian heretics, they became suspicious of his gospel and gave it a critical re-evaluation' (Fung).

same line as Paul, they might *be zealous*[46] for the false teachers.

18. It might be thought from what he has just said that the apostle is objecting to people being zealous. He removes any such inference by saying plainly, *It is good to be zealous always.* Zeal is a necessary ingredient in the Christian life; no church that is apathetic is a live church and no Christian who is apathetic is a real Christian. The Galatians should understand that zeal is an important part of being Christian. But the zeal Paul commends is zeal for *what is good,* and the apostle's complaint is that the zeal of the Galatian converts was misplaced. This had not always been the case. While he was among them they had shared his zeal for authentic Christianity. But their zeal had lasted only for the time that he had been with them, and such a temporary zeal is of little worth. *Always* is an important word.

19. The conclusion of this paragraph is emotional; Hamann speaks of it as 'a cry torn from Paul as from one in anguish'. The apostle's concern and anguish find expression in his address *My children* (a form of address Paul uses only here, though a number of times he speaks of his converts as his children, *e.g.* 1 Cor. 4:14, 17; 2 Cor. 6:13; several good MSS have 'My little children' here, as a number of times in 1 John), and in his likening his experience to that of being *in pains of childbirth.* Elsewhere he likens himself to a father of his converts (1 Cor. 4:15) or to a nurse (1 Thes. 2:7); he cheerfully changes his metaphors! That they were his *children* points to the fact that it was through him that they had been born into the Christian faith. He had been the means of leading them out of their false religion into saving faith in Christ.

But his converts had now accepted ideas that the apostle could not reconcile with genuine Christianity and that, coupled with his earnest desire that they should be true Christians, now leads him to say that he finds himself once more *in pains of childbirth.* His *again* points to the fact that he had been through all this once before. When he had preached in Galatia he had brought people to see that being Christian meant more than picking up a few new ideas. It meant dying to a whole way of life and being reborn into a new way. This had not been easy for the preacher, and Paul had *pains of childbirth* as he gave himself over to bringing the converts into newness of spiritual life.

But birth pangs are over when the child comes to birth; it is unnatural that the mother should have them all over again. Paul's

---

[46]Robertson notes that this is one of only three places in the New Testament where *hina* occurs with the present indicative (p. 984). But he insists that in all its wide range of usage *hina* expresses 'the pure telic idiom' (p. 985).

language means that it is unnatural for the Galatians to behave in such a way that he has birth pangs twice! It is also unnatural that *he* should be having the birth pangs, but *Christ* is to be formed in them. But if the physiology is unusual, Paul's meaning is clear. Through his anguish, no less than Christ is formed in the Galatians. Blackwelder has the striking phrase, 'Christmas in Galatians' (*IB*).

But now he faces the birth process all over again. He is undergoing anguish once more like that when he first preached to them, and that pain, he says, will last *until Christ be formed in you.*[47] This is an interesting way of referring to being truly Christian. The believer is not only one who professes faith, but one who is transformed into the likeness of Christ; indeed Christ indwells the believer and this means a complete change. Paul is not looking for a few minor alterations in the Galatians but for such a transformation that to see them would be to see Christ. The apostle leaves no doubt about the depth of his feelings on the matter, or about the importance of what he was urging. So far from the Galatians going on to an advanced form of Christianity, they were in danger of needing to start all over again.

20. Paul would like to be present with the Galatians once more.[48] He seems to be thinking that it would be better to engage in face-to-face dialogue than in a discussion at a distance. He speaks of wanting to change his *tone* or 'voice'; he wants such a change in the Galatians that he would be able to speak to them in a different way. Or we might understand the verb in the sense 'exchange' (a meaning it has in Rom. 1:23). In that case he would like to exchange the letter for a voice. Perhaps he felt that the trouble that had arisen would be much more easily settled if he could have a conversation with his converts than by the process of letter-writing. The Galatians might not appreciate the significance of something he wrote, but if he were present the tone of his voice might well convince where they missed the point of the form of words he used. Paul was *perplexed* (Moffatt, 'I am at my wits' end about you!'). He could not understand why people who had responded to the gospel in the way his Galatian converts had done should so soon be tempted to go off into some form of legalism. Hendriksen remarks that this passage 'is one of the finest practical applications of 1 Cor. 13 . . . Though the Galatians have failed Paul, his

---

[47]Luther comments, 'He saith not: Of whom I travail in birth until my form be fashioned in you, but "until Christ be formed in you"' (p. 412). They are not being urged to accept Paul, but Christ.

[48]He uses the form *ēthelon*, where the use of the imperfect in the sense of the present is 'a polite idiom' (Robertson, p. 919).

love toward them never fails, for love is longsuffering and kind, and even now hopes all things.'

9. Two covenants, 4:21–31

[21]Tell me, you who wish to be under law, don't you hear the law? [22]For it is written that Abraham had two sons, one from the slave girl and one from the free one. [23]But he who was born of the slave girl was born according to the flesh, but he who was born of the free one was born through promise. [24]Which things are allegories; for they are two covenants, one from Mount Sinai bearing children for slavery, which is Hagar. [25]Now Hagar is Mount Sinai in Arabia and corresponds to the present Jerusalem, for she is in slavery together with her children. [26]But the Jerusalem that is above is free, which is our mother; [27]for it stands written:

> *Rejoice, you barren one who did not bear,*
> *Break forth and cry out, you who did not give birth;*
> *For many are the children of the desolate,*
> *More than those of her who has the husband.*

[28]Now you, brothers, are children of promise like Isaac. [29]But as then, he who had been born according to the flesh persecuted him born according to the Spirit, so also is it now. [30]But what does the Scripture say? 'Cast out the slave woman and her son; for the son of the slave woman will not inherit with the son of the free one.' [31]Therefore, brothers, we are not children of a slave woman but of the free one.

Paul drives home his point with an allegorical treatment of Hagar and Sarah and their sons which enables him to bring out an important point. Duncan says, 'By an *allegory* he means something more than an *illustration*: it is a spiritual truth embodied in history, a shadow from the eternal world cast upon the sands of time' (on verse 24).[49] In Paul's day (and in Abraham's) there was a great difference between the treatment accorded a slave woman and her offspring and that given to

---

[49]Those who see the words as an illustration nevertheless see them as conveying important truths. Calvin speaks here of 'a fine illustration'. He adds, 'As an argument it is not very strong, but as confirmation of his earlier vigorous reasoning, it is not to be despised.' Cf. Allan, 'As an illustration it is by no means ineffective. Its vivid use of imagery serves to express a fine scorn for those who can dream of adhering to a slavish sect and a splendid aspiration after a heaven-sent freedom. There breathes through the passage a thrilling sense that our liberating Gospel is as old as Abraham.'

those who were free. Paul makes the point that believers in Christ, like the free woman and her son of old, are free and therefore inheritors of the blessing. As Stott puts it, 'Abraham's true children are not those with an impeccable Jewish genealogy, but those who believe as Abraham believed and obey as Abraham obeyed.' The Jews made a good deal of the Sarah-Hagar story (see the passsages adduced by Longenecker, pp. 200–206); the apostle is treading on what would be familiar territory for the Judaizers. We see this in the fact that he does not name two of the important people in the incident to which he is referring, namely Sarah and Ishmael. He can assume that his readers will know who are in mind.[50] But if he can refer to an event that was very familiar to teachers, he gives it an interpretation that was devastating. The Jews were in no doubt that they were the children of Sarah, but Paul claims that distinction for men and women of faith, Gentiles though they might be. The Jews he sees as the spiritual children of Hagar.

Andrew C. Perriman has an interesting treatment of the passage.[51] He makes the important points that 'it is the specific quotation in v. 30 of Gn. 21:10 that has determined the development of the argument', and that this verse 'stands as the basic answer to the question with which the pericope began: "Do you not hear the law?"' (p. 32).

21. Paul addresses those who were inclined to accept the teaching of the Judaizers, speaking of them as *you who wish to be under law*.[52] He asks whether they in fact *hear the law*, and the article shows that it is the law of Moses that he has in mind. Paul asks them whether they are really listening to what the law actually says. They had evidently taken up the position that the Judaizers were validly teaching the word of God as laid down in inspired Scripture, but Paul is sure that they do not really understand what is written in the books of the law. A superficial acquaintance with it under the guidance of inspiring leaders is not at all the same thing as a genuine understanding of what the law teaches and what it demands.

---

[50]Ramsay sums up in this way: 'The Jews, though Sarah's sons, are described as the offspring of Hagar, because they, like Ishmael, are descendants by nature; the Gentile Christians are described as the offspring of Sarah, because they, like Isaac, are descendants by promise of God.'

[51]'The Rhetorical Strategy of Galatians 4:21 – 5:1' in *EQ*, LXV, 1993, pp. 27–42.

[52]*Thelontes* points to the action of the will and while there is no article with *nomon* there is no doubt that the apostle is referring to the law as practised by the Jews. Fung holds that Paul addresses 'those who wanted or desired to be under law . . . as a religious principle' and that the apostle goes on to challenge them to give heed to what the law says.

22. *For* introduces the reason for his doubts, and *it is written* is the usual formula when citing from Scripture. Here, however, it is used to introduce not a quotation from holy writ, but a summary of certain things contained in Scripture. It is interesting that Paul does not refer to passages that specifically mention circumcision or to any of the rules of conduct laid down in the law. He goes back to *Abraham,* and points out that that patriarch *had two sons* (actually he had several other sons, Gn. 25:1–2, but these were not relevant to the argument). This would have been a most unexpected use of the law. The Judaizers would have made much of the law's demand for circumcision and the observance of holy days and feasts, and it is highly unlikely that they would have paid a great deal of attention to Abraham's offspring. But Paul points to the significance of the fact that one of Abraham's sons was born *from the slave girl* and the other from the free woman. The mother determined the status of the children (not the father), so the son of the *slave girl* was necessarily a slave.

23. The *But* that begins this verse is the strong adversative, which, Guthrie says, 'is intended to bring out a deeper contrast between these two sons of Abraham. It was not merely a difference in the status of their respective mothers, but also in the circumstances of their birth.' It mattered to Paul that the baby *born of the free* woman came *through promise.* That is to say this child was one whom God had promised to Abraham (Gn. 17:15–16; 18:10), and he had made the promise when it seemed quite impossible for the old couple to have children: Abraham was a hundred years old and Sarah was ninety (Gn. 17:17). The child by the slave, Paul says, *was born*[53] *according to the flesh.* When Sarah could not bear a child she asked Abraham to go in to Hagar, her Egyptian slave girl, saying, 'It may be that I shall obtain children by her' (Gn. 16:1–2, RSV). When Paul says that Hagar's child was born *according to the flesh* he is pointing to this human device and contrasting it with God's gift to Abraham and Sarah when Sarah was past the age for bearing children. The *promise* of God was very important.

24. Paul finds *allegories* in these things[54] (NIV, 'These things may be taken figuratively'). This does not mean that the stories are not to be taken as factual. Rather, Paul is dealing with a situation in which his oppponents seem to have used allegory in their understanding of the

---

[53]'The perfect with reference to an OT event can mean that this event still retains its (exemplary) meaning'; the expression 'approximately = *gegraptai hoti egennēthē*' (BDF, p. 342 [5]).

[54]Lenski sees *hatina* rather than *ha* as meaning '"things of this nature or character," implying that the ones just mentioned belong to an entire class, that more of them are found in Scripture'.

story and the apostle is responding in kind. The Judaizers would have argued that they were the descendants of Isaac, the ancestor of God's free people, whereas the Gentiles were outside the covenant as the slave woman's son was. But Paul turns this interpretation on its head. The spiritual descendants of the slave woman are those who are in bondage to the law, whereas the spiritual descendants of the free woman are those who live in the freedom of the gospel. The slave woman *Hagar* points him to the covenant God made with his people at Mount Sinai, a covenant which he describes as *bearing children for slavery* (the child of a slave woman would be a slave). The old covenant involved obedience to a multiplicity of regulations both in the way its adherents worshipped and in the way they lived out their daily lives. In comparison with Christianity with its absence of such regulations, this seemed a form of slavery.[55] Cf. Burton, 'As applied to the Sinai covenant it refers to the fact that they who came under this covenant were in the position of slaves as being in bondage to the law.'

25. Paul carries his symbolism further. *Hagar*, he says, *is Mount Sinai*[56] *in Arabia.* Mount Sinai was, of course, the mountain on which the law was given, that law which the Judaizers were emphasizing in their attempts to enrol the Galatians among their followers. Paul is apparently viewing Arabia as the land of Hagar's descendants and the land of slaves; it was not the holy land that God gave Israel. He proceeds to link this slavery with Jerusalem, the centre from which the Judaizers emanated. This would have seemed a shocking interpretation to those teachers, but Paul is making the point emphatically that their teaching means slavery just as much as Hagar's offspring meant slavery. *The present Jerusalem* means that the apostle is not referring to something in the past. At the time of writing there were those whose

[55]Bruce points out that Paul 'is not thinking of allegory in the Philonic sense . . . he has in mind that form of allegory which is commonly called typology: a narrative from OT history is interpreted in terms of the new covenant'. Meyer, however, argues that allegory must be distinguished from typology. Betz comments, 'What (Paul) calls "allegory" is really a mixture of what we would call allegory and typology.'

[56]The neuter *to de Hagar*, rather than the feminine, indicates that Paul is not speaking here of the woman named Hagar, but of the word 'Hagar'. This may mean that the mountain was sometimes given a name that could be represented in Greek by Hagar. Chrysostom tells us that Hagar 'is the word for Mount Sinai in the language of that country' and others draw attention to an Arabic word very similar to 'Hagar'. This could give the meaning that Hagar means Sinai and thus refers to the giving of the law. *Hagar* is not read in some MSS (REB has 'Sinai is a mountain in Arabia'), but it has good attestation and should be accepted. However we take the expression, it is clear that Paul is associating Hagar with slavery. He is saying that what happened at Sinai leads to slavery, not freedom.

teachings brought people into the slavery of which he writes. It is a way of saying that the message they brought, and which some at least of the Galatians were inclined to view favourably, is no more than a continuation of the slavery that is to be seen in Hagar.

Paul proceeds to underline this with his addition *she is in slavery together with her children*. The eminent teachers of the law were in Jerusalem at the time he writes, and their teaching with its multiplicity of regulations meant slavery, not the glorious compliance with the will of God which they said it was. *Together with her children* catches up all those who follow the way advocated by the Judaizers. As Fung points out, Paul is linking together (as characterized by bondage) Hagar, Ishmael, the Sinaitic covenant of law, the present Jerusalem and all who 'adhere to the law as the means of justification and the principle of life'. Submission to the way of law means accepting slavery instead of the glorious freedom of the gospel.

26. Paul contrasts the *slavery* in which the Judaizers find themselves with *the Jerusalem that is above* which, he says, *is free. Jerusalem*, of course, was the capital of the Jewish state, and, as Paul is speaking allegorically of holy things, this stands for the holy city, the place where God's people delight to worship. The description *that is above* points us to heavenly realities. Paul is not talking about the Jerusalem in Palestine that was the chief city of the Jewish nation at that time, for that city was not free. It was under the rule of the Romans. But the spiritual or heavenly Jerusalem is not in bondage; it *is free*. This probably means more than that it is not subject to human bondage. It is not unlikely that Paul is also suggesting that sin has no sway there. Those who belong to the heavenly Jerusalem have through Christ a victory over the forces of evil. The apostle goes on to say that this Jerusalem *is our mother* (for the imagery, *cf.* Is. 66:8); that is where we belong and the place to which we look for spiritual sustenance, just as the child on earth looks to his human mother for all that he or she needs to sustain this earthly life. A number of good MSS read 'mother of us all' and, whether this be read or not, it conveys an important truth. Paul is then claiming that all believers, Jewish or Gentile, belong to the one heavenly family.

27. Paul proceeds to quote Isaiah 54:1, words which seem to apply to Jerusalem at the time of the exile and in the days that followed. At the time of the Babylonian exile the city could be likened to a *barren one who did not bear*.[57] It was overthrown by the enemy and its

---

[57]'*Hē tiktousa* is common in tragedy . . . as a practical synonym of *hē mētēr*, the title of a continuous relationship' (MI, p. 127). We should notice that here it is negatived with *ou*, not *mē*.

population carried away. Well might it be likened to a woman who did not bear children. But God had not abandoned his people and in due course the exile was brought to an end, a time of great joy for the people of God. So the prophet calls on them to *Break forth and cry out*; that is to say, in place of the mourning that characterized their state during the time of their oppression they are to burst forth into joyful song. The reason given is that *many are the children of the desolate* and that they will be *more than those of her who has the husband*.[58] The number of people in Jerusalem after the people came back from the exile was in time greater than that in earlier days, but more importantly for Paul those descended from Isaac were more than those from Ishmael. There will also be the thought that those who followed the way Paul was outlining would in due course considerably outnumber those who followed the way of strict Judaism. Indeed at the time of writing there were more Gentile Christians than Jewish believers and in due course Gentile believers would considerably outnumber Jews.

28. Paul links his readers with the blessed ones of the Old Testament, here singling out Isaac. He addresses them warmly as *brothers* and speaks of them as *children of promise like Isaac*. God had promised Abraham that he would have a son (Gn. 15:4), and this promise was to be fulfilled literally. Sarah in her barrenness gave her maid Hagar to her husband, saying, 'The LORD has kept me from having children. Go, sleep with my maidservant; perhaps I can build a family through her' (Gn. 16:1–2, NIV). But this was not the way God would fulfil his promise, and in due course Sarah became pregnant and bore a son whom Abraham named Isaac (Gn. 21:1–3). Paul sees believers, including those in Galatia, as *children of promise like Isaac*. He is referring not to physical birth but to spiritual birth; when people put their trust in Christ they are born into the heavenly family and become children of God. Notice that he is assuming that his readers will see themselves as belonging with Isaac, not Ishmael, and thus as accepting the freedom that Paul espouses, not the bondage to which the Judaizers would confine them.

29. Being born *according to the Spirit* is a great blessing, but it is not an unmixed blessing. Paul points out that Isaac was not well treated by Ishmael, whom he does not name but characterizes as *he who had been born according to the flesh*. The persecution in question should

---

[58]Luther comments, 'The people of faith have not the law for their husband, they serve not in bondage, they are not born of that mother Jerusalem which now is; but they have the promise, they are free, and are born of free Sarah.'

probably be understood of the mockery accorded Sarah's son (Gn. 21:9).[59] The Hebrew verb that usually signifies 'laughed' may mean 'mocked'; some such meaning is demanded by Sarah's anger and the fact that the occasion was one for honouring the child Isaac. Or, of course, Paul may be referring to some other occasion, not recorded in Scripture; Jewish tradition held that there were other occasions of conflict between the two. Paul sees in this the kind of opposition that invariably occurs. Those whose lives are *according to the flesh* are always opposed to those *born according to the Spirit*, a truth believers have experienced in every age. 'Legal bondage and spiritual freedom cannot coexist' (Bruce, on verse 30). And, as Duncan puts it, 'a legalistic religion cannot be other than a persecuting religion, for it knows that it cannot endure unless its regulations are kept in the letter'.[60]

30. But Paul is not laying down his own view of what happened: he proceeds to appeal to Scripture, quoting from Genesis 21:10. From Abraham's point of view both Ishmael and Isaac were his sons, and he was unhappy that Sarah had demanded that Ishmael (and Hagar) be sent away. But while Sarah's action may be viewed as less than kind, in the providence of God it opened the way for it to be made plain to everyone that it was Isaac and not Ishmael, the older son, whose descendants were to be born the people of God. Ishmael would indeed be the ancestor of a people, but those of Abraham's descendants in whom the divine purpose would be fulfilled were to be those descended from Isaac.[61]

Perriman holds that 'Paul has demonstrated both the manner in which he intends Gn. 21:10 to be interpreted and the grounds for applying it to the Galatian situation. The injunction to "throw out the slave woman and her son" refers primarily neither to the Judaizers nor to the Jews but, according to the terms of the allegory, to the Sinaitic

---

[59]Ridderbos comments, 'In this context the word *persecuted* means – as is evident from the comment *so also is it now* – not so much a threat to life as one to freedom and security. It was so that Ishmael had persecuted Isaac. He did not leave Isaac in peace, grudged him his priorities, his privileges.'

[60]Boice points out that 'the remarkable thing' about the persecution of Christians 'is that this will not always be by the world but also and indeed more often by their half-brothers – the unbelieving but religious people in the nominal church.'

[61]Moulton sees the double negative here as 'most naturally classed as imperatival' (MI, p. 177). Fung cites A. T. Hanson for a summary of the argument in this place: 'Hagar the slave bears a son who persecutes the son of Sarah, the free woman. She and her son are cast out by divine command. The unbelieving Jews, enslaved to the Torah, persecute believing Christians, who are free in Christ. The unbelieving Jews are rejected by God.'

covenant and its tradition of enslavement. The reason for rejecting the Sinaitic covenant is that inheritance is not through the law and the flesh but through promise and the Spirit' (p. 41). It seems that this is the way the passage should be interpreted.

31. From all this Paul deduces that *we* (*i.e.* 'we Christians'; he classes himself with the Gentile believers, not with the Jews) *are not children of a slave woman but of the free one.*[62] Clearly the divine purpose that Paul has in mind was worked out through Isaac's descendants rather than those of Ishmael. To accept the thinking of the Judaizers was on his view to take the line of binding believers to slavery, whereas they were called to freedom. Christians are born to be free. Freedom from the bondage which the apostle saw in keeping all the commandments in the law meant a great deal to Paul, and he wants his correspondents to find the same liberty that he had found, a liberty that mattered so much to him. Barclay makes the point that anyone who makes law central 'is in the position of a slave; all his life he is seeking to satisfy his master the law'. But when grace is central, the person 'has made love his dominant principle . . . it will be the power of that love and not the constraint of law that keeps us right; and love is always more powerful than law.'

---

[62]The absence of the definite article before *paidiskēs* and its presence before *eleutheras* should be noted. We are not children of any slave woman, but of 'the' important free one.

GALATIANS 5

IV. Christian freedom, 5:1 – 6:10

It is clear from all his writings that Paul put a high value on Christian freedom. When he looked back on his pre-Christian life he saw it as fenced in by a multitude of restrictions so that the simplicity of the Christian life came to be very important to him. He saw now that there was no place for striving to acquire merit before God, for Christ had died for him and had thus taken away all his sins. Life did not mean a constant endeavour to acquire merit before God. Rather, becoming a Christian meant entering a life of freedom, a life in which sin had been dealt with by Christ's death, a life in which the believing Paul now experienced the indwelling of the Holy Spirit. There was no pressure to keep a set of rules, no compulsion to earn merit in the sight of a God who was himself perfect and who demanded wholeheartedness from his worshippers. That the believer is called to live his or her whole life in obedience to the will of God did not, for Paul, constitute bondage. It was the natural outcome of the fact that the believer is set free from the slavery to evil that is the characteristic of unbelieving humanity.

It grieved the apostle to find that some of his converts in Galatia who had begun the Christian way by experiencing Christian freedom should now be in danger of becoming legalists. They had apparently not recognized that the acceptance of circumcision meant the acceptance of the obligation to keep the whole law. As Paul saw it, this meant turning their backs on freedom and giving themselves over to bondage, bondage because life now meant keeping a series of legal obligations. So at this point in his letter Paul turns his attention to the meaning of Christian freedom and to the significance of the bondage which he saw as the inevitable consequence of accepting circumcision with all that that entails.

Perhaps we should notice that in the opinion of many, verse 1 belongs with the previous chapter. A number of translations print it as a little paragraph on its own, which perhaps indicates that it has affinities with what precedes and with what follows, but belongs exclusively with neither.

1. Freedom and the bondage of circumcision, 5:1–12

¹For freedom did Christ set us free; stand firm therefore and do not be loaded down again with a yoke of slavery. ²Look, I Paul tell you that if you get yourselves circumcised Christ will profit you nothing. ³I testify again to every man who is circumcised that he is under obligation to keep the whole law. ⁴You have been alienated from Christ, you who are being justified by law; you have fallen from grace. ⁵For we in the Spirit, by faith, eagerly await the hope of righteousness. ⁶For in Christ Jesus neither circumcision nor uncircumcision is of any force, but faith working through love. ⁷You were running well; who hindered you from obeying the truth? ⁸That persuasion is not from him who calls you. ⁹A little yeast leavens the whole batch of dough. ¹⁰I am persuaded about you in the Lord that you will not think otherwise; but he who troubles you will bear the judgment, whoever he may be. ¹¹But I, brothers, if I still preach circumcision, why am I still being persecuted? Then the stumbling-block of the cross has been nullified. ¹²Would that those who trouble you would castrate themselves!

Paul devotes the last major section of the letter to the subject of Christian freedom. Some of his Galatian converts had clearly been led to see conformity to the Jewish law as a wonderful advance on what they had earlier learned about the Christian way. For them this was a great step forward in their service of God. For Paul it was sheer tragedy. It meant that the converts were abandoning what was of central importance for an understanding of Christianity and for living the Christian life. Christian freedom was not a side issue. It was at the heart of the Christian way as Paul saw it.[1] That there were many important truths to be learned from a study of the books of the Old Testament was not in doubt for the apostle, nor that such a study would give helpful guidance as to the way we should serve God. But that believers should seek the essence of Christianity in what they learned from those books was a serious misunderstanding of essential truth. In the previous section the apostle has examined the place of the law. Now he turns his attention to the meaning of Christian freedom.

1. Paul emphasizes the importance of *freedom* in his opening words. He uses the definite article: *the* freedom, that is, the significant Christian freedom. He is not talking about the abstract concept of

---

[1]'The danger which the Galatians are in is that they will lose their freedom in Christ if they do not exercise it' (Betz).

freedom, or about the kind of freedom the lordly Romans enjoyed, but specifically about Christian freedom, the freedom Christ died to bring about. This is a subject to which Paul gives a good deal of attention,[2] and here he gives it emphasis: it is *for freedom*[3] that Christ brought salvation. Further, that *Christ set us free* shows that salvation is to be understood in terms of freedom. Paul could have spoken of any one of a number of aspects of the Christian life: he could have emphasized the importance of forgiveness, of justification, of the indwelling of the Holy Spirit and much more. His letters leave us in no doubt but that he saw the Christian salvation as many-sided, and in other places he puts emphasis on various other aspects of salvation. But here it is freedom that looms large in Paul's assessment of the Galatian situation; 'he freed us . . . so that we should have, maintain, exercise, enjoy this freedom' (Lenski).

Paul leaves his readers in no doubt about the importance of liberty in the Christian life. The Galatians were in danger of accepting circumcision, and that meant taking upon themselves the obligation to make the Jewish law central to their understanding of the Christian way. This would mean slipping away from the position into which Paul had led them when he evangelized Galatia. In his view that would be disaster.

So the apostle makes this fundamental liberty the basis of an appeal: *Stand firm therefore* (for other calls to stand firm *cf.* 1 Cor. 16:13; Phil. 1:27; 4:1; it is important). His converts had moved their ground considerably since he had preached among them, and he calls on them to stop this. His *therefore* is important: Christ has set us free and this act of liberation has consequences. Because of it, believers should resist any attempt to bring them into bondage of any sort. A great price has been paid to bring about their freedom: let them then live in the freedom into which Christ has brought them. It is perverse for free people to seek bondage. *Do not be loaded down again,* Paul writes,

---

[2]He uses *eleutheria* 7 times (4 times in Galatians is the most in any one writing), *eleutheros* 16 times and *eleutheroun* 5 times, a total of 28 uses of the freedom words. In all the rest of the New Testament the total is 13; it is Paul who, more than any other New Testament writer, insists on liberty.

[3]*Tē eleutheria.* A. Deissmann sees in this a reference to the formula used in sacral manumission, when a slave was purchased by the god 'for freedom' (*Light from the Ancient East* [London, 1927], pp. 322ff.). That meant that, while technically he was the slave of the god, as far as people were concerned the former slave was now free. Another meaning of the words might be 'with this freedom (lit. "the freedom") Christ set us free' as Burton argues, though he admits that 'For freedom' is possible. JB has 'he meant us to remain free'. Whichever way we take it, there is an emphasis on freedom.

changing his metaphor. Now he is thinking of a beast of burden with its *yoke* that fastens the burden to the animal so that it cannot shake it free (*yoke* was 'used figuratively in antiquity for any disagreeable burden that was unwillingly tolerated, like slavery', Longenecker). The particular burden to which his converts were in danger of attaching themselves is that of *slavery*. This emphasizes the unrewarding way of life which the converts were seeking to undertake. They saw the acceptance of what the Judaizers were offering as the entrance into a more wonderful way of serving God; Paul saw it as a descent into slavery. The multitude of regulations (the Jews found 613 commandments in the Law, the books Genesis to Deuteronomy) was such that even to remember them all was a burden, and to keep them all bordered on the impossible. Small wonder that Paul referred to subjecting oneself to them all as entering into *slavery*.[4]

2. *Look,*[5] Paul says, thus putting some emphasis on what follows, and he backs this up with *I Paul tell you*. He leaves the Galatians in no doubt but that what follows is important. The next words could be understood as *if you get yourselves circumcised* or as *if you are circumcised*. Perhaps it is more likely that we should take it as the former. The apostle himself was circumcised and he accepted circumcision for the sons of Jewish believers (Acts 21:20–24), though he regarded the rite as in itself unimportant (*cf.* verse 6). But when it was made a demand on Gentile converts to Christianity, that was quite another thing. Paul is now warning his readers that the most serious consequence will follow if they take the action they are contemplating. That consequence he states in the words *Christ will profit you nothing*. In becoming Christians converts pledged themselves to follow Christ and they looked forward to receiving his blessing now and in the life to come. But Paul is now telling them that to undergo circumcision was to remove themselves from the sphere of Christ's own. The salvation that Paul had preached to the Galatians was salvation by grace, but the undergoing of circumcision signified that those who received this rite no longer looked for grace as the way of

---

[4]Cole sees Paul as referring to 'the change brought about by the "freedom" of the gospel, combined with the gift of the Spirit' as 'a change in character which all the restraints or "bondage" of the Jewish law had utterly failed to produce. In these last two chapters Paul will hammer this home in order to clinch the matter' (p. 186). Lightfoot comments, 'Having escaped from the slavery of Heathenism, they would fain bow to the slavery of Judaism.'

[5]*Ide* is properly the imperative of *eidon*, but is used as a particle to give emphasis to what follows. This is the only place in the New Testament where it is used outside the gospels. A number of translations render 'Mark my words!' and NRSV has 'Listen!'

salvation. Rather they emphasized the keeping of the law. These two ways are incompatible. The undergoing of circumcision could not be seen as a further stage in the outworking of grace. Its significance was that those who received this mark entered into an obligation to perform works, not that they came to rely on grace.

3. *I testify again* presents a little problem, for Paul has not hitherto in this letter testified in the terms that follow. He may mean that he has said in other words what he is now about to enunciate. Or he may be referring back to the earlier times when he had preached among them. *To every man* admits of no exceptions. Paul is making it clear that everyone who undergoes the rite of circumcision by that very fact places himself under the obligation to keep the whole law. This is but one rite, but it carries with it the inference that the person accepting it has by that acceptance pledged himself to keep all the other provisions of the law.[6] This would be all the more the case in that people like the Galatians who accepted circumcision were not baby boys without any knowledge of the significance of what was happening. They were doing it of their own volition, knowing that it was a fundamentally important part of the law. They were not quite in the same position as Jewish men who had been circumcised in infancy without any volition of their own. They too were under the obligation to keep the whole law, but those who voluntarily submitted to the rite in adulthood had by their own choice placed themselves under a binding obligation and Paul leaves them in no doubt about that. They had apparently conformed to some of the teachings of the law (4:10), but had evidently not realized the significance of undergoing circumcision as a rite of initiation. It laid on the recipient the obligation to embrace a whole way of life. Paul is warning them that accepting circumcision meant binding themselves to keep the whole of the law. It would seem that the Judaizing teachers had not insisted on the obligation to keep the whole law. They seem to have advocated keeping certain holy days (4:10) and the sign of circumcision. But Paul wants his converts to be clear that the acceptance of circumcision was more than the undergoing of an edifying ceremony. It was the acceptance of an obligation to live their whole life in obedience to the law.[7]

---

[6]It is sometimes suggested that Paul was exaggerating or misrepresenting Judaism. But Longenecker has gathered a not inconsiderable group of references from official Jewish sources which make it clear that it was widely accepted that the whole law must be kept.

[7]*Cf.* Bruce, 'He who submits to circumcision as a legal requirement, necessary for salvation, accepts thereby the principle of salvation by law-keeping, and salvation by law-keeping implies salvation by keeping the whole law.'

4. The apostle turns his attention to those who had accepted the Judaizers' teaching. He speaks of them as *you who are being justified by law*, which perhaps would more accurately reflect Paul's thinking if we understand it as 'you who are trying to be justified by law'. To seek justification in this way was really to *have been alienated from Christ*. It is fundamental to Paul's position that justification can come about only because of what Christ has done. Therefore to seek it *by law* is to reject God's way of justification; it is to bring about alienation from Christ. A rejection of God's way of justification necessarily means alienation. 'You cannot have it both ways. It is impossible to receive Christ, thereby acknowledging that you cannot save yourself, and then receive circumcision, thereby claiming that you can' (Stott).

The same spiritual disaster is put in the words *you have fallen from grace*. *Grace* is one of Paul's important words (he uses it 100 times out of 155 times in the whole New Testament). Over and over again he insists that salvation is due entirely to God's grace, so it is not surprising that he points out here that the position of the Judaizers meant falling away from the central truth of the Christian way. It was spiritual disaster.[8]

5. *For* introduces a reason for what Paul has just said and his *we* is emphatic, 'we Christians, as opposed to others who hold to legalism of some sort'. He goes on to lay down three important points about the Christian salvation. First, it is *in the Spirit*.[9] It is not something we bring about by human striving, whether by keeping the law or any other way. It is sheer miracle, something that takes place only in the sphere of the divine Spirit, and, of course, by an activity of the divine Spirit.

Secondly, salvation is *by faith*. This is a truth that reverberates throughout the New Testament. Faith is not a human merit, as though we are rewarded for faith by being granted salvation. Rather, faith is the means by which we receive the gift. It is a refusal to see our merit as deserving salvation as a reward for our attitude, and it is a reliance on God alone to bring us out of our sin and into salvation.

---

[8]*Cf.* Luther, 'If thou retain Christ, thou art righteous before God: but if thou stick to the law, Christ availeth thee nothing.' Cousar remarks, 'There is simply no way to tack circumcision on to the gospel of grace' (p. 113; he has a significant section on Christian freedom, pp. 102–111).

[9]It is, of course, grammatically possible to understand *pneumati* to refer to the human spirit, in which case Paul would be saying that our salvation is something that takes place in our spirit, rather than in some other part of our being. But this is not a Pauline thought and it is most unlikely in this place.

Thirdly, Paul can say that we Christians *await the hope of righteousness*. That we *eagerly await* this hope shows that it is much to be desired, though not yet present. Paul is speaking of the future consummation of the Christian salvation. That is implicit also in the word *hope*. Elsewhere Paul points out that 'in hope were we saved' (Rom. 8:24), and that is his meaning here also. At the time any believer is saved he or she enters a wonderful experience. But that is only a beginning. The New Testament is full of the thought that there is much more to come. But here the apostle does not leave *hope* to stand by itself; he speaks of *the hope of righteousness*. Believers know something of righteousness here and now. They have been called out of their sinfulness into a life which they live strengthened by the Holy Spirit. But at our best we do not reach the pinnacle at which we aim. That is saved up for the life beyond this one, which means that no matter how far we have advanced in the Christian way we still look forward in hope for better things to come. Fung examines a number of possible meanings and settles on 'the hope to which the justification of believers points them forward'.[10] Hamann reminds us that this is true of more than righteousness: 'Every gift of the Gospel is described in some passages as present, in others as future.' The whole of the Christian life is the present possession of blessings which will be realized in fuller measure in the life to come.

6. Paul explains a little further. *For* introduces a reason for what he has just said. *In Christ Jesus* here clearly indicates being a real Christian; the essential thing about the state of the believer is that of being *in Christ Jesus*. This way of putting it emphasizes the importance of vital fellowship with the Saviour. The Christian is not simply someone who has heard about Christ and is loosely attached to him. The Christian is wholly committed to Christ, so wholly that he or she does not merely stand 'for' him or 'by' him, but is really 'in' him, surrounded by him. Paul never defines what the expression means, but clearly it points to the closest of unities.[11]

The apostle dismisses the idea that getting oneself circumcised, or for that matter an insistence on being uncircumcised, matters in the slightest. Neither *is of any force*.[12] For the Jews of that day circumcision

---

[10]Guthrie reminds us that *hope* 'is not simply a pious wish as it has come to mean in modern English usage: rather it is a strong assurance'.

[11]When he is using the two names he prefers the order 'Christ Jesus' to 'Jesus Christ'.

[12]*Ischuei*. In this passage BAGD translate it as 'means anything'.

was of the greatest importance; indeed, the Jews could be called 'the circumcision' (as in verses 7, 9). To deny that there was any force in circumcision was to take up a radical position. *But* is the strong adversative: far from the presence or absence of this ceremonial rite, what matters is the practice of Christian qualities, of which Paul singles out two, *faith* and *love*. Faith is absolutely fundamental. It is basic to the Christian understanding of salvation that it comes to the person who trusts Jesus Christ, who believes in him. It is not a matter of our earning our salvation by what we do, but of receiving it as a free gift, of trusting Christ for now and for eternity. But we are not to think that the fact that we receive salvation by faith in Christ, not by any good deeds of our own, means that the Christian life is a life of blessed idleness. The way this faith is put into practice is by *working through love* ('expressing itself through love', REB).

This is the first of three occurrences of *love* in this letter, a virtue Paul mentions altogether 75 times (the most of any other New Testament writer is 28 in the Johannine writings). As used here it underlines the truth that, if there is a genuine faith, then there will be love, Christian-style. That is to say the believer loves, not because he or she has found people worthy of being loved, but because she or he has become a loving person. As Christians, we love because of what we have become when we believe, not because of the attractiveness of the people we meet. Saving faith inevitably issues in love.[13] It is important to be clear about this. Sometimes Christians have been so concerned with a zeal for rigid correctness in doctrine, which they have identified with faith, that they have overlooked the warmth of love that is inevitably the outcome of faith as Paul understood it.

We should notice the conjunction of *faith* with *love* in this verse and of faith with hope in verse 5; Paul links these three a number of times (*cf.* 1 Cor. 13:13; Col. 1:4–5; 1 Thes. 1:3; 2 Thes. 1:3).

7. The apostle looks back to the earlier days of the Galatian Christians when they were *running well*, and he has earlier spoken of himself as 'running' (2:2). In such passages he is using a metaphor taken from the Games, a metaphor that points to the importance of speedy progress. Paul can also use the metaphor of walking for one's whole manner of life, sometimes in a bad sense (2 Thes. 3:6, 11), but more commonly of those who are living out their faith (Eph. 4:1; Col. 1:10, *etc.*; this metaphor is mostly Pauline in the New Testament).

---

[13]It would be possible to take *energoumenē* as passive with the sense 'faith wrought by love', *i.e.* faith brought about by love, *i.e.* the love of God. But the middle is much more likely.

Perhaps *running* points to more rapid progress. Paul had been well pleased with the way the Galatians had begun along the Christian way. But things are now different. He does not think that this lack of progress arises out of their own ideas and reasonings but asks, *who hindered you . . ?*[14] There had to be some interference by some other teacher. The NIV renders, 'Who cut in on you?' which brings out something of the wrongness in what the false teachers had done.

The thrust of this interference was to keep the converts from obeying *the truth.* Paul has earlier referred to 'the truth of the gospel' (2:5, 14), and this is in mind here: the Christian gospel is *the truth.* Before the Judaizers made their appearance, the Galatian converts had had *the truth.* The effect of adding to the saving truth of the gospel the claim that it is necessary to keep the Jewish law was to turn the believers away from *the truth.* If all that is necessary for salvation is to accept the gospel message and trust Christ, then the additions made by the Judaizers must necessarily deny or at least obscure the truth. To live one's life in conformity to the Jewish law was certainly to reject the simplicity of the call to trust Christ alone for salvation.

8. *That persuasion* (actually Paul says 'The persuasion')[15] refers to the new teaching the Galatians were being asked to accept; they were being persuaded to move away from simple trust in Jesus to a position of trust in Jesus plus the keeping of the Jewish law. This, Paul says, *is not from him who calls you.* This might be understood in the sense 'not from me, who called you to believe in Christ'. But more probably he is referring to the call of God in the gospel message (see on 1:8 for the thought of God's call in this epistle). The new teaching which the Galatians were in danger of accepting was no part of the gospel and indeed was not compatible with the gospel.

9. A warning follows in what may well have been a proverbial saying (it occurs again in 1 Cor. 5:6; *cf.* Mk. 8:15; NIV puts it in quotation marks here). Bread would have been baked in most households, and people in general were very familiar with the process of making bread. It was common knowledge that when a little piece of

---

[14]There is a change of tense from the imperfect 'you were running' to the aorist, 'Who hindered you?'; the former indicates a continuing activity, the latter a sudden throwing up of a hindrance.

[15]*Peismonē* occurs only here in the New Testament and Bultmann tells us that it is not found in any previous literature (*TDNT*, VI, p. 9; he thinks 'the true sense' here is 'This following, or obedience'). There is a play on words following *peithesthai* that ends the previous verse. BAGD note that some understand the meaning 'obedience', but those who do 'must depart fr. the Gk. text as handed down by the great majority of witnesses' (they give 'persuasion' as the meaning).

fermented dough from a previous baking was placed in a batch of dough it would in due course affect the whole mass.[16] Paul is warning that, although the new teaching had apparently been accepted by only a very small number of people, unless it was vigorously repudiated, it would in time affect the whole church.[17]

10. Paul has recognized the danger of the false teaching and he has given warning of its possible consequences. But he now expresses his confidence in his converts. His *I* is emphatic: whatever be the case with others, Paul expresses his view that the church as a whole will not follow the false teaching. And his verb is in the perfect tense, indicating that he had no doubts; he was fully persuaded.[18] *In the Lord* indicates that this is an assurance that rests on a relationship to Jesus Christ. Paul was himself 'in Christ' (an expression he uses frequently), as were the genuinely converted Galatians. As they were all *in the Lord*, Paul can express his confidence in them; those who have a genuine faith in Jesus are not going to be persuaded to adopt a totally different way of seeking God and living for God. So the apostle expresses his confidence that in the end the Galatians *will not think otherwise*. They have been too well grounded in the saving work of Christ.

But what of anyone who was preaching the false way? Paul speaks of such a person as *he who troubles you*. Meyer points out that the singular does not mean the class of troublers, but 'the troubler *in each actual case*'. That teacher thought he was leading immature converts into a deeper understanding of the ways of God, but in fact he was doing no more than lead the converts who took notice of him into trouble. To pervert the teachings of the gospel was a serious matter and Paul is sure that the guilty person will *bear the judgment* (*i.e.* that of God; the expression may well be understood as 'bear the penalty'). And it does not matter who he is; he may be highly acclaimed in the community where he teaches, but if he is perverting the gospel he is a

---

[16]It appears that it was fermented dough from an earlier baking that was normally used in New Testament Palestine rather than yeast in the strict sense. Yeast could be made, but as a general rule leaven was used (see my commentary on *The Gospel according to Matthew*, IVP, 1992, p. 353, n. 83).

[17]Schmoller rejects the view of some that the leaven here refers to false teachers: 'It is not the number of the false teachers that is of account, but the influence of their teaching.'

[18]If we insist on the meaning of the perfect as indicating the present consequences of a past action, Paul is speaking of his confidence in the Galatians when he was among them as continuing up to the time of writing. His *egō* is emphatic: whatever be the case with others *I* have confidence in you.

guilty person and his rank and reputation will not shield him.

11. *But I* (with the use of the emphatic pronoun) sets Paul in sharp contrast to such false teachers, and the address *brothers* is a warm one. He is writing to people he regards as friends. *If I still preach circumcision* presents a problem. We do not, of course, know the exact terms in which Paul had preached the gospel in Galatia, but as we read his letters we get to understand the things he held to be important. We also discover some of the things he opposed, and from all this we are driven to see that no-one was less likely to preach circumcision than Paul. But his circumcision of Timothy (Acts 16:3) may indicate that he was ready to accept circumcision where it was seen as conformity to ancestral custom, though not, of course, where it was held to be necessary for acceptance before God. Perhaps some of his opponents, seeking to gain acceptance for their teaching, pointed out that Paul had himself been circumcised and suggested that in the matter of circumcision his teaching was much the same as theirs. Or the expression may look back to his pre-Christian days, when as an outstanding advocate of Judaism he had preached circumcision. Whether that is the way to understand it or not, Paul strongly repudiates any suggestion that he now 'preached circumcision'. He could recount the fact that he had been circumcised 'on the eighth day' among things of which he might well have been proud (Phil. 3:5), but that no ritual act availed before God was central to the gospel he preached and by which he lived. He preached Christ crucified, not circumcision.

So he draws attention to the fact that he was *still being persecuted*, and asks why this should be the case if he advocated circumcision. The point of this is that to preach circumcision was to engage in an orthodox Jewish line of teaching and that was permitted by the authorites. What was not given official permission was the new Christian teaching, and for engaging in that teaching Paul underwent persecution. Had he taught as he was accused of teaching, he now says, *the stumbling-block of the cross* would have *been nullified*. There would have been no objection to his essential teaching if he had endorsed this significant bastion of Judaism. He speaks of the cross as the *stumbling-block*.[19] The message about the cross means that people

---

[19]*Skandalon* strictly signifies the bait stick of a trap; that which springs the trap when it is touched. Metaphorically it can signify *'that which gives offense* or *causes revulsion, that which arouses opposition, an object of anger* or *disapproval, stain* etc.' (BAGD). Loane reminds us that Christians have often 'tried to soften or remove the offence. People like hymns with a sentimental appeal; architects like a cruciform style for a church

can do nothing to bring about their salvation, nothing at all. It insists that Christ has done all that is necessary by laying down his life in place of sinners. This message has not been popular through the centuries, and from these words of Paul we see that this has been the case from the beginning. Had preachers like Paul told their hearers to do something to acquire merit before God (such as complying with the provisions of the law), they would have been acceptable. By saying that Christ had done all that was necessarily, they aroused opposition. To change from preaching the cross to preaching the law, Paul says, would be to 'nullify' the stumbling-block. These two ways of understanding the Christian message are mutually exclusive.

12. Paul goes on to refer to the preachers who opposed his teaching as *those who trouble you*. This was not how it seemed to those tempted to accept the new teachers, but for Paul it was clear that people were troubled when their simple faith in Christ was disturbed by their being told that they must supplement that faith by submission to the law. For teachers to do this was, for Paul, such a wicked thing that he utters the horrific desire that these teachers *would castrate themselves*.[20] This was a dreadful thing to wish, but then the teaching was a dreadful thing to inflict on young Christians. We should notice also that castration meant exclusion from the assembly of God's people (Dt. 23:1). Paul probably has in mind also the practice of priests of Cybele who castrated themselves in the service of their deity. He is pointing to the lengths to which self-mutilation could go.[21]

2. Love, 5:13–15·

13For you were called on the basis of freedom, brothers; only do not use that freedom as an opportunity for the flesh, but serve one another

---

building. A cross may be ornamental, decorative, fashionable. But that was not how St Paul spoke of the Cross; he thought of it in its stark reality' (Loane, p. 38).

[20]Phillips translates, 'I wish those who are so eager to cut your bodies would cut themselves off from you altogether!' And Ramsay accepts the rendering in the AV. But such softening of the expression is scarcely true to the Greek. It is possible that the false teachers had suggested that their teaching of circumcision was no more than Paul taught and that he now suggests a way in which they could go beyond anything he said.

[21]'Such a mutilation of the gospel stands for Paul on one and the same level as the most despicable pagan practices, by means of which men tried to assure themselves of the favor of the gods' (Ridderbos). Lightfoot makes the point that castration 'was a recognised form of heathen self-devotion', and as such 'it could not possibly be shunned in conversation'. Paul's words would not have seemed as shocking to the Galatians as they do to us.

through love. [14]*For the whole law is fulfilled in one word, namely,
'You shall love your neighbour as yourself.'* [15]*But if you bite and
devour one another, beware, lest you be consumed by one another.*

It is Paul's habit to finish a letter with an exhortation to his readers
to live out some aspect of the Christian faith. 'To Paul a theology was
not of the slightest use unless it could be lived out in the world'
(Barclay). So now he reminds the Galatians of the importance of
freedom and of love. We have seen that Paul insists, above all the other
New Testament writers, on the importance of both these qualities. So it
is not surprising that he should now revert to the importance of love in
the Christian life, or that he should point out that, while the freedom
believers have in Christ is important, as he has just been insisting, that
freedom is not to be seen as an exercise in selfishness; it must be
exercised in love. It was the love of God that brought us salvation, and
it is essential that believers reflect that divine love by manifesting love
in their own actions. Christian liberty does not mean that the believer
is free to do anything. The believer is always under the constraint of
love.[22] But we should not miss the point that Christian love means
Christian freedom. We live in a world where all too often we
Christians fail to give the impression that we are free. People tend to
categorize us for the things we do not do rather than for the loving
deeds we accomplish. They see us as inhibited and our lives as limited
by harsh, cramped boundaries. Indeed, we are not thought to be free
at all, or particularly loving. But Christian freedom and Christian love
are important. Both need emphasis in our teaching, but more
especially in our way of life.

13. *For* introduces an explanation[23] and *you* is emphatic: the apostle
has been denouncing false teachers, but he insists that his converts are
not lightly to be associated with those false teachers. *You* are different,
he is saying; *you were called on the basis of freedom.* There are two
important things here. The first is that the believers were *called.* Paul
does not see them as people who of their own volition decided to
become Christians. They became Christians in the first instance
because God was at work in them; God called them. If becoming
Christians had been purely a matter of personal choice, then it might

[22]Cousar quotes Jacques Ellul, 'The glorious liberty of the children of God is not the
happy fluttering of a butterfly from one attractive flower to another. It is joyous, but it
is also radical, hard and absolute . . . Giving us our burden, God launches us into an
unsuspected adventure . . .' (p. 125).
[23]' "For" at the head of a paragraph = "in order to elucidate still further." The
elucidation now offered concerns the use of Christian freedom' (Lenski).

well be that personal choice could now lead them on to something quite different. But they could not modify the divine call. They could respond to that only by obedience; they could not modify it into something they now thought might be better.

The second important thing is that that divine call was *on the basis of freedom*.[24] God did not take them out of their pre-Christian bondage, of whatever sort it was, simply to entangle them in another sort of bondage. It matters a great deal to Paul that Christians are freed people. He is not saying that a certain measure of liberty was grudgingly accorded believers. He is saying that freedom is of the essence of being Christian; it is the fundamental basis of all Christian living, a thought which often comes to the surface in the apostle's writings (see the note on 2:4).

We should not miss the importance of the address: *brothers*. Paul is not writing to people who are firmly held in bondage to an élite who command them to go in a certain direction. While sound teaching is important, it is also important that Christians are brothers. There is no hierarchy which will authoritatively command all believers as to what they must do. Christians are as free as brothers with one another.

But if Paul can insist on the importance of freedom, he does not mean by it libertinism. He can also insist that freedom[25] is to be used rightly (actually Paul does not employ the verb *use*, an omission which, as Guthrie points out, makes the Greek 'more vivid than the English'). The freedom Christians know is not an exercise in selfishness; it does not mean that the believer can do anything that he or she chooses. Specifically, freedom is not to be the starting-point for *the flesh*, an excuse to pander to our sinful self.[26] It comes naturally to us, when we find that we are not compelled to walk in a certain path, to

---

[24]Ramsay points out that the freedom words are found in this letter 11 times, whereas in Romans they occur only 7 times, in 1 and 2 Corinthians 8 times and in all the rest of Paul's epistles twice. The concentration in Galatians is striking.

[25]There is an article with *eleutherian*; it is *the* freedom, the Christian freedom, of which he writes.

[26]Fung comments, '"Flesh" denotes not merely the bodily passions and lusts, nor even strictly speaking a "lower nature" contrasted with a "higher nature" in a person, but rather the human individual in his or her sin and depravity". He cites Barrett's criticism of NEB's rendering, 'our lower nature', as 'a most unfortunate rendering, not least because it implies that we have a higher nature which if left to itself would be intrinsically good. Paul knows no such higher nature.' BAGD speak of the flesh in Paul's thought as 'the willing instrument of sin' and as 'subject to sin to such a degree that wherever flesh is, all forms of sin are likew. present, and no good thing can live in the *sarx*' (BAGD, 7).

stray on to other paths which are easier or more enjoyable.[27] Paul counsels his readers to remember that there are things more important than selfish indulgence. So he calls on them to *serve*[28] *one another* and to do this *through love*. There are two points here: (a) believers are called to serve others rather than to seek some eminent place for themselves, and (b) in doing this they make it manifest that they are loving people. That Christians serve in love is of the utmost importance. Paul uses the article: it is *'the* love' of which he writes, the distinctive Christian love. Christians enjoy freedom indeed, but it is the freedom to serve other people in love.

14. The Galatians were evidently quite interested in the law[29] recorded in Scripture, and Paul now draws their attention to it. He does not regard the law as binding in the way his Jewish opponents saw it, but he recognized that God has spoken in the law and that, for example, the commandment to love comes to us with all the force of a divine initiative.[30] *For* introduces a reason for the preceding statement, and the apostle goes on to point out that one of the precepts in the law is all-embracing, namely the command to love (Lv. 19:18; *cf.* Rom. 13:8–10). The *neighbour* is, of course, not simply the person who lives next door, but anyone with whom one comes in contact. The duty of the servant of God is to be a loving individual and thus to treat each person with love. The precept accepts the truth that everyone has a certain concern for himself or herself,[31] and enlarges that concern to embrace those other people with whom we have to do. Paul is saying that if we live in love then other precepts are not needed. Our whole duty to other people will be met if we act in love towards them. We are reminded of Jesus' words that all the law and the prophets hang on the commandments to love God and to love our neighbour (Mt. 22:37–40). The rejection of law-keeping as the way of salvation does not alter the fact that the law gives us a useful guide to the way we should live.

---

[27]'It is so easy to interpret *liberty* as "the right to sin," and to construe *freedom* as "the privilege to do whatever one's evil heart *wants to* do," instead of looking upon it as *the Spirit-imparted ability and desire to do what one should do'* (Hendriksen).

[28]Schmoller speaks of *douleuein* as 'in happy antithesis to the *eleutheria* of Christians'. There is a paradox here: Christians are called to be free and that means being slaves to one another!

[29]Bruce points out that the order *ho pas nomos* (in verse 3 we have *holou ton nomon*) yields the meaning 'the law as a whole – the spirit and intention of the law'.

[30]'Paul could distinguish between aspects of the law which were obsolete and aspects of continuing validity' (Frank Thielman, *NTS*, 38, 1992, p. 252).

[31]'Basic to this thought is not the notion that we must love ourselves also, but rather the thought that self-love is natural, instinctive, to man. Just as directly and unhesitatingly as he loves himself, one must love his neighbor' (Ridderbos).

15. Paul points to what is left if his readers do not live in love (*But* marks a contrast). The construction introduced by *if* supposes the condition to be fulfilled, and the present tense points to continuing action.[32] The alternative to living in love is to live self-assertively, and the apostle sketches this graphically with *bite and devour* (Moffatt, 'snap at each other and prey upon each other'). The loveless life is a life lived on the level of animals, with a concern only for oneself, no matter what the cost to other people. But the end result of the self-centred life is that those who live it are *consumed*[33] *by one another*. As one wise man has remarked, any man wrapped up in himself makes a very small parcel. To be self-centred is to cut oneself off from a great deal that makes life worth living. And it invites hostile action from the people around us whom we refuse to help. Selfish people are thus *consumed by one another*.

3. The Spirit and the flesh, 5:16–26

> [16]*But I say, Walk in the Spirit and you will not fulfil the lust of the flesh.* [17]*For the flesh lusts against the Spirit and the Spirit against the flesh, for these are in opposition to one another, so that you do not do the things you want to do.* [18]*But if you are led by the Spirit you are not under law.* [19]*But the works of the flesh are manifest, which are fornication, uncleanness, licentiousness,* [20]*idolatry, sorcery, enmities, strife, envy, angers, rivalries, dissensions, factions,* [21]*jealousies, drunkennesses, carousings and things like these, of which I tell you in advance, just as I told you before, that those who do such things will not inherit God's kingdom.* [22]*But the fruit of the Spirit is love, joy, peace, longsuffering, kindness, goodness, faithfulness,* [23]*meekness, self-control; against such things there is no law.* [24]*But those who are Christ's have crucified the flesh together with its passions and lusts.* [25]*If we live by the Spirit let us also keep in step with the Spirit.* [26]*Let us not become conceited, provoking one another, envying one another.*

When Paul lists evil deeds to be avoided and good qualities to be practised, he is writing in a way that would have been widely accepted. In many writings in antiquity there are lists of virtues or vices or both, and such lists are found in the Old Testament, and

---

[32]'It would but slightly exaggerate . . . to translate, "If ye continue your biting and devouring of one another"' (Burton).

[33]*Analoō* (or *analiskō*) is used of destruction by fire in Lk. 9:54.

elsewhere in the New. But the lists here are perhaps the most spectacular and best known. We should not regard them as exhaustive or even as listing all the most important qualities (murder and robbery, for example, are not listed among the vices, or loyalty and humility among the virtues). They simply remind the reader of the kind of conduct to be eschewed and the kind of conduct that is to be followed. Commentators often arrange the qualities in groups, listing the first three as sexual sins, then religious errors, and so on. But Paul gives no indication that he has any such classification in mind, and it seems better to consider individually the various qualities he lists.

Paul is very conscious of the fact that it is not easy to live the Christian life. Human nature being what it is, there are always temptations to do the things we should not do and to leave undone the things we should do. The apostle now exhorts the Galatians to be aware of this conflict and to be aware, too, that the Holy Spirit is always with us guiding and strengthening us. There is always strength available if we would only use it. When we follow the leading of the Spirit a wonderful group of qualities follows, which Paul calls 'the fruit of the Spirit'. Longenecker reminds us that 'the truly unique feature of Pauline ethics is the role assigned to the Spirit'. The apostle will not let us forget that the Christian life must be lived and can be lived, but it can be lived only as the Spirit directs and empowers.

16. Paul follows his paragraph on the right and wrong uses of Christian freedom with a command to his readers to *walk in the Spirit*. Walking is a metaphor used from time to time in Scripture to denote spiritual progress. People in the first century could not travel as fast as we do, with our cars, planes, trains and the like, but even so, for them as for us, walking was the slowest way of going places. But even though walking was slow and unspectacular, walking meant progress. If anyone kept walking, she or he would certainly cover the ground and eventually reach the destination. So for the apostle walking was an apt metaphor. If any believer was walking, that believer was going somewhere. Paul is anxious for his Galatian friends to be making progress in the right direction, though he is aware that it is quite possible for them to be moving along the wrong road.

Walk in the Spirit (or, *by the Spirit*), he says, which points to lives lived in close connection with the Holy Spirit; the present imperative has the force of 'keep walking in the Spirit', which seems to imply that they are in fact walking in the Spirit (Paul is using the verb of the walk of life). Elsewhere Paul often speaks of being 'in' Christ, so we should not understand the expression to point to a relationship exclusive to the Spirit; perhaps we can say that the Spirit is the atmosphere in which the believer lives and moves and has his or her being. The believer relies on the guidance and the strength of the Spirit at every turn.[34] And that guidance and strength are adequate for the needs of believers. As Longenecker puts it, 'the Spirit opposes the flesh and replaces its works (cf. vv 19–21) with his own harvest of virtues' (p. 247). We should not miss the point (which Cousar, for example, makes) that Paul constantly speaks of what the Spirit does, so that believers are 'led' by the Spirit (5:18), he refers to 'the fruit' of the Spirit (5:22), and of 'reaping life eternal' from 'sowing to the Spirit' (6:8). The apostle is telling his readers what the Spirit does in them, not what they themselves can accomplish if only they try hard enough.

The contrary way of living is to *fulfil*[35] *the lust of the flesh*. The *flesh* is the physical part of our being and stands accordingly for that which is opposed to our spirit as well as to the divine Spirit. Our *flesh* is characterized by *lust*, which stands for the strong, but sometimes evil, desires that are associated with bodily living. Boice sees the term as used by Paul as meaning 'man as a fallen being whose desires even at best originate from sin and are stained by it'.[36] To *fulfil* those desires signifies to carry out what the *flesh* desires, to make the *flesh* the norm by which we live. The defence against this is not some outstanding striving of our own, but the strength we derive from the Holy Spirit as we *walk in the Spirit*.[37]

17. The mention of *flesh* evokes an explanation introduced by *For*; Paul explains why *the flesh* is to be resisted. *The flesh* (see on 5:13) *lusts against the Spirit*. There is that in *the flesh* which is totally opposed to all that the Holy Spirit stands for and, of course, the Spirit is totally opposed to what is merely flesh.[38] Thus Paul speaks of a continuing

---

[34]Schmoller sees the meaning as that the Spirit is 'not the path in which' they walk, but 'the power, through which they walk'. Lenski maintains that throughout this passage we should understand 'spirit', not 'Spirit' (*i.e.* the human spirit, not the Spirit of God), but his argument is unconvincing.

[35]*Teleō* means something like 'bring to its appropriate end' and the appropriate end for *the flesh* is at the furthest remove from the end at which those saved by Christ must aim. The double negative is emphatic: 'you will certainly not fulfil . . .'

[36]Chrysostom says that Paul 'is wont to call the flesh, not the natural body but the depraved will' (on 5:17).

[37]Luther comments, 'Thou seest many things in me which offend thee, and I again see many things in thee which mislike me. Here if one bear not with another through love, there shall be no end of dissension, discord, envy, hatred and malice' (p. 498).

[38]Calvin asks, 'What else then is the flesh but the old man?' and proceeds, 'And so, since the whole nature of man is rebellious and obstinate against the Spirit of God . . .'

conflict. The heavenly side of the conflict is, of course, that *the Spirit* is totally opposed to *the flesh*. The Holy Spirit is active in promoting all sorts of goodness and it is impossible for the Spirit to countenance the things *the flesh* strives for. The Spirit and the flesh *are in opposition to one another*: what the flesh so passionately wants the Spirit rejects outright, for the flesh is concerned with the basic drives of this life and the Spirit is concerned with ultimate and heavenly realities.

The result[39] is that *you do not do the things you want to do*. Paul does not, of course, mean that we never manage to long for what is right and to do it. With the help of God's Holy Spirit this can happen and, when it does, it brings about the wonderful joy that is part of Christian service. But this is what the Holy Spirit does in the believer. Paul is saying that in our *flesh*, that is, when living according to our own best insights and in our own best strength, we do not want to do the right things and, of course, as we lack the desire we also lack the accomplishment. We do not do the good things we ought to do (and in our best moments would like to do).

18. *But* introduces a contrast: we are not left in a situation where we can never do the things we know are right. Paul speaks of being *led by the Spirit*.[40] The Spirit, so to speak, goes ahead of the believer, leading him or her in the right path. The verb indicates that the Spirit leaves the believer in no doubt as to what the right course is. This does not mean that the believer never goes astray and is never in doubt. It is simply the antithesis of the position outlined in verse 17. *Flesh* and *Spirit* being what they are, none of us could ever walk in the right way if left to ourselves. But we are not left to our own devices. The Spirit is with believers and this transforms the whole situation.

The way Paul puts the resultant situation is *you are not under law*, that is, not under law's dominion. The word *law* lacks the definite article, which means that it is not limited to the Jewish law, though, of course, it is the Jewish law that is primarily meant. But subjection to any law means condemnation, for we are not able to keep all the law's prescriptions. If we are left with nothing but law, we are left with a situation in which we know what is right, but are powerless to do it. Paul had known this from his own experience and he counsels his Galatian friends to bear the real situation in mind. The way of law is

---

[39]*Hina* here indicates result rather than purpose; Robertson cites Lightfoot approvingly for this view (p. 998).

[40]The construction implies that the condition has been fulfilled: 'if (as is the case) you are led by the Spirit'. Burton sees nothing implied as to the fulfilment of the condition (*Moods*, 242), but Moule does not agree (Moule, p. 142).

the way of failure, but believers are not *under law*. There is no reason to live in the frustration and defeat of those who saw the law as setting standards that people ought to attain, but which by their own efforts they cannot. Paul's readers are not *under law*.

19. Paul proceeds to detail two kinds of conduct, and he begins with *the works of the flesh*, the deeds people do when controlled by their sinful impulses.[41] These works, he says, are *manifest*, they are plainly to be seen. There is no arguing about them. He does not say that all of these evil deeds are committed by everyone who is subject to the flesh, but he lists them as the kind of thing that people dominated by the flesh will certainly do. He begins with *fornication*, which strictly means the use of the harlot, but comes to be used for a wide variety of sexual sin.[42] *Fornication* was so widespread that it was apparently accepted as a normal part of life (unless it was carried to excess). Paul cannot accept any such view of the practice; he sees it as totally wrong. He goes on to *uncleanness*, a term which could mean what is literally unclean (such as the contents of a tomb, Mt. 23:27) and which comes to be used of 'dirty' conduct ('esp. of sexual sins', BAGD, 2; JB, 'gross indecency'; *cf*. Bruce, 'the tendency of vice to spread its corrupting influence'). With that Paul links *licentiousness*, a disregarding of accepted rules,[43] and often used, as here, of sexual misbehaviour, of conduct that knows no restraint. In these first three words Paul is comprehensively listing sexual sins.

20. He moves to *idolatry*, which was an accepted feature of most of the religions of antiquity. The making of a visible god seems to have satisfied people in general much more than the worship of a deity who could not be seen and for whom there was no visual representation. As Paul uses it, the term stands for practically all of the religions of his day except Judaism. To replace the real God by a piece of wood or

---

[41]Betz sees these deeds as 'a random collection of terms, describing the ordinary occurrences of evil among men'. He goes on, 'The seemingly chaotic arrangement of these terms is reflective of the chaotic nature of evil; this chaos is to be contrasted with the oneness of the "fruit of the Spirit" and its orderly arrangement (v 22–23).'

[42]Barclay cites Demosthenes, 'We keep mistresses for pleasure, concubines for the day-to-day needs of the body, but we have wives in order to produce children legitimately and to have a trustworthy guardian of our homes' (*Flesh and Spirit* [London, 1962], p. 24; this book examines each of the terms in verses 19–23). He reminds us that Paul 'lived in a world in which such sin was rampant, and in that world Christianity brought men an almost miraculous power to live in purity' (*ibid.*, p. 28); 'It has been said that chastity was the one completely new virtue which Christianity introduced into the pagan world' (*ibid.*, p. 27).

[43]'A man may be *akathartos* and hide his sin; he does not become *aselgēs* until he shocks public decency' (Lightfoot).

stone could, for Paul, come only from the fleshly impulse. We should bear in mind that the apostle probably has in mind more than engaging in specific acts of worship. As Lührmann puts it, 'the problem of idolatry did not lie in pagan worship, which could fairly easily be avoided, but rather – as 1 Cor. 8:1–13, for example, shows – especially in the religious permeation of life as a whole'. The passage mentioned refers to the common practice of selling meat that had been part of a sacrifice made to an idol. Idolatry was so widespread that one could give countenace to it without actually making an offering in a temple.

The word I have translated as *sorcery*[44] means 'the use of any kind of drugs, potions or spells' (LSJ). First-century medical knowledge was not profound, and the terms came to be used not only for drugs which had therapeutic value but also for magical ways of healing and then for magic of any kind (*cf.* Rev. 9:21; 18:23). It is this reliance on magic that Paul is denouncing (NIV has 'witchcraft'). *Enmities* renders a word which might also be understood as 'hatred'; whichever way we take it, it marks an evil. It may be used of hostility to God (Rom. 8:7). *Strife* ('a contentious temper', REB) fits in with *enmities* as an obvious evil. Barclay points out that in four of the six examples of the word in Paul it refers to the church, and comments that it is strife 'which has split the church, and which has brought enmity where there should be love' (*Flesh and Spirit*, p. 44).

With *envy* Paul moves on to the motivation for such activities, though we should notice that sometimes the word can refer to the good quality of zeal (*e.g.* Rom. 10:2; 2 Cor. 7:7). But the word can also signify *envy* and that is clearly the meaning here. With this Paul links *angers*.[45] *Rivalries* might be understood as 'ambitions'.[46] *Dissensions* and *factions* are obviously activities that should have no place among

---

[44]*Pharmakeia.*

[45]Abbott-Smith defines the word's meaning as 'passion, hot anger, wrath', and sees the plural as signifying '*impulses* or *outbursts of anger*'. Barclay points out that the word may on occasion be used in a good sense: 'It is like an explosive which can equally well be used to blast a way through obstacles in the way or to blast a town into ruins' (*Flesh and Spirit*, p. 51). Here, of course, it is used in the bad sense, of 'the blaze of temper which flares into violent words and deeds and just as quickly dies' (*ibid.*, p. 52). As I have written elsewhere, '*thymos* more readily denotes passionate anger, arising and subsiding quickly, whereas *orgē* is adapted to a more settled emotion' (*The Apostolic Preaching of the Cross* [London and Grand Rapids, 3rd edn. 1965, p. 180). NIV and REB have 'fits of rage'.

[46]LSJ see the word (*eritheia*) as meaning initially 'labour for wages', then as 'canvassing for public offence, intriguing' and 'selfish or factious ambition'. Here they suggest 'selfish or factious ambition'. Burton sees the meaning as 'self-seeking'.

the people of God, even if, tragically, they have made their appearance from time to time through the history of the church (and are not unknown in modern times!).[47]

21. *Jealousies* translates a word which seems always to be taken in a bad sense, unlike *envy* of the previous verse which can sometimes be used in a good sense. *Jealousy* is always an evil. *Drunkennesses* and *carousings* ('drinking bouts', REB; 'orgies', Phillips) are sins of a different type, and incidentally they let us see that the early church was not made up people whose pre-Christian lives were of the highest standard. The gospel made its appeal to people much given to self-indulgence as well as to those who lived on the highest level. Paul recognizes reality and reminds his readers that whatever kind of sin they had favoured in their pre-Christian days should be decisively abandoned. He is probably indicating also that his readers must expect to be tempted to go back to the sins in which they had indulged before they had come to know Christ. But such evils have no place in the life of the Christian. Paul's list is not exhaustive and he concludes it with *things like these*. His readers can fill in what is necessary.

He reminds his readers that this plain speaking is not new. He has told them this before, but evidently thought that his earlier teaching had not been heeded. So he now repeats it. And he sums up the consequences of the loose living he has denounced: *those who do such things will not inherit God's kingdom*. His list is not exhaustive, for people may do other *such things*; it is the kind of thing he has denounced and not simply the specific evils he has denounced that puts people outside the sphere of God's blessing.[48] Paul speaks of this in terms of *God's kingdom*, which reminds us of the frequent topic in Jesus' teaching, though here, of course, it is the future kingdom that is in mind. *Inherit* brings out the point that people in the kingdom do not earn their place; it is a gift to them from him who died.

22. The apostle turns from his catalogue of evils and considers *the fruit of the Spirit*,[49] qualities which are to be found in believers because of the change the Spirit of God has made in them. If there is an intentional contrast with the 'works' of the flesh, Paul may be suggesting that these virtues are produced by the Spirit rather than

[47]'There is all the difference in the world between believing that we are right and believing that everyone is wrong. Unshakable conviction is a Christian virtue; unyielding intolerance is a sin' (Barclay, *Flesh and Spirit*, p. 60). *Hairesis* may be used in a good sense (*e.g.* Acts 24:5), but here it is factionalism that is in mind.

[48]*Do* represents a present participle, 'people doing such things', and it carries the implication that they do them constantly.

[49]The adversative conjunction *de* introduces a contrast.

by human effort.[50] It may be significant that the word *fruit* is singular; Paul is not speaking of a series of fruits that would be shared around, so that one believer has one, another another. Rather he is referring to a cluster, such that all these qualities are to be manifested in each believer.[51] Further, 'the imagery used is particularly suggestive to convey the idea of spiritual growth, in striking contrast to the deterioration which follows the activities of the flesh' (Guthrie).

The apostle begins with *love* (for which see the note on 5:6; *cf.* 5:13–14). The first quality to be mentioned when speaking of the fruit the Spirit produces in believers is *love*. It is important for Paul that Christians should be loving people, and he comes back to the thought again and again. We should be clear that he is writing about the love that proceeds from people in whom the Holy Spirit has been at work so that they have become loving people, not love elicited by attractiveness in the loved ones. It has been said that this kind of love means loving people you do not like! There is a sense in which all the other virtues in the list flow from this one. *Love* is very important.

Paul follows this with *joy*, a quality he mentions 21 times (nobody else in the New Testament has it more than John's 9 times). *Joy* is for Paul 'a basic aspect of Christian piety' (Hamann). The gospel he preached has about it a great solemnity, for Paul is clear that unrepentant sinners face a bleak future. But we should not understand him to mean that salvation is a gloomy affair. To become a Christian means to pass from the domain of Satan, which is ultimately all gloom and doom, into the blessedness of the saved, which means love and joy. It means other important qualities as well, but it is significant that Paul begins with these two.

Next comes *peace* (43 times in Paul; next is Luke with 13; the word is found in every book of the New Testament except 1 John). *Peace* as we use the term can mean the absence of strife, but in the Bible it means more; it is a rich and positive concept. It is not the absence of anything, but the presence of the rich blessing of God. The word is used in the Greek translation of the Old Testament to render the Hebrew *šālōm* with its implication of wellbeing under the blessing of God. The peace for which Paul looks is peace with both God and

---

[0]'The word *fruit* indicates more plainly even than *work* that the issue in this matter is not what man himself can do. A fruit is not something that is made or done' (Ridderbos).

[51]Osiek misses the significance of the singular with her comment, 'The desirable traits are rightly called "fruits" of the Spirit . . .'

people, a peace that preserves the believer from the inner strife that can tear people apart. Hendriksen points out that peace 'is a natural result of the exercise of love, for "Great *peace* have they that *love* thy law" (Ps. 119:165 . . .)'.

Longsuffering[52] points us to the importance of patience with other people. In other places Paul can speak of the forbearance of God with the use of this word (Rom. 2:4; 9:22), and also of that of Christ (1 Tim. 1:16). We are to be imitators of God in refusing to be irritated by the wrongs people do to us. As Barclay puts it, we 'must reproduce God's undefeatable patience with people and God's undiscourageable patience with events' (*Flesh and Spirit*, p. 97).

With that goes *kindness*,[53] a most important feature of the Christian life. *Goodness* is not far distant in meaning from the preceding word (BAGD give the meaning of the word here as 'generosity'; so NRSV, Phillips). There appear to be no examples of the use of the term in the classical writers, and Trench sees it as 'one of many words with which revealed religion has enriched the later language of Greece' (*Synonyms*, p. 231). Fung sees it here as representing 'a magnanimous kindliness which issues in practical generosity'. It is not a quality which many modern people would claim, but it is important in the living out of the Christian faith. And in a world like ours there is plenty of room for its exercise.

Faithfulness renders the word that is usually translated 'faith' (as AV does here), though most agree that here it refers to *faithfulness* or *fidelity* (as in Mt. 23:23, *etc.*, *cf.* JB, 'trustfulness'). Either way, it is, of course, of central importance in the Christian understanding of things (and Paul uses the term 142 times). But in this context it is more likely that the apostle is saying that the Spirit brings about *faithfulness* in believers (all the other terms in this list denote ethical qualities and accordingly we expect this one to do so also). The ability to serve God faithfully through the years and through the temptations of life is not something we achieve by heroic virtue. It comes from the Spirit.

23. *Meekness* (a number of translations have 'gentleness') is another virtue that is not highly regarded in this self-assertive age, but it points us to a quality that is very important in making life run smoothly. It is not easy to tie the meaning down closely and, for example, one lexicon

---

[52]*The Shorter Oxford English Dictionary* includes a word 'longanimity', which might be regarded as a suitable equivalent, but this term has not passed into general usage.

[53]*Chrēstotēs*. The word may signify 'goodness' (*e.g.* Rom. 3:12), but as Trench points out, it is the goodness shown in Jesus' reception of the penitent woman (Lk. 7:37–50) rather than that in his driving of the traders out of the temple (Mt. 21:13) that is in mind (*Synonyms*, pp. 234f.).

says it means 'gentleness, humility, courtesy, considerateness, meekness in the older favorable sense' (BAGD). It is important for the Christian to see that the self-assertiveness that is so much part of twentieth-century life should not be valued highly. It is much better that each of us curtails the desire to be pre-eminent and exercises a proper meekness (or gentleness) in the situations in which we find ourselves.

The final virtue in Paul's list is self-control (BAGD give this meaning and add, 'esp. w. ref. to matters of sex'). In every age this has been honoured as a virtue, but in practice it has been frequently neglected. The self-made person, the one who gets to the top of the tree no matter what the cost to those who are trampled or pushed aside, is the one who is honoured in our day, and for that matter at most times. But Paul is aware of what we owe to God and of our duty to our fellows. If we insist on asserting ourselves whenever we can secure an advantage, we are out of step with the Christian way.

Paul rounds off his treatment of the qualities the Holy Spirit brings about in believers with the comment that against such things there is no law. This is a masterly understatement. It draws our attention to the fact that the kind of conduct that Paul has outlined is that which law-makers everywhere want to bring about.

24. People who belong to Christ[54] will have nothing to do with the evils Paul has listed earlier. He makes this point by saying that they have crucified the flesh, a strong way of saying that they no longer respond to the temptations arising from the physical nature. Crucified is an interesting way of putting it. It is a vivid metaphor for bringing out at one and the same time the importance of the crucifixion of Christ and the effect that that crucifixion has on the way the followers of Jesus live as well as on what he did for them in his death.[55] We should not miss the point that this crucifixion is something believers do. Stott emphasizes the importance of this: 'This is something we did decisively at the moment of conversion. When we came to Jesus Christ, we repented. We "crucified" everything we knew to be wrong. We took our old self-centred nature, with all its sinful passions and desires, and nailed it to the cross.' Paul's addition, with its passions and lusts, underlines the feelings associated with the body. A few verses back he has indicated some of the sins that arise from surrender to the desires that spring from bodily life. There is no need to list them again.

---

[54]Some very good MSS read Christou Iēsou (א ABC, etc.) but Iēsou is omitted by P46 DFG and others.

[55]'The Christian stakes everything on the reality of God's grace, on the victory of Calvary, on the offer to himself to share in the grace of that victory' (Warren, p. 101).

It is enough that believers have made a decisive break from them.[56]

25. Paul has spoken of the fruit of the Spirit (verse 22) and he puts a similar thought in different words.[57] Now he speaks of believers as those who *live by the Spirit*; his 'if' introduces a clause with the implication 'If (as we do) . . .' This underlines the thought that the power of the Spirit manifest in the life of the believer is not an occasional thing, manifesting itself now and then in times of special need. The believer's whole way of life is dominated by the divine Spirit. That is the profession believers make and Paul exhorts them to make it good in their manner of living: *let us also keep in step*[58] *with the Spirit*, i.e. 'let us live our lives with the help and direction of the Spirit' (REB, 'If the Spirit is the source of our life, let the Spirit also direct its course').

26. Having made an exhortation to living 'by the Spirit' Paul puts the negative: *Let us not become conceited*. It is easy to assume that because we are Christ's we will always say and do the right thing. Paul is warning his readers that believers can be too confident that they are right in what they are contemplating. He singles out two things: *provoking*[59] and *envying*. It is easy for the believer to be so intent on what he or she sees as service that she or he does not take notice of the fact that the proposed course of action will certainly provoke someone else into doing what is wrong. And even if we do not succumb to this temptation it is also easy to be jealous of what some other believer is doing. To be *conceited*, to be sure that we are always right (even if that means other people are always wrong!) is a perennial temptation to believers.

[0]Duncan comments on the crucifixion of the flesh that 'the flesh is not merely treated as dead, but becomes as a matter of fact as good as dead'. He goes on, 'How different it is with the non-Christian, as we see him, e.g., in the modern novel or play, a creature who apparently never expects to be able to do anything except what his lusts and selfish ambitions dictate for him.'

[57]Commentators differ as to where the section should end. Some make the break at the end of verse 24, others at the end of verse 25, others at the end of verse 26. In the absence of any convincing reason to make the break earlier I follow the chapter division and end this section at the end of verse 26.

[58]The verb *stoicheō* means '*be in line with, stand beside* a pers. or thing, *hold to, agree with, follow*' (BAGD). The present imperative indicates that this is to be the habitual practice (MIII, p. 75).

[59]'This does sound suspiciously as though there was party strife in the church of Galatia of the type familar to us from Corinth' (Cole).

GALATIANS 6

4. Mutual helpfulness, 6:1–10

> [1]Brothers, if a man is caught in any transgression, you who are spiritual, restore such a one in a spirit of gentleness, considering yourself, lest you also be tempted. [2]Carry one another's loads and so fulfil the law of the Christ. [3]For if anyone thinks he is something when he is nothing, he deceives himself. [4]But let each one prove his own work and then he will have matter for glorying in himself alone and not in another. [5]For each one will carry his own load.
>
> [6]Let him who is instructed in the word be a sharer with his instructor in all good things. [7]Don't go astray, God is not mocked. For whatever a man sows, this he will also reap; [8]for he who sows to his own flesh will of the flesh reap corruption, but he who sows to the Spirit will of the Spirit reap life eternal. [9]Let us not be weary in doing good, for in due time we will reap if we do not grow slack. [10]So then, as we have opportunity, let us do good to all people, especially to the household of the faith.

1. Paul proceeds to urge his converts to live genuinely helpful Christian lives. He uses the warm address, *Brothers*, and follows this with an *if* clause which makes no supposition as to whether anyone was in fact guilty of the offence in question or not. *A man* is quite general; it points to any believer. *Is caught*[1] seems to imply that the brother is not intentionally doing wrong; he is 'caught' by the sin and goes astray. The verb does not imply any particular sin. Nor is *transgression* specific; it signifies any sin a person may commit.[2] Paul addresses his readers as *you who are spiritual*, which clearly classes believers as people indwelt by the Holy Spirit (*cf.* 3:3; 4:6; *etc.*). When such believers become aware of a sin that a fellow believer commits,

---

[1]*Prolambanō* sometimes retains the temporal force of the *pro-*, but this is not the case here. Paul may be thinking of believers as becoming aware of, or detecting, a fault in another believer. Or the verb may signify that a believer 'finds himself inadvertently involved in some wrongdoing' (Bruce). MM cite its use in the papyri in the sense of 'entrapped', used of a girl 'against whom a plot had been formed'.

[2]'*Paraptōma* contains the idea of falling. It is not the deliberate, the planned, aspect of sin that is stressed here, but rather the unwitting element. Mistake rather than misdeed is the force of the word, though without absolution of responsibility' (Ridderbos). It 'is not a settled course of action but an isolated action which may make the person who does it feel guilty' (Bruce).

they are not to regard this as a matter for gossip or a means of seeing themselves as in some way superior. Rather, they are to restore[3] the sinner and to do so *in a spirit of gentleness* (or *meekness*).[4] The test the church must use is whether what is done will help to restore the sinner to the place from which he or she has fallen.[5] The thought is that of assistance, not punishment. And the helpers are not to adopt any attitude of superiority but to *consider* themselves; they are to bear in mind that they, too, might *be tempted*. We should notice that Paul changes from the plural, *you who are spiritual*, to the singular, literally 'considering thyself', which makes this personal to each believer.[6] Calvin points to this and remarks, 'However acute we may be in observing the faults of others, we do not see, as someone says, "the wallet that hangs behind our own back."' Fallible sinners must never assume that they will not do something as bad as the sin they discern in other people. As much as they can they should avoid being in situations where they will be tempted. Being *tempted* may mean being tempted to do the same sin, but more probably to being tempted to see oneself as superior or the like.

2. Far from standing aloof in judgment on others, Paul counsels the Galatians to *carry one another's loads*. He puts *one another's* first in the sentence, which gives it emphasis. People carry a variety of burdens through life and Christians should be noted for helping one another with whatever burden the other believer may be compelled to carry. The tense of the imperative is present, which conveys a meaning like 'keep carrying'; Paul is not counselling believers to perform an occasional helpful act, but to live their lives as helpful people, always ready to lift the burden from other people's shoulders.

In this way they are to *fulfil the law of the Christ*. *Fulfil* is a strong word;

---

[3]Lightfoot points out that the verb is used 'especially as a surgical term, of setting a bone or joint'.

[4]E. A. Judge points out that the gentleness in question was originally that of the powerful towards those in lower stations. In the present passage he sees the meekness Paul has in mind as 'still an attribute of those with authority' (in Horsley, *New Documents*, 4, p. 170). If this is the case Paul may well be thinking of the function of the leaders of the local church.

[5]Cousar comments, 'The very idea of restoring one "caught in any kind of wrong-doing" [GNB] sounds a bit strange to modern ears. The current mood is more one of live-and-let-live, of staying out of other people's business, of avoiding friends who seem constantly to want to take care of us . . . But Paul describes the restoration as bearing burdens: sharing the pain of failure, assuming a portion of the guilt and judgment . . .'

[6]The change from a plural verb to a singular participle serves to remind the individual of his responsibility' (Chamberlain).

it points not to a half-hearted fiddling round the edges of a task, but to accomplishing it wholeheartedly. *The law of the Christ* is an unusual expression (found here only in the New Testament, though *cf.* Rom. 3:27; 8:2; 1 Cor. 9:21). The article with *Christ* perhaps adds a touch of formality, as it directs attention to the messianic function of Jesus. We generally associate grace and forgiveness with Christ, but we must never forget that he demanded wholeheartedness in those who followed him. He called on any who wanted to be his disciples to take up their cross if they would follow him. This is not a *law* in the sense of part of a legal code, but it points to the necessity for lowly service if we would truly be followers of Jesus (*cf.* the demand for the washing of other people's feet, Jn. 13:14). Lowly service is not just an option that some Christians might like to follow. It is an obligation resting on all believers, and it is so important that it can be said to define the whole duty of the believer (*cf.* Mt. 20:25–27). We are reminded that a little earlier Paul has said that love for one's neighbour fulfils the whole law (5:14; love for one another is a command of Christ, Jn. 13:34).[7]

3. It is easy to deceive ourselves about our own importance. We can think that we are *something*,[8] when in fact it is basic to the Christian understanding that we can do nothing at all for our salvation. All we have and all we are we owe to God. Christ came to this earth and lived and died so that there would be a way of salvation. For salvation we can do nothing at all. We are called on simply to believe, to trust Christ alone. And when it comes to living out the Christian life we are wholly dependent on the strength and guidance of the Holy Spirit. We may (or, of course, may not) amount to something in the earthly circles in which we live and move and have our being. But where it counts, in the issues of eternal salvation, we are *nothing*.[9] To hold otherwise is to *deceive* ourselves (we certainly do not deceive anyone else).

4. Paul turns to another aspect of Christian service. He counsels *each*

---

[7]'Paul's meaning is that Christ's law is one of love, not rituals, and the only way to fulfill it, that is, express its true meaning, is to behave lovingly towards one another' (Osiek). Dunn comments, 'At any one time all members of a Christian congregation would have such burdens to shoulder, and when such burdens outgrew the individual's strength, it was important that there should be a supportive family-community to help out.'

[8]*Cf.* Meyer: such a man 'imagines himself possessed of peculiar moral worth, so that he conceives himself exalted above such a mutual bearing of burdens'. The Greek word order follows 'something' immediately with 'nothing', thus making a sharp contrast between the two.

[9]'There is nothing wrong with being "nothing" or a "nobody," because that is what one actually is. It is wrong, however, to be deluded into thinking one is "somebody"' (Betz).

one to *prove*[10] *his own work.* We must not look at the appearance and achievement of others and fancy ourselves as in some way superior. It is important that we make our own work the best we can possibly make it. If we are concentrating on ironing out the imperfections in what we are doing, we are unlikely to be critical of what other people are accomplishing. Paul is not, of course, advocating that Christians be habitually boastful; he is saying that they should so live that their lives will give evidence of praiseworthy qualities.[11] He is making strongly the point that each must concentrate on improving what she or he is doing and not imagine that he or she is doing well because of a fancied comparison with someone else. In the end we stand or fall according to what we are and have done, not in the person and deeds of somebody else. Chrysostom emphasizes the importance of scrutinizing our motives: 'If thou hast performed a good deed, consider whether it was not from vain glory, or through necessity, or malevolence, or with hypocrisy, or from some other human motive.'

5. The same point is put in other words. *Each one* applies the saying to every Christian as Paul moves to the imagery of carrying burdens. His word for *load*[12] is used literally for the cargo of a ship (Acts 27:10), and figuratively for the burden of the law (Mt. 23:4). In this passage 'everyone is to concern himself about his own burden, rather than to compare himself complacently w. others' (BAGD). The guilt of another person does not justify me in committing a sin. Paul is urging believers to concentrate on their proper task in the service of God, and not allow themselves to be distracted by fanciful comparisons with how other people are serving him. Phillips translates, 'every man must "shoulder his own pack"', which brings out some of the force of the original. And K. Weiss sees the word as meaning 'the "achievement" or "work" that each will bring with him for evaluation in the judgment' (*TDNT*,

---

[10]*Dokimazō* means 'put to the test, examine' and thus 'prove by testing', 'accept as proved, approve' (BAGD).

[11]His word is *kauchēma*, not *kauchēsis*; BAGD see the meaning here as 'a reason for boasting'. It is not the act of boasting but the possession of a quality that one could boast about were one boastful. Burton sees it as 'a less opprobrious term than the English word "boast"', and says that the context here 'demands the more common and proper meaning, "ground of glorying"'.

[12]*Phortion* (in verse 2 *barē* was used for 'burdens'). It can denote a heavy or a light load, whereas *baros* seems always to be burdensome. Guthrie finds it 'suggestive that the same word used here for load (*phortion*) is used by Jesus of the burden of his yoke, which he himself describes as light (Mt. 11.30)'. Boice says with reference to the two Greek words, 'It is difficult to establish a precise distinction between *barē* . . . and *phortion* . . . But such distinctions as there are seem to be between a load that is burdensome and one that is a man's normal work to carry.'

IX, p. 86). There are some things we cannot push off on to other people. There is a Christian duty which each of us must perform.[13]

6. Paul moves to the duty rank-and-file believers owe to those who teach them about holy things. With our elaborate ecclesiastical organizations and specifically with our time-honoured way of providing for the needs of our ministers, it is easy for us to overlook the fact that in the early church Christian teachers led precarious lives. There were no elaborate schemes for seeing that even their elementary needs were met, no guaranteed clergy stipends. In this passage we see something of the way provision was made. *Him who is instructed in the word* is a description of a member of the rank and file of church membership. None of the members of the church in its earliest days had been to Sunday school as a child. All were converted in adulthood and thus were in need of a good deal of instruction about the Lord they had come to serve, about what that Lord had done to bring about their salvation, about the kind of people they ought to be and about the kind of things they, as Christians, ought to be doing. So the giver of instruction in Christianity was an important person. Here Paul speaks of instruction *in the word*, which points to teaching about Christ (who could be called 'the Word', as in Jn. 1:1), and about the divine revelation that underlay the Christian understanding of life and salvation. It does not require a great deal of reflection to see that in the early church the person who taught new believers the essential things to know about God, about Jesus, about the way of salvation and about the way the saved ought to live was doing a very important work.

So Paul says that the person *who is instructed in the word* has a responsibility to his teacher. He is receiving priceless instruction from a person who (as far as we know) had no regular source of income. Accordingly he is called on to be *a sharer . . . in all good things*.[14] We have no information about whether the early Christians gave money or food

[13]David W. Kuck argues that Paul is referring to final judgment: 'The present realities of tensions in the community, ethical uncertainties, disappointed expectations, flagging endurance, and disconcerting sufferings are to be resolved or endured with a view to the final judgment of God. In this judgment not only will all Christians as a group reap the harvest of eternal life, but also individual Christians will know the joy of appropriate praise and reward for the burden of their work in the Lord's church' (*NTS*, 40, 1994, p. 297). This is possible, but there is nothing in the context to indicate that Paul is speaking of God's judgment at the end of the world.

[14]Stott quotes Stephen Neill, 'This is not to be regarded as a *payment*. The word "shared" is a rich Christian word, which is used of our *fellowship* in the Holy Spirit.' Lenski understands the sharing to be the other way: the teacher shares his good teachings with his hearers. But this does not seem to be what Paul is saying, for it is the hearer who is to do the sharing.

or lodging or all of these things (Paul does say *in all good things*!). But what is clear is that Paul is exhorting his readers to take good care of those who taught them important things about the Christian way of life. Ramsay reminds us that this duty 'was quite novel in ancient society'. He further says, 'There was no system of instruction in the Pagan religions. The favour of the gods was gained by acts of ritual, not by moral conduct. Every prayer for help was a deliberate bargain; the worshipper promised certain gifts to the god, on condition that the god gave the help implored.' To people used to this kind of religion, a good deal of instruction had to be given before they were used to the Christian way. The teacher was thus very important, and Paul insists that care be given to provide for such teachers.[15]

7. Paul moves to the general manner of life of his readers. *Don't go astray* will have the force of 'Don't be deluded'. He goes on to point to some undeniable truths, beginning with *God is not mocked* or perhaps 'treated with contempt' or 'outwitted' (see BAGD; the verb means something like 'turn up the nose at').[16] Sinners may assure themselves that what they desire will come to pass, but they cannot outwit God. It is a serious mistake when people assume they can ignore the commands God has given and go their own way with impunity. It comes easily to us to think that the way that we want things to happen is the way they will happen. Paul is reminding us that God has his purposes and that these will assuredly work out.

Specifically, Paul cites what looks like a proverbial saying: *whatever a man sows, this he will also reap.* This is obviously a truism of agriculture. If a farmer sows wheat he will not reap barley.[17] Paul is saying that this has an important application to the way people live. It is what we sow that determines our ultimate harvest. We may not like it. We may prefer some very different outcome. But life is a continuing process of sowing and reaping. We have constant reminders of the truth of what Paul is saying.[18]

---

[15]'Christian giving, for Paul, is never a mere payment, but is an essentially spiritual act in which it is a privilege to be allowed to share (cf. 2 Cor. viii.1–6), one way among many in which Christians can show their fellowship in the gospel (cf. Phil. i.5)' (Duncan).

[16]'The reference is not to verbal scoffing but to the despising of God by a man's being, by his whole manner of life' (H. Preisker, *TDNT*, IV, p. 796).

[17]Cf. Stott, 'It is not the reapers who decide what the harvest is going to be like, but the sowers.' To get the harvest we want we must sow the right seeds.

[18]Barclay reminds us of 'a grim truth', namely that 'in the end life holds the scales with an even and a scrupulous balance. If a man allows the lower side of his nature to dominate him, in the end he can expect nothing but a harvest of trouble. But if a man keeps on always walking the high way, and always doing the fine thing, he may have

8. Paul applies his proverb to the ultimate issues. The person who *sows to his own flesh* is the person who concentrates on life here and now. He may not be a grievous sinner (or, of course, he may be!), but if he concentrates on limiting himself to horizons dictated by his bodily interests then in the end he can reap only what is of concern to those bodily interests. And, as in the end the body dies and decays, Paul goes on to point out that this means that the ultimate harvest of the flesh-oriented life is *corruption*.[19] This word may be understood in a number of ways, but here it surely points to ultimate loss; it is the opposite of *life eternal*.

The apostle moves from the person who concentrates on this earthly life to the one *who sows to the Spirit*. This person, he says, *will of the Spirit reap life eternal*. There is quite an emphasis on the Spirit in these last chapters of the letter. Paul has spoken of 'walking' in the Spirit (5:16), being 'led' by the Spirit (5:18), 'living' by the Spirit (5:25) and now of 'sowing to the Spirit'. 'Sowing to the Spirit' is an unusual expression, but it clearly points to a concentration on those aspects of life which involve interaction with God's Holy Spirit. It signifies concentrating on what will produce 'the fruit of the Spirit'. It means seeing our spiritual life as more important than our secular experiences and devoting time and energy to it accordingly. And as we live Spirit-oriented lives Paul assures us that we *will of the Spirit reap life eternal*. The thrust of this is, of course, with respect to the afterlife, *life eternal*. Paul is reminding the Galatians that they should get their priorities right and give time and energy to that which concerns ultimate issues and not merely the passing things of here and now. There will also be the thought that believers here and now experience something of what that life will be. Their life in fellowship with God is a richer and fuller life than that of the worldly-minded or the worshipper of idols.

9. It is easy for the servants of God to become discouraged: the opposition they meet is so constant and the good they are trying to do is so hard to accomplish. Paul recognizes this and exhorts the Galatians not to *be weary*,[20] though we should notice that his *we* brackets the apostle with the Galatian converts. He, like them, found the temptation to slacken in *doing good* and, just as they did, he needed

---

to wait long, but in the end God repays. Christianity never took the threat out of life.'

[19]Paul 'forcibly reminds his readers that the glorious status of sonship does not imply an easy-going God' (Allan).

[20]Hendriksen reminds us that 'well-doing requires *continuous* effort, *constant* toil; but human nature, being fond of ease, lacks staying-power, is easily discouraged'.

to look forward to the time when *we will reap*.[21] He does not say what the harvest will be, but we should surely understand it in part at least as the leading of sinful people into the salvation Jesus brings (*cf.* Jn. 4:35–38). There is probably also the thought of the development of Christian character. That, too, takes time and effort. And, Paul assures his readers, this reaping will be done *if we do not grow slack*. It is fatally easy for the Christian to lose concentration on the daily struggle and say, 'I have done enough!' Paul reminds his readers that they must not give in or even slacken off. Reaping the harvest is too important for slackness in the reapers.

10. The apostle draws a logical conclusion.[22] Because of the importance of reaping the harvest of which he has been writing, Paul stresses the necessity for making the most of our *opportunity*. From the nature of the service to which he goes on, it is clear that the *opportunity* of which he writes occurs throughout our lifetime. He is saying in effect that while we have life we have opportunity and we should make the most of that opportunity. And specifically we should *do good to all people*. In every age the temptation to all the human race has been to do the things that bring benefit to the person doing them. Doing good to others is demanding; we are all tempted to limit it to helping people who may be expected to reciprocate. Paul's exhortation means that we must not confine ourselves to doing the things that bring benefit to ourselves or the things that we simply enjoy doing. We must enlarge our horizons. Doing good to others is often a thankless activity. But it is an important part of the Christian life and Paul leaves his readers in no doubt that it is eternally significant.

Doing good to all sorts of people is then the duty of Christians. But Paul sees of particular importance one group of people who may be helped, as he goes on, *especially to the household of the faith*. This had a great significance in the first-century Roman empire. Christians were often poor and they could not expect help from the non-Christian state. Rather the opposite. The state did not want people to be Christians and it placed all sorts of obstacles in the way of believers. Helping the poor was a duty taken very seriously in the early church. Moreover, Christians understood the obligation of taking the gospel to people who did not know it, and this meant travelling. And for

---

[21]'Which in class. Greek must be *if we do not faint*; but by Paul it is intended as a fact' (MIII, p. 285).

[22]'*Ara oun*, "so then", where *a.* expresses the inference and *oun* the transition' (BAGD, *ara*, 4).

Christians who were not travelling evangelists, it could involve providing accommodation for travellers who came to preach the gospel.

There was plenty of room then for people in the church to do good to their fellow believers. It is of interest that these people are called *the household of the faith* (or, *of faith*). We could understand this to mean people who had faith or people who belonged to a community which could be called 'the faith'. Either way, the emphasis is on the fact that Christians are believers. What distinguished Christians from other people was their faith. They were people who had put their trust in Jesus as their Saviour and this was the most important thing about them. Paul sees all Christians as united by the bond of their common faith and therefore it is important that they do good to one another as they have opportunity. Notice that the apostle sees believers as making up one great family, one *household*.

V. Conclusion, 6:11–18

[11]*See with what large letters I write to you with my own hand.* [12]*As many as wish to make a good impression in the flesh are trying to compel you to be circumcised, only so that they may not be persecuted for the cross of Christ.* [13]*For not even those who are circumcised keep the law, but they wish you to be circumcised so that they may boast about your flesh.* [14]*But as for me, may it not be that I should glory except in the cross of our Lord Jesus Christ, through whom the world has been crucified to me and I to the world.* [15]*For neither is circumcision anything, nor uncircumcision, but a new creation.* [16]*And as many as will walk according to this rule, peace be upon them and mercy, even upon the Israel of God.*

[17]*Let no-one henceforth trouble me, for I bear the marks of Jesus in my body.*

[18]*The grace of our Lord Jesus Christ be with your spirit, brothers. Amen.*

Paul is coming to the end of his letter. There are just a few more remarks to be made, and a greeting. Betz sees this section as 'most important for the interpretation of Galatians. It contains the interpretive clues to the understanding of Paul's major concerns in the letter as a whole and should be employed as the hermeneutical key to the intentions of the Apostle.' Longenecker doubts whether Betz is correct in seeing this passage as a *peroratio*, but agrees that the passage is very important: 'More directly than in any of his other letters, Paul's subscription in Galatians brings to a head and highlights the central features discussed within the body of his letter.'

11. It seems to have been Paul's habit to dictate his letters to an amanuensis, but to take the pen himself and write the concluding section, possibly because this would authenticate the letter. Elsewhere he tells his readers that this was his custom (2 Thes. 3:17) and, while he does not always draw attention to it, we need not doubt that he did it as his general rule.[23] It seems that it is at this point that he takes up the pen, though it is not impossible that he had written some of the earlier words, or even the whole letter. The AV implies this as it reads, 'how large a letter I have written' and Duncan holds that 'from first to last, Galatians was not dictated, but came direct from the hand of the apostle'. But not many have been convinced. It seems much more likely that Paul is here referring to the closing words of the letter.

He did not use the small letters professional scribes would use, but wrote in large characters. He wants there to be no doubt in the readers' minds that this letter comes from Paul. It is properly authenticated. The aorist tense of the verb is usual in such cases: when the letter was read the writing of it would be in the past.[24] Why he wrote in large letters is not clear. Some have suggested that Paul's eyesight was poor and that he wrote in large letters to see what he was writing, others that he was not an efficient scribe and that his clumsy letters came out large, or that his hand had been hurt in one of his brushes with opposition. Such views scarcely seem probable and it is more likely that he wanted to give the passage emphasis (*cf.* the use of capitals or bold type for emphasis in modern writing).

12. The apostle gives a reason some people are advocating circumcision for the Galatians. There are those who *wish to make a good impression in the flesh*, a description which brings out the point that the false teachers were more concerned with the *impression* they

---

[23]The practice is attested in the papyri. Thus A. Deissmann reproduces a letter which he dates 12 September, AD 50, in which the body of the letter is written in one hand and the farewell and date in another (*Light from the Ancient East* [London, 1927], pp. 170–172). There seems no doubt that this second was the hand of the author and that he had dictated the earlier part to a scribe. Paul is following a contemporary custom.

[24]Moule sees the use of the aorist tense as 'an understandable idiom – and a rather gracious one, though it causes more ambiguity than the English – whereby the writer courteously projects himself in imagination into the position of the reader, for whom actions contemporaneous with the time of writing will be past' (p. 12, and see n. 1).

were making and with matters that had to do with *the flesh* than they were with the essential Christian message.[25] Circumcision was a physical action, something necessarily performed *in the flesh*. It was not to be compared to the important spiritual truths that the apostle and others like him so constantly set forth. That these false teachers were still *trying*[26] to bring about circumcision for the converts seems to show that they had not yet succeeded. But *compel* points to pressure; these teachers were not saying that circumcision was a helpful rite for people who chose to accept it, but that it was necessary for true Christian initiation.

Paul switches to the reason that motivated these teachers. His *only* indicates that this was the driving force, as he sees it. That they should not *be persecuted for the cross of Christ* seems to indicate that preachers like Paul, who emphasized the centrality of the crucifixion, were under pressure to give up preaching this gospel. To advocate circumcision was to align the new movement with Judaism, a religion that had official Roman sanction, and therefore one that avoided persecution. The preachers Paul was opposing may have included the cross in their proclamation, but by adding the necessity for circumcision they avoided persecution.

13. Keeping the whole law was a difficult task and Paul is clear that the false preachers did not succeed in doing this. They had themselves[27] been *circumcised*,[28] but they did not reproduce in their lives the keeping of the law that their acceptance of this rite involved. This may mean that keeping the whole law is so difficult that the teachers in question, like everybody else, could not manage it. Or Paul may be saying that they were hypocrites: they did not try to keep the whole law. But even though they did not keep the law, they wanted the Galatian believers *to be circumcised*. This meant asking them to accept the yoke of the whole law, but the apostle does not see this as their primary motive. Rather than putting their emphasis on the uprightness of life demanded by the law, they were ready to *boast*

[25]Boice points out that *euprosōpēsai* 'carries overtones of insincerity'.

[26]Turner sees here a 'conative present' with the meaning 'try to compel' (MIII, p. 63).

[27]Moule stresses the importance of the article. He says that this passage 'means *for not even the very ones who get circumcised keep the law*, whereas, if the article had been omitted, the sense would have been *for not even* when they *get circumcised do they keep the law themselves*' (p. 107).

[28]This takes *peritemnomenoi* as passive. But Bruce argues that the term should be 'taken as middle voice with causative significance ("causing to be circumcised")'. Cf. JB, 'want to force circumcision on you'.

about your flesh. Indeed, Paul says, this was their motive.[29] They were evidently glorying in the number of people they could induce to undergo circumcision. The reference to *your flesh* shows that they were concentrating on the physical instead of bringing people to the spiritual challenge that the gospel presents.

14. Paul distances himself from any such approach. *But as for me* signifies a decisive taking up of a different position.[30] The apostle declines to *glory* in anything *except in the cross of our Lord Jesus Christ.* It is easy for us to miss the shocking nature of this assertion. Bruce can say, 'The word *crux* was unmentionable in polite Roman society . . . even when one was being condemned to death by crucifixion the sentence used an archaic formula which served as a sort of euphemism: *arbori infelici suspendito,* "hang him on the unlucky tree" . . .' But Paul not only used the unmentionable word: he gloried in it. He saw with clarity that the central truth of Christianity is that the Lord Jesus Christ went to the cross for the salvation of sinners, of whom he saw himself as chief (1 Tim. 1:15). No matter how unpalatable this was to the people of his day, he saw that it was a truth that must be proclaimed with emphasis. So he gloried in it.[31]

When that great central truth is grasped all else pales into insignificance before it. That does not mean that godly living is unimportant, but that godly living can be done only in the strength that God supplies, and that God supplies it to all who put their trust in the crucified Saviour.

Paul brings this out by going on after his reference to the cross of Christ, *through whom the world has been crucified to me and I to the world* (*cf.* Phil. 3:7–8).[32] The apostle's identification with the crucified Christ

[29]*Hina* introduces a clause of purpose.

[30]*Emoi* comes first with emphasis and *de* is adversative, while *mē genoito* marks an emphatic repudiation. The expression 'strongly deprecates something suggested by a previous question or assertion. Fourteen of the fifteen New Testament instances are in Paul's writings, and in twelve of these it expresses the apostle's abhorrence of an inference which he fears may be (falsely) drawn from his argument' (Burton, *Moods*, 177).

[31]This reference to the cross 'clearly stands for much more than the mere historical fact that Jesus was crucified. It stands for the whole significance of the event, not only for mankind in general but for Paul in particular. He could understand how the cross was a stumbling-block for Jews, but he could never understand how Christians could ever fail to see it as their greatest glory' (Guthrie). He adds, 'It may well be that a major part of the weakness of much of the witness of the modern Church lies in a failure to boast in the cross, whether or not its opponents treat this message with contempt or hostility.'

[32]'They are dead to me, and I to them, neither can they captivate and overcome me,

meant that for him *the world* was dead; it *has been crucified*. And the other side of that coin is *and I to the world*. As far as the world was concerned, Paul was dead; it evoked no reaction from him. Paul leaves his readers in no doubt as to the wholeheartedness with which he gave himself to the crucified Christ. His acceptance of the crucified Christ was not simply an interesting episode: it was a death to a whole way of life and a rising to a new mode of existence.[33]

15. *Circumcision* was of critical importance to Jews and to those Christians who were Paul's opponents in Galatia. They saw it as something divinely commanded and therefore as something that must be taken with the fullest seriousness. But while Paul did not minimize it in its rightful place he could yet say *neither is circumcision anything*. He immediately adds, *nor uncircumcision*, so that he is denying that either the observance or the non-observance of this ritual requirement is important in the scheme of salvation. Rather, what matters is *a new creation* (*cf.* 2 Cor. 5:17). Paul was quite ready to practise circumcision in the right situation, as his circumcision of Timothy shows (Acts 16:3). But he was not prepared to acquiesce in a situation where some people were apparently claiming that circumcision was a necessity for anyone who wanted to belong to the people of God. The false teachers in Galatia were demanding, not that Jewish Christians be circumcised, but that Gentile believers should undergo this rite. That was teaching that Paul could not accept for a moment. It contradicted the central truth of the gospel.

So the apostle goes on, *but a new creation*. When a sinner comes to trust in the crucified Saviour that sinner is wholly remade, there is a 'new creation' (2 Cor. 5:17). This was at the heart of the gospel Paul proclaimed, and the contrast with what the Jews saw as the all-important circumcision makes clear its central importance. It is in the light of this divine work in the repentant sinner that Paul can deny that either *circumcision* or *uncircumcision* is *anything*. Circumcision is irrelevant to salvation.

16. Paul pronounces a blessing on those who live in the light of this truth. *As many as* is comprehensive; all whose lives are lived in dependence on the crucified are included. *Walk*, as often in the New Testament, is used for the manner of living. It points to steady but unspectacular progress in the right way. Some MSS have the present

---

for they are dead once for all, nor can I desire them, for I too am dead to them' (Chrysostom).

[33]Turner argues that Paul means that he had been literally crucified (Turner, p. 94). But the language used does not support such an unlikely hypothesis.

tense, 'walk', but it seems that the future *will walk* is the right reading.[34] Paul is looking to the ongoing nature of the Christian life. It is interesting that he goes on: *according to this rule*, for he has been opposing people who subjected believers to strict rules. But *rule* (= 'straight rod', BAGD) points us to the authentic way, the one right path on which to walk. The person who has received the Christian salvation is one who has come to see that the 'new creation' is the heart of the Christian way. And in trusting Christ for salvation, that believer has eschewed the kind of rules the Judaizers were seeking to impose on believers.

So Paul prays: *peace be upon them and mercy. Peace* is important, for sin makes sinners into the enemies of God. When Christ saves them from their sin he saves them from divine hostility and so brings them *peace*. And this, of course, comes about through *mercy*. It is fundamental to the Christian way that our salvation rests entirely on what God has done in Christ, and this means his showing of mercy to sinners who did not deserve mercy. Both concepts are frequent in Paul and they combine to sum up the way of salvation for sinners.

Upon the Israel of God is an unusual addition (Paul has it only here). But *Israel* was well known as the name of the people of God and Paul has just been outlining the way sinners can become members of that people. So it follows easily enough that he prays for peace not only on his correspondents in Galatia, but on all God's people wherever they may be. The expression 'stands here not for the faithful converts from the circumcision alone, but for the spiritual Israel generally, the whole body of believers whether Jew or Gentile, and thus *kai* is *epexegetic*, *i.e.* it introduces the same thing under a new aspect' (Lightfoot).

17. *Henceforth*[35] indicates that Paul has come to the end of his argument. We might perhaps translate the words as 'in conclusion'. He has just a few remarks and his letter is ended. The whole letter indicates that he has had considerable opposition and he has argued strongly against the positions of his opponents. Now he asks that no-one should *trouble* him. He is ready to argue strongly with anyone who opposes the truth of the gospel, but he does not look for arguments. He wants to remain in peace.

He gives a reason (*for*) and begins with the emphatic *I*: what he is about to say is intensely personal. Paul bears *the marks of Jesus* in his

---

[34]The aorist subjunctive *stoichēsōsin* is read by P46, but *stoichēsousin* by ℵ BC*, *etc.*, and is usually accepted.

[35]*Tou loipou*, 'from now on'. The expression may, of course, be understood as 'finally'.

body, an expression which seems to indicate that he had been physically abused during his work for Jesus and that his body still showed the scars.[36] What he had suffered as he preached the gospel, often before hostile audiences, showed the extent of his commitment. No man who had suffered so much should be regarded as a trifler. His body showed plainly his deep commitment to Christ. Those scars testified to his readiness to suffer for Christ if need be and they showed him to be Christ's own.

18. In his extant letters Paul invariably has a prayer for *grace* for his correspondents in the closing section. It was fundamental to him that believers owe all their spiritual blessings to the unmerited favour of God, and this is the note on which he delights to end his letters. Allan sees this as particularly appropriate in this letter: 'The epistle must close with "grace", for the whole theme is an appeal to live by grace.' Paul invariably links this *grace* to *our Lord Jesus Christ*, where the full title brings out something of the majesty of the Saviour.[37] Sometimes he adds to this (as in 2 Cor. 13:13, where he refers also to 'the love of God and the fellowship of the Holy Spirit'), but here he concentrates on the Saviour. The reference to *your spirit* rather than 'you' or the like indicates that Paul has a religious approach in mind. He is mindful of the spiritual need of his correspondents. *Brothers* is an affectionate address and one which is found only here in Paul's final benedictions. Coming at the very end of the letter as it does shows that, despite all the problems to which he has referred in this vigorous epistle, and the undoubted forcefulness of his opponents, Paul still sees himself as at one with his correspondents. They are all members of the heavenly family and are bound by family ties. *Amen* is far from invariable at the close of Paul's letters, and when it is used it imparts a devotional tone. The letter has some of the characteristics of a prayer.

---

[36]BAGD give the meaning of *stigma* as 'mark, brand' and point out that a master would put a *stigma* on his slave and that 'religious tattooing also played a great role in antiquity'. Here, 'Paul is most likely alluding to the wounds and scars which he received in the service of Jesus.' Moffatt translates, 'I bear branded on my body the owner's stamp of Jesus.'

[37]Cf. Hendriksen, 'The solemnity with which the apostle utters this full name deserves attention. As *Lord* he owns us, governs and protects us, and we belong to him and should do his bidding. As *Jesus* he, he *alone*, is our Savior... And as *Christ* he was appointed and (as to his human nature) gloriously qualified to be, in his capacity as our Mediator, "our chief Prophet, only Highpriest, and eternal King."'